The Secret Inner Teachings of Daoism

WILLIAM BODRI

First Edition – March 2024
Second Edition – July 2024 (Revised and Expanded)

Top Shape Publishing LLC
1135 Terminal Way Suite 209
Reno, NV 89502

Library of Congress Control Number: 2024931674
ISBN-13: 978-1-7370320-4-5

DEDICATION

This book is written on behalf of everyone who wants to follow the Daoist pathway leading to enlightenment, and for those ardent practitioners trying to re-establish Daoist practice in China and throughout the world without rejuvenating useless or superstitious ways. This information clearly places Daoism in a new light and condenses the religion into an understandable pathway that leads to personal elevation as well as enlightenment or salvation that entails liberating you from the earthly realm and spiritual ascension to the highest heavens. May this hidden information guide you more speedily and surely in your personal cultivation practice. Additions, clarifications, corrections and emphasis are sure to be made by later generations and are welcomed.

CONTENTS

FORWARD

Much of Daoism in ancient times was taught in riddles, and its deeper truths (stripped of any masquerading confusion) were only taught to qualified adepts.

Most men are now more educated than in the past. They tend to be more virtuous too since they are constantly tested by worldly temptations and ethical trials they pass whereas the mettle of religious functionaries is rarely tested due to their protected environments. Scientific thinking has also come to permeate society, and the public has ready access to spiritual teachings from countless traditions that provide a much fuller picture of the cultivation path and what it entails. You can explain its principles using the lives of saints from many spiritual traditions, which is what is done here since much Daoist documentation is lacking, and thereby realize its non-denominational structure. Therefore the spiritual mysteries of the past are fast dropping away.

This is happening for Daoism today, which is seeing a modern resurgence in China. Its mysteries are no longer secrets or superstition when understood through the universal principles of spiritual cultivation. If you understand these non-denominational principles you will make tremendous progress with your Daoist practice and the spiritual work of internal mind-body-energy purification necessary for spiritual progress. It is hoped that this information will help many more people attain the Tao of spiritual ascension.

INTRODUCTION

This is not an ordinary book on Daoism with information you can find anywhere. This is about the secret basis of Daoism concerning how you cultivate practice to attain enlightenment and become a Daoist sage like Lu Dongbin. Hence, it does not have the main purpose of transmitting Daoist philosophy or internal alchemy lessons since you can find those materials elsewhere. The purpose is to unveil heretofore secret Daoist mysteries that were previously taught in riddles, and then guide you to even deeper, hidden aspects of the true Daoist path of achievement.

Should you fail in joining the ranks of the Daoist Immortals in this life, it will still help to prepare you for this achievement in a subsequent life in four ways:

1 – It emphasizes that you can only achieve enlightenment if you are virtuous and have merit. Therefore it encourages you to purify your personality, conduct and behavior, and perform many good deeds of merit in life. In fact, it points out that the purpose of becoming an Immortal is not to escape the lower realm planes of existence but to take on the occupation or vocation of Immortals like Lu Dongbin (who represents the Third Pure One Taishang Laojun) and help people in the world with your many long-lived transcendental spiritual bodies and their powers. In other words, the purpose of Daoism is similar to that of Buddhism, which is to actualize the

Bodhisattva ideal rather than simply escape the lower realms of existence by becoming an enlightened Arhat.

2 – Therefore it also introduces you to various Daoist fields of knowledge you might start to master in order to develop specialized skills and understanding (wisdom) so that you will then have them upon your attainment. Daoism states that naturalism and non-resistance are models for human behavior but does not eschew advancing scientific knowledge or working out the best ways to approach situations (or methods to use) such as in medicine, agriculture, marketing and so on. Innovation and invention are not against Daoism but *are Daoism*, which is responsible for the development of many of the sciences within China. One accepts conditions as they are but walks step-by-step to purposefully create whatever you want in life without battling against it.

3 – It teaches you that the real path of Daoist practice involves inner Qi purification techniques where you wash your body's Qi by stimulating various emotions (that change its texture and tone) and then guide internal Qi movements that churn it in different ways while holding onto the feeling of those different energy qualities. It outlines various *neijia* inner alchemy techniques across the world's religions that do this with or without the involvement of emotions as the stimulant to change the texture, quality or sensation of your Qi.

4 – It explains the Daoist ranks of spiritual achievement, which are stages of Immortal body attainments. This unlocks many secrets as to why spiritual masters act in puzzling ways and explains a variety of strange cultivation phenomena that will happen to you at Daoist temples and on the spiritual path in general. To make clear the principle that the spiritual path is non-denominational it will use ample examples not just from Daoism but from Christianity, Hinduism and Buddhism to illustrate these principles.

CHAPTER 1:
THE THREE PURE ONES AND
THE MODEL DAOIST IDEAL

The message of Daoism is represented within the symbolism of the *San Qing*, the "Three Pure Ones," Three Purities, or Three Divine Teachers that are depicted as throned elders. Many Daoist temples contain statues of the Three Pure Ones who represent a triumvirate comparable to Christianity's Father, Son and the Holy Spirit.

The Holy Spirit represents the all-encompassing fluctuating energy of the universe that Daoism calls *Taiji* while the Father represents the fundamental substrate or substratum of the universe, namely *Wuji* that is the ultimate, absolute source of Creation. The Son represents any phenomenon within the manifest cosmos – any of the "ten-thousand transformations" that appear within *Taiji*. Our minds therefore are the same as the fundamental essence of the universe as are all aspects or attributes of our physical existence. Everything at its core is the fundamental essence of existence.

You can find statues of the Three Pure Ones within many Daoist temples such as Taiwan's famous Sanqing Temple, the Daoist temple on Mount Sanqing of Jiangxi Province, the Dongshan Sanquing Temple as well as the more modern Green Pine Daoist Temple in Deagon, Australia.

The first of the Three Pure Ones represents the most fundamental substrate of the universe. This is the absolute, singular, purest "substance," substratum, ground state or essence of the cosmos. You can consider this the ultimate nature of the universe is a singular all-encompassing substrate that cannot be further decomposed into other components but is just one thing. Thus it is unchanging, infinite, eternal, non-active, and homogeneous or pure. You should consider it the most fundamental primordial form of the universe, its absolute substratum as a singular substance or essence without qualities or attributes other than just itself before it becomes manifested as innumerable forms and energies.

The second of the Three Pure Ones represents the actual physical universe of manifestation rather than its absolute singular substratum.

The third of the Three Pure Ones represents an accomplished celestial master of the Tao, namely a human being and his potential for celestial activity within the universe.

The first of the Three Pure Ones (Three Purities) is known as Yuanshi Tianwang or Yuanshi Tianzun, the Heavenly Worthy of Prime Origin. He represents the absolute primordial nature, fundamental essence or ground state of the universe of which all things are essentially composed. This substance or essence was not created from anything else but is a self-so entity. It has always been there because it is the unmoving ground state that doesn't come from anything else.

Daoism calls it the "Nameless One" because it lacks perceptible attributes just like empty space does. In western religions it is often referred to as "God" while Buddhism calls this the fundamental essence or Emptiness (because it lacks any phenomena), Judaism calls it Ein Sof, Hinduism calls this Nirguna Brahman or *Purusha,* Islam calls this Allah and so on it goes.

This is *Wuji*, the Great undifferentiated formless Tao where there is no existence of *Taiji* (manifestations). Although all-encompassing the fundamental substratum *Wuji* is unfathomable because it is void of phenomena so you cannot perceive It, and because It is empty of manifestations various religious injunctions across the world tell us not to make any image of it because they cannot denote It. If you make an image of It then it is just as Laozi says, "The Tao that can be described is not the eternal Tao."

Yuanshi Tianwang is described as the lord of the origin of things, or lord of the primordial beginning. He represents this fundamental singular substrate of the universe and his title denotes that somehow the complex universe of forms is born from this pure, uncreated, undifferentiated (unconditioned) singular essence that, because It is eternal and pure, never actually changes into anything else. Everything that appears still remains It. He is lord of the beginning, lord of the creation of all things, and lord of the beginningless non-manifestation substratum that is *true existence and true beingness.*

The second of the Three Purities is Shangqing, the Supreme Pure One who is also known as Lingbao Tianzun. He is "The Celestial Worthy of Numinous Treasure" who represents manifest existence. He represents the created universe called *Prakriti*, Shakti or Saguna Brahman in Hinduism. In Buddhism the manifest universe of karmic formations or energies is called the "Triple Realm" that arises out of the Tathagatagarba (matrix womb of creation), and in Daoism it is the Queen Mother of the West (Xiwangmu or Wusheng Laomu) who is the infinite mother or creational origin of all things. In Christianity the universe that is all realms of manifestations is called "Creation."

Lingbao Tianzun represents the universe of manifestation that arose out of its undifferentiated substratum substance that lacks qualities like empty space. He represents a frothing, fluctuating cauldron of ceaseless transformations that we call the universe. It is always transforming from one appearance to the next because of ceaseless transmutations that encompass all existing multiplicities of energies and forms. There are laws of cause and effect that comprehensively specify all these transformations and because everything affects everything else the entire cosmos is always in a state of vibration, transformation or indeterminacy. The laws of nature are the laws of cause and effect that specify how phenomena transform into other phenomena, and Buddhism calls the macro set of all causality rules "dependent origination" or "interdependent arising."

All the phenomena of the universe are a simple fabric or singular body and at the same time they are its absolute substance or substratum that has somehow become *differentiated in appearance* into the realm of universal manifestation. Because Shangqing represents the frothing universe of ever-fluctuating manifestations, which is an illusion to our sense organs since it is really just the one fundamental substratum, Shangqing is considered the principal disseminator of Daoist teachings. The Daoist "teachings" here represent all the phenomena of the universe, which Buddhism calls forms and labels.

To prove this we can see that Shangqing is also called Jingbao, the "Treasure of the Laws of Nature" or "The Universally Honored One of Divinities and Treasures" since the universe is differentiated into all sorts of forms, phenomena, energies, processes or functions that are here called divinities and treasures. Shangqing therefore represents the entire field of manifestation - the "All of Creation" - and everything within the universe are the treasures. In other words, Shangqing represents the cosmos of creation and everything within it.

The third of The Three Pure Ones is Taishang Laojun or Daode Tianzun. He is also known as "The Universally Honored One of Tao and Virtues," "The Celestial Worthy of the Way and its Power" (Daode Tianzun) or "The Heavenly Worthy of Tao and its Virtue."

His other names include Daode Zhizun and Daojiao Zhizu ("The Daoist Ancestor"). He is called the Taiqing or Great (Grand) Pure One and he is the one most appropriate to us in terms of instructions for our life. He is the "Lord of Man" because he represents the human being who cultivates self-mastery and mastery of the cosmos, which is the goal of Daoist aspirants. He represents mastery because he has consciousness and it is through consciousness (through a mind) that we have awareness, cognizance, knowledge, and understanding. Because we have a mind we can develop awareness as well as control of our self and our actions to produce whatever we want in the universe.

As Daojiao Zhizu ("The Daoist Ancestor") he actually represents the ideal of becoming an accomplished Daoist master, namely a Daoist Immortal. His title as Taishang Laozun, the "Highest Elder Lord" or "Grand Supreme Elder Lord," denotes that he is a highly accomplished individual, namely a master of virtues and excellences. He represents mastery of sentience (oneself) and mastery of activity within the field of manifestation (Creation) so he serves as a teacher or leader of mankind. He represents us – human beings with minds who can learn to control our consciousness, learn the laws of cause and effect in Nature and human affairs, and then employ those laws of consequence to produce whatever we want in the cosmos.

Pictures of Taiqing usually show him holding a fan to indicate that he has mastered thinking and activity as well as *his own internal energy*. These are all movements in the field of manifestation and aptly represented by waving a fan, which additionally symbolizes mastery of the energies of universe that are the forces or attributes of the manifest cosmos. Of particular note is that he symbolizes mastery of the Qi life force energy within the human body that is linked to our breathing (and hence the fan), and which is the basis, or composition, of our internal spiritual body. We must cultivate our inner Qi energy and learn to control it in order to attain the higher spiritual bodies of enlightenment that turn us into spiritual Immortals because they are composed of energy. He is an accomplished spiritual master who has attained these higher celestial spiritual bodies which he also indicates by holding a fan.

Because we are living beings with higher consciousness rather than inert insentient matter, survival charges us with this task of mastering ourselves *and our environment or circumstances* in order to thrive. You can word this, as Daoism does, as meaning that we must learn to be in harmony with the cosmos as well as master the various aspects of the universe. This is what Daoism is all about, which is how to live in harmony with the universe while also accomplishing our own unique goals within it. Since we are to master cause and effect not just to survive but in order to make progress and thrive, it becomes evident that religions which thwart the development of science, math, invention, innovation and progress are clearly in error. There is certainly a focus in Daoism on naturalism but this does not mean mankind should refuse to develop itself and make progress in various fields by conducting research and innovating in the fields of science, medicine, farming and invention in general.

The fan in Taiqing's hand can cause wind, which means that he can create phenomena or events (by his pushing or activity) because of possessing a consciousness that understands the cause and effect laws of nature. Insentient matter, on the other hand, cannot think so it cannot produce self-directed activity. Fanning his fan is also a symbol for pushing around the Qi inside one's body.

Since Taiqing can master the laws of interdependent origination that rules the realm of manifestation, he is said to preach the Laws of Nature – how things are "meant" to be – as well as how we should develop in life since development follows the same laws of causality. He represents the highest possible achievement of human beings. He is someone who cultivates his mind and body according to the science of nature to become a Daoist Immortal, and he masters the laws of phenomenal change and transformation to order to help the world and bring well-being to it by creating great benefit for others through his activities.

In conventional terms, Taiqing represents a *sentient* being that evolves within the universe and acts according to its own self-will due to the property of having a mind. Humans, for instance, have minds and sensory awareness so we can form thoughts to become aware of ourselves and our environment. Because of having consciousness we can develop understanding and wisdom that enables us to even predict the patterns of transformation of phenomena and gain control over those changes. This is the wisdom (understanding) we need for our lives.

Our goal in understanding the causality of human affairs and the cosmos is so that we can use an understanding of cause and effect, and its regular patterns of predictability, to manage situations, "control Nature," "control natural forces," "control material reality" or "guide (master) the changes of phenomena." We do this in order to make things better for ourselves. We want to control Nature and domesticate it under human rule so that it becomes more manageable, more beneficial to us and much less unpredictable and frightening. We do this for purposes of survival and to flourish. We use rational, logical thinking to investigate Nature to discover its principles, laws and innumerable transformations in order to use that information to improve our own lives.

Consciousness lets us do this. We can do this only because we are sentient and have a mind capable of higher thinking. We grow by developing our consciousness and cognitive skills in various ways to gain control of Nature and make our lives better, and Taiqing represents the guide of Daoism that helps us do this. He not only represents proper, effective, skillful activity but self-mastery over ourselves and the elevation of our thinking and behavior – our virtues, skills or excellences.

Our consciousness (knowing, knowledge or awareness) is not just a movement of energy within our heads because you can think of its continuous nature as a moving string of energy in the cosmos. Taiqing represents the moving aspect of Creation embodied in a sentient being that can manage its own functions, properties and aspects through self-decision and thereby direct them however he wishes through self-will rather than just robotically, automatically responding to Nature due to predictable laws like the chemical reactions of inert matter.

Taiqing is also described as the "educator who brings civilization," which is because through his mind and actions he then acts for culture and society and teaches the people how to act and behave. This is like the Bodhisattva in Buddhism. Taiqing's highest behavior is disseminating civilizing influences throughout the world such as ethics in society, technical skills (like farming, cooking, medical treatment or manufacturing), scientific and economic improvements, and knowledge of the pathway to Tao (how to attain our higher spiritual bodies that take us out of the lower realms forever).

As an educator who teaches or transmits, Taiqing represents gaining control over the forces of transformation in the field of manifestation. But in which direction should we take things? He learns the transformations of phenomena and uses his knowledge of how to change things to make situations better, thus enriching the world and human civilization in the material and ethical, moral, cultural or spiritual spheres. *He improves matters!*

He tries to enrich the lives of people everywhere by trying to create value for them with his efforts to create a brighter future. He helps to magnify their spirit, protect their interests, end their sufferings and difficulties, and gives teachings that serve their happiness and well-being. He teaches the highest methods of cultivation for our bodies, minds, internal energy and behavior and also advises society in many areas. He corrects the elites,[1] corrupt institutions and those in power who try to oppress or exploit the people and he tries to help the poor, sick, elderly, widowed, orphaned and less privileged by engaging in auspicious activities wherever he goes. He intervenes in people's lives in service to the highest principles, acting out of love, and strives to produce prosperity for everyone he meets.

We are advised to emulate Taiqing by developing ourselves in terms of ethics, virtue and good deeds as well as in the personal cultivation of our own personal physical health, self-discipline and mastery of our consciousness. He represents someone who cultivates mastery of his body, consciousness, behavior and activities to control external phenomena which he tries to do in the most skillful, easiest possible way. He represents the human endeavor to learn new bodies of knowledge and skills to help society grow and develop so he represents the continual impetus for human evolution.

As a general rule for life we must transcend our animal nature and train ourselves to develop our bodies, minds, virtues, skills and activities in order to elevate our personal lives and the conditions for society. This is the primary occupation of a Daoist Immortal. Taiqing therefore represents the grand ideal of Daoism, which is someone

---

[1] No matter the form of government it takes a nation will develop a governing ruling class of elites at its top that gradually plunders the wealth of the other classes and is then eventually deposed in response. Empires bring national stability in the form of a parasitic court of elites, religions produce national social cohesion at the expense of having a parasitic priestly class, nationalism raises the power to a nation at the expense of a parasitic military, socialism brings more equality to the citizenry at the expense of burgeoning debts and a parasitic bureaucracy, and capitalism brings efficiency and prosperity at the expense of parasitic financiers and an elite class of the wealthy. Countries grow wealthy when they restrain the powerful from plundering people, such as by enforcing the rule of law that protects peoples' assets. Man-made constraints such as traditions, laws and institutions also compel a ruling elite to promote the common good rather than its own good.

who cultivates all his own attributes to become a Daoist Immortal. He is someone who achieves the higher spiritual bodies of existence that are already inherent in the unpurified energy matrix of our physical body. Once those spiritual bodies become untangled and free then a true Daoist Immortal acts as a guide for humanity and as a benefactor who helps others with the powers he thereby attains.

To the Daoist, Jesus is an example of Taiqing because he is a trinity of God, the Holy Spirit (Shakti or the manifest universe of vibrations) and himself (a phenomenon) or essence, body and mind. The savior ideal of the Buddhist Bodhisattva – who takes vows to perform beneficial actions on behalf of mankind – is also an example of Taiqing as are the kami protector spirits and deities of Japan, orisha of Africa, and *tudigong* protectors of cities and communities. These deities all refer to human beings who achieved the higher spiritual bodies of existence, which means they attained enlightenment, and then work to serve mankind.

Some religions describe enlightenment, liberation, spiritual ascension or "being saved" in terms of purified realms of consciousness while Daoism describes it as a physical body achievement that ascends to a different (more transcendental) realm of existence where your ordinary consciousness, which becomes a bit more clear with each new progression, simply comes along with your new body attainment. Daoism is thus more accurate, or we should say less misleading in its description of what "enlightenment" actually entails because it has to do with body achievements and the attendant state of consciousness for that new body.

Daoists aspire toward a stage of accomplishment called "becoming a sage or Immortal," which is someone who actually possesses these higher spiritual bodies. They are taught that to attain the higher spiritual bodies – to enter the ranks of the Daoist Immortals – you must engage in spiritual cultivation efforts to purify your internal vital energy (Qi) so that it gradually differentiates itself into purer (higher) and less pure (impure or denser) components that can be left behind. The purified Qi aspect ascends by separating itself from the denser impure matter of the physical body, and this is achieving the first stage of the Daoist Immortals. That is why most beneficial Daoist practice deals with purifying your physical body (which is composed of your Qi), personality (which expresses your Qi), behavior (which comes from activating your Qi), and internal energy (which is your Qi that when purified separates as a new stage of life).

Some describe this by saying that we *differentiate* or untangle the lower from higher energies of the body to attain the higher spiritual bodies and become a Daoist Immortal, or that we *separate and purify* our body's Yin and Yang components through spiritual cultivation, or that we raise the *frequency* of our transcendental etheric components and thereby separate the elevated fractions from our denser nature through an arduous purification process of spiritual cultivation, or that we purify our energy, actions and personality, and so forth.

Essentially, to become a Daoist Immortal means that *we are becoming pure spirits or pure energy* where each new rank of attainment represents a more transcendental state of existence that is more energy-like in composition than the previous one. Eventually you can say that the bodies become like light because of its capabilities. Thus the various spiritual schools of the world say, *since their adherents also attain these same non-denominational stages of spiritual attainment* (otherwise the attainments wouldn't be true) that through spiritual practice we can stop identifying with our physical body and carnal urges, *transcend* our lower nature and rise above the lower planes of existence within the universe of vibrations. This is because we can attain higher spiritual bodies composed of more transcendent materials whilst alive. Thus becoming a Daoist Immortal is a process of spiritual ascension, and therefore it also requires the cultivation of inner virtues and merits.

What is surprising is that the Three Pure Ones also stand for the three earliest links within the Buddhist chain of the Twelve Links of Interdependent Origination. According to the Twelve Links the singular Unmanifest, pure, undifferentiated, unconditioned, self-so, eternal and unchanging foundational ground state substance of the universe (base reality) somehow turns into the manifest cosmos. Since the absolute ground source is changeless, (1) we do *not understand* how this singular substratum can manifest a universe of phenomena so Buddha refers to this impossibility of understanding as "Ignorance," which is the first link in the chain. We don't understand how Yuanshi Tianwang generates the universe, which is represented by Lingbao Tianzun. The existence of the primordial, uncreated and changeless eternal Tao is self-so, hence it actually precedes the first link of Ignorance regarding how the cosmos was created.

The second link in the Buddhist chain of dependent origination is Lingbao Tianzun who represents (2) the development of "karmic formations," which just means the creation of the universe of manifestation and all its various contents. The pure fundamental substratum of the universe is there in a changeless unmoving mode free of phenomena and then it somehow generates this universe of uncountable manifestations. Hinduism calls the manifest universe Shakti, Saguna Brahman, *Prakriti*, Creation and other terms that basically denote an endlessly vibrating universe that is constantly transforming in all sorts of ways. We see (observe) it in a certain way that isn't the way in which it really exists.

In Daoism the universe is symbolized as a cauldron of "transformations" and the *I-Ching* describes it using the word "change" since it is always changing into some sort of new appearance. Buddhism describes it using the term "impermanence" to denote that no state within it stays the same, thus we should not attach to any. Hinduism uses the term "movement (dancing),"

Shaivism uses the term "vibration" or "scintillation," physics uses the terms "fluctuation" or "cause and effect," and Islam describes the universe using the term "complex interactions" that are all comprehensively connected to one another. You yourself are always continuously changing and rarely remain the same even for a short period of time.

Taiqing charges us to learn the laws of cause and effect that rule these transformations and then to use them in virtuous, beneficial actions. This is the basis of Daoism that has had a developmental influence on medicine, agriculture, political science, warfare, martial arts, astrology, economics, and the sciences in Chinese culture. A true Daoist tries to move society ahead by discovering the laws of transformation that rule a body of karmic formations and then teaches others how to apply them for human benefit.

Within the universe of ceaselessly evolving transformations, life eventually formed and in time it developed into complex life that has consciousness. We are that revolutionary development of sentient life and are (3) represented by Taishang Laojun (Daode Tianzun). This is the third link in the chain of dependent origination. As a form of complex life we are capable of higher consciousness because we have the ability to perform advanced reasoning and can control the abilities of our consciousness, our internal energy, and our movements to some extent. In the universe we are forms of living sentient existence that have minds and bodies that must be maintained in order to survive, and our species must also procreate in order that it does not become extinct.

The great miracle of our existence is consciousness that is the rarest, most precious and miraculous treasure of the universe. Because we have self-consciousness and advanced cognitive and reasoning abilities we can learn to control and perfect our mind, body, and behavior and guide ourselves through self-cultivation efforts to attain spiritual bodies that transcend the lower planes of existence. Those who attain these achievements are honored as saints and sages when they become the spiritual guides of mankind.

Each of the Three Pure Ones is denoted as a deity but each one represents a sequential role in the process of Creation. In summary there is the (1) the pure, infinite, eternal, empty, original spotless substratum of the universe or *Wuji*, (2) its transformation through a process we don't understand into the manifest universe that we call Shakti, Purusha, Saguna Brahman, the Triple Realm, cosmos or *Taiji*, and (3) individual phenomena including the human being who can cultivate his own elevation to become master of himself and the cosmos because he has the rare and miraculous attribute of consciousness that is lacking in most of the universe. He can become a Buddhist Bodhisattva, Daoist Immortal or Japanese kami and so on who performs specific functions with his various spiritual bodies and skills to help human beings. This trio is actually the Father, Holy Spirit and Son of Christianity.

Consciousness, or Knowledge, gives rise to comprehension that enables us to attain mastery of ourselves along with the laws of cause and effect that rule manifest existence. The third deity, Taiqing (Taishang Laojun or Daode Tianzun), represents the ultimate model of what we are striving for as human beings, which is self-knowledge (awareness), understanding, mastery of ourselves and mastery of phenomena and the energies of the universe.

Through consciousness and self-mastery we can ponder the causes of suffering and unsatisfactoriness that afflict human lives, eliminate and ameliorate those conditions, and use our minds, behavior and activities to pursue and experience happiness, prosperity, flourishing and bliss. This is the goal of Daoism.

CHAPTER 2:
THE NON-DENOMINATIONAL STAGES OF ENLIGHTENMENT AND THE SPIRITUAL RANKS OF THE DAOIST IMMORTALS

Daoism offers a philosophy for how to properly manage your consciousness (your senses, thinking, emotions, will and viewpoints/perspectives), how to run your life so that it flows in tune with nature, and how to become an enlightened spiritual Immortal.

Because the world is filled with books on Daoist philosophy we need not spend precious time with information that is readily available everywhere. Instead we will concentrate on what is *not normally known* within Daoism yet is *the very heart and soul* of Daoism. You can go to Wikipedia and find nearly anything else you want to know about Daoism except this information since it is usually considered an initiate's transmission.

The enlightenment of the Daoist sages is actually the attainment of higher spiritual bodies that they achieved due to spiritual cultivation exercises, especially the inner alchemy of Qi cultivation. When we die our spirit leaves our physical body shell and this new spiritual, subtle energy, astral, deva or angelic body is considered the first of the higher spiritual body attainments. Buddhism says that individuals who are coarse and unpurified become *asuras* or angry (unpurified) devas after they die while the more cultivated and angelic of humans simply become devas. Other schools call those who die spirits, disembodied beings, or simply say that your soul is released upon death which once again means you become a deva. It's all the same thing and this couldn't be any other way because it happens to *all* human beings. The physical world is not the prime reality.

The lowest rank of the Daoist Immortals is when you achieve this deva body while alive so that it is tethered to your physical nature and you can use both bodies – one for interacting with the physical world and one that lives in the heavenly earthly plane all around us. This subtle body takes refuge within the shell of your physical nature as a home or resting place. Your physical shell is then considered the lower, denser or most impure part of your total physical nature. Your deva body - composed of Qi, subtle energy or the "wind element" - is considered the higher, more spiritual part of your nature which is why Christians say that your soul leaves your body at death. This higher body is then the real you, but the actual "truest you" or "real man" is locked within its corporeal matrix until you release it through the processes of further spiritual cultivation.

Your mind and life continue only as long as your vital Qi force remains within you, which means that the basis of life is not purely material chemistry and physics. Matter is not the sole principle of the universe and physical energy is not its sole mover. You are not just the cells of your body. Life involves a higher transcendental (spiritual) component that science hasn't discovered yet, but which is recognized by spiritual traditions. The subtle body endows the physical body with life. Robots and computers do not have this core that transcends the material world so can never be considered a form of life or as something with actual consciousness.

If you didn't have an inner Qi body, namely an inner subtle energy body that we call the deva body or soul, you would neither live nor have consciousness. In some sense it really is as Manichaeism says that a supernatural light, the subtle body or soul (the divine essence of humans), is imprisoned or ensnared within the darkness of the material world that restricts its true essence and longs to be released through liberation from the world so that it can return to its heavenly home, so there is no reason to fear death. All the secret tantras of Vajrayana relating to Hevajra, Guhyasamaja and Chakrasamvara practice etc. are simply elaborate methods for cultivating the Qi of your body so that you can attain the stage of being a deva while alive. The same goes for secret Daoist or other Yoga techniques.

Within the matrix of the angelic deva body composed of subtle Qi energy is the potential of yet higher spiritual bodies that must be decoupled from within it. Our human condition is like that of a Russian Matryoshka doll where various shells are stacked within one another that Hinduism calls *koshas* and Buddhism calls *skandhas*. Various higher transcendental energies interpenetrate with one another in a human shell and can separate out as independent bodies when you engage in the proper practices and processes of spiritual cultivation. This is the process of becoming a Daoist Immortal or sage. Each higher body is invisible and intangible to the lower body out of which it immediately arose because it resides on a higher transcendental plane of existence, which for simplicity's sake you might think of as a plane of higher frequency.

While our physical human body is composed of flesh that originates from a union of egg and semen (Jing), the next highest body is composed of Qi, which is our vital internal energy that keeps us alive. From within that subtle body composed of Qi you can release a yet higher spiritual body composed of Shen energy, which is then known as the Causal body in Hinduism or Anagamin stage of Buddhist Arhat. So the life force of the subtle Qi body is called Shen. From within the Causal body of Shen you can release a higher Supra-Causal body composed of Later Heavenly Energy through even more cultivation effort, which is the Buddhist stage of the full Arhat and

Daoist stage of the Celestial Immortal. Most schools use terms like wisdom and dharma, or light and rainbow, to describe this body because these are good analogies for some of its capabilities.

This body achievement is considered "enlightenment with a *remainder*" for the "remainder" means that there is one more body to go, and thus more purification work can be performed on the energies of that body to generate a yet higher body vehicle. From within the Arhat's body of Later Heavenly Energy, which is the stage of Daoist Celestial Immortal, you can release the highest possible spiritual body attainment, which is to achieve the Great Golden Arhat, Immanence body or Tathagata body attainment of the pure *atman* or *jiva* that is composed of Primordial Heavenly Energy. This is considered the *true man or real human being*.

When Daoism or the Zen school talks of the "real man" or "true man" it is referring to this highest spiritual attainment – your highest and longest living spiritual body that is inherent within the human shell. Once you cultivate and attain the lowest of these spiritual body attainments while alive, which is the astral deva body composed of Qi or "subtle energy," you automatically become an enlightened "Daoist Immortal" or *xian*. When you achieve the highest body you are considered fully and completely enlightened for having achieved the highest stage possible for a Daoist Immortal.

In Hindu thought, the true soul, *jiva* or *atman* of humans is this highest innermost core, and our *material* self has the spiritual task of becoming one with Brahman through the processes and practices of moral refinement and spiritual cultivation that take you to this achievement. To become one with Brahman - the foundational essence, substratum or ground state of the universe (our base reality) - simply means liberating from within oneself the potential of the Immanence body attainment that is composed of the highest possible etheric energy encased within the matrix of living matter. Buddhism says that all beings have the "seed of Buddhahood," which simply means that within the matrix of dense living matter is a very high (transcendental or pure) type of energy that can be purified and released as an immortal spiritual body that resides on the highest etheric planes of the universe. This is why everyone has the potential for enlightenment. To attain this Immanence body is to attain the highest possible rank of Daoist Immortals or sages beyond the Celestial Immortal attainment and thus is considered the highest stage of enlightenment. This is the highest possible sage – the Universal Immortal.

The way you achieve the higher spiritual bodies is by purifying your Qi through the frictional process of stirring it just as in the Hindu story of the Churning of the Ocean of Milk (*Samudra Manthana*) from the *Vishnu Parana* that generated all sorts of spiritual beings from within it. This is why Daoism employs countless internal energy circulation exercises in its *qi-gong* and *nei-gong* practices. To achieve the stage of an Immortal all the modalities of your Qi have to be washed through internal *neijia* churnings that purify them through friction.

The Daoist Ge Hong (d. 343) has written, "people reside within *Qi* and *Qi* resides within people. From heaven and earth down to the ten thousand things, each one requires *Qi* to live. As for those who excel at circulating their *Qi*, internally they are able to nourish their body; externally, they are able to repel illnesses."

The basic principle is that there is a subtle body of Qi within us, and this is what becomes released at death to become a deva spirit. You need to cultivate this Qi in order to live a longer, healthier life by improving its circulation, but a higher achievement is to attain an independent spiritual deva body composed of Qi that can leave your physical shell at will whilst you are alive. If you are a deva, which is the Buddhist stage of the Srotapanna, you must also exercise your Qi to purify it to become a Sakadagamin, and then proceed significantly enough in purification that you can release a new body from within it is to achieve a new Anagamin or Spirit Immortal body made of Shen, which is the next higher form of life force energy inherent within Qi. Buddhism says this body resides in a higher etheric Realm of Form, and divides the realm into several gradients to denote degrees of purification of this Causal body (Anagamin) attainment. Every time you see a scheme where a heaven is divided into higher and lower partitions you should simply think of them as notable stages of progress one can achieve in purifying their internal energy until they attain the next higher spiritual body.

Daoism is about working with the natural energies of your body, which is called "nurturing life," in order to transform your body and mind. This is a process of physical, mental, emotional and spiritual purification. You also want to learn how to use the natural energies of the universe to improve your life, and be in harmony with the world by following the natural way of things, or Tao.

You can purify your Qi to some extent on your own (which is the preoccupation of a Human Immortal) through various exercises. Please reference *Correcting Zen* (which is especially good for Daoist monastics), *Arhat Yoga* and *Neijia Yoga* for suitable techniques. However, to succeed at the process to the extent of generating this new and independent life (and become an Earth Immortal) requires the assistance of countless higher Immortals and their students helping you for years in order to revolve your internal Qi and circulate it in various ways so that it becomes refined through the friction of higher energies rubbing against lower, less purified energies. Thus you also require virtue, merit and personality purification.

Your internal vital energy (Qi) will gradually differentiate into a purer (higher) and less pure (impure or denser) aspect through this churning just as milk resolves into denser and lighter components when continuously stirred. A better analogy is when a heavy liquid is stirred in the middle of a vat so that denser dregs accumulate at its sides producing a differentiation in viscosity, and this same type of Qi differentiation happens in the body due to *nei-gong*. We must *differentiate* the lower from higher energies from within our corporeal physical body to attain the higher spiritual bodies because this *is* the process of purification. We must purify our body and its internal energy in a way where the various qualities of our internal energy are activated and washed through a long purification process that takes years of continuous effort rather than simply just living without doing any cultivation practice at all. You might say that we must *separate or clearly differentiate and purify* all of our body's Yin and Yang energy aspects through spiritual cultivation. You can also say that we must raise the *frequency* of our transcendental etheric components by separating the higher from the lower aspects of our energy nature.

There are many ways to alternatively describe this process. Basically, the higher your body of spiritual attainment the closer it is to becoming pure energy that lacks any denser components. Thus, spiritual cultivation is the process of becoming more and more like pure energy in your corporeal composition. What activates the various Yang tonalities of your energy are positive emotions (such as joy, love, courage, happiness, amusement, optimism, sunniness, etc.) and what activates or energizes the Yin tonalities of your energy are negative emotions (such as fear, sadness, grief, embarrassment, depression, etc.) or negative body states such as cold, pain, exposure to electronic EMF and sickness.

When through spiritual practice you achieve a new spiritual body it automatically becomes the new center of your life while the previous body out of which it arose then becomes just a shell-like appendage used to interact with its own particular plane of being. When the full individual with all his bodies is withdrawn into his physical body then it seems like he is there, otherwise it can seem to very observant people as if he is absent (hint: a stiffer body and vacant eyes which some masters hide by wearing dark sunglasses), When his spirit bodies are gone his physical body can still be operated from afar like an appendage, or possessed and operated by a local deva or master when he is away, which may or may not cause troubles. This is why some masters in India take vows of silence to prevent troubles during long interludes away from their body or just stay in retreat. Or, an absent master might simply remain motionless in meditation when he is gone, which is not some "state of samadhi" but simply the fact that his higher spirit bodies are absent.

As stated, sometimes a master's human body will be possessed by another enlightened person to operate while he is away and in those instances the master using his body will simply repeat an old lesson he reconstructs from the memories in the brain. That, then, keeps both the students and the visiting master occupied while also giving that visiting master an opportunity to practice and show off his own skills. Sometimes a master will send his own *nirmanakaya* to take over.

You transcend each new plane of existence, or "heavenly realm," by attaining a new spiritual body whose energy composition transcends that of the lower realm from which it was distilled or purified out. However, since your lower body remains connected to that new higher body unless it dies or you sever the connection, you can continue to use that lower body (and all others) as a shell or appendage to do things on that lower plane of existence and see it as the beings within it experience them. Your higher bodies can move to any of their previous body shells and occupy them so that you can do things on each of the lower realms of existence and respond to people in need. You can therefore give teachings to a lower plane of existence from a higher realm, or manifest miracles in a lower realm by using a body from a higher realm to perform the miracle that is demonstrated in the lower realm. The miracle would not be anything special on the higher plane of existence but would appear as miraculous to those on the lower planes even though it would just be an ordinary skill that everyone could learn on the higher plane through ordinary practice.

By attaining the higher spiritual bodies you thereby "transcend" or "ascend above" the physical world, thus escaping the lower planes of existence. This is liberation from our material realm of carnality and desire. As long as your physical body is alive but your new center of life is a higher spiritual body you can "live in the world while transcending it." When you attain any higher body there is then no reason to attach to anything in the lower planes of existence so it is easy to preach about detachment, charity, celibacy, bear poverty and so on because *the truest you* is living on a higher plane of existence where this realm is a throwaway existence that can be compared to a dream. For instance, it is easy to talk about *bramacharya* (celibacy) to people when you have a wife in heaven.

Daoism calls the non-denominational ranks of spiritual achievement "Immortals" to denote their longevity because the higher spiritual bodies all live for much longer periods of time than an ordinary human life.

According to the *Zhong Lu Chuan Dao Ji* there are five ranks of Daoist Immortals, who as a group were usually called *fang shi* before Daoism became formalized in China. Of these five ranks the Human Immortal *(renxian)* is an ordinary person who simply cultivates the methods of health, vigor and longevity, presumably due to following Daoist or other wise philosophies and methods, to thereby live a virtuous, long, healthy, and prosperous life. You just cultivate the wisest methods of the world, and wisest ways of living, acting or being, to become healthy and live a long life. That's a Human Immortal. The designation of being a Human Immortal applies to most everyone who lives according to Daoist philosophies in the world. You don't have to be Chinese or go to China to be a Daoist.

Anyone who lives like a Daoist according to its philosophies and perspectives or who uses its methods of cultivation for health and longevity can claim they are a Daoist or Human Immortal.

The Earth Immortal (*dixian*), which is the next stage of achievement, is a man or woman who cultivates spiritual exercises and then becomes able to separate off from themselves their independent inner spirit body made of Qi that normally detaches from their physical body upon death. This astral body of Qi resides on the earthly heavenly plane where all human spirits reside after the transition of death. Then humans become known as devas, *asuras* or spirits. The astral body is known as a deva body or subtle body, but it is an "impure" subtle body because as subtle bodies go there are higher bodies possible on more ascendant planes of existence. They require more purification for you to achieve them so this bottom stage is the most impure of them all.

In any case, death is a definite migration of the soul where our inner subtle Qi body is released from its mortal frame so that we can afterwards meet deceased old friends in the earthly heavenly plane of existence (if they have not yet reincarnated). So there really is something within us that belongs to the transcendental! We are not totally annihilated upon death nor absorbed into the totality of the universe at that time. It is simply that our soul, or inner subtle body, escapes the matrix of the physical shell within which it is imprisoned and begins a post-mortem life. Terrestrial beingness with a material body ends but personhood in a subtle Qi body remains for a period of time before its own death and reincarnation. That process of reincarnation is managed or administered by higher enlightened masters who help insert souls into karmically appropriate wombs otherwise there really would be permanent extinction due to the entropic degradation of the spirit body.

Hence, our material body is made of Jing, our subtle spiritual body is made of Qi (this is the basis of the *dixian* Earth Immortal stage of accomplishment), and its own internal life force energy is Shen that can be purified and released as an independent life, too, which is then accomplishing the stage of the Spirit Immortal (*shenxian*). Above the Spirit Immortal is the stage of the Celestial Immortal (*tianxian*) that is the typical stage people think of as enlightenment because this is the stage of the Buddhist Arhat, Chinese *luohan*, or Supra-Causal body attainment of Hinduism. When the Shen spirit "merges" with emptiness this simply means the attainment of the Supra-Causal body that is "beyond the Realm of Form," and thus "formless" due to shape-shifting capabilities available because of its composition as nearly pure energy.

This information you have just read is far above the teachings you will normally receive in ordinary Daoism.

Our inner subtle body is like a life of its own, which is why it is released upon death as our form of living beingness. We have life and consciousness on this material plane of existence only because our material corporeal shell is "powered" by the presence of an internal subtle body (soul) composed of Qi energy so it is ludicrous seeing individuals insist that computer neural networks, robotics and AI systems are actually "life forms," alive and conscious, when they are just programming code. The idea is as ludicrous as "the inevitable merging of humans and technology like the Borg," or the idea that cybernetic enhancements would somehow remain a prized addition to you rather than detriment in the afterlife, or that you will be able to upload your consciousness to a computer or robotic avatar and live forever.

Those are the views of silly people who have watched too many science fiction movies or read too many sci-fi books. On the other hand, many individuals have reported out-of-the-body near-death experiences that prove the existence of their Qi soul body attested to by the spiritual masters of many traditions. The problem is that this inner body of ours constitutes unpurified energy unless we perform lots of spiritual practices that purify its nature. This is why Tibetan Buddhism calls it the "impure illusory body." It is impure because it isn't composed of refined energy-matter, and illusory because it still isn't the real human being or innermost highest body core.

The stage of the Earth Immortal, or independent subtle body attainment, is equivalent to the impure illusory body of Tibetan Buddhism, the deva body of Hinduism, astral body of western lore, (Srotapanna and) Sakadagamin stage of Arhatship, and the 1st and 2nd bhumi of Buddhism, *Sukshma deha* in Nath Yoga, *Suddha deha* of the Tamil Siddha tradition, "Beauty" stage of Confucianism, pranayama *kosha* (energy body made of Prana) of Vedanta, and so on. Once you attain this body it becomes the new center of your life and it enables you to do various things that we would normally call small superpowers. Once people die they go through an orientation process lasting several weeks to learn how to use their subtle body and are taught how the world really works as regards reincarnation, higher body attainments, the truths and falsities of religion and so on. They obtain this information because they have spirit bodies but can see the human world all around them, which they can pass through, and also observe the processes of reincarnation and so forth.

The subtle deva body composed of our Qi energy is the reason we are alive as it resides within our mortal shell until death frees it. Thus Christianity calls it our soul. As a spiritual body it is capable of the eight *siddhi* of Yoga: *anima* (ability to shrink one's body), *mahima* (the ability to increase one's body size), *laghima* (the ability to become lighter), *garima* (the ability to become denser/heavier), *vasitva* (the ability to possess a human and take control over them), etcetera. No one ever tells people this information but the *siddhi* superpowers pertain to the deva body. You can access them once you attain the deva body but the higher transcendental spiritual bodies have even greater *siddhi.*

Daoism needs to incorporate these lessons into its fold because all it has are pieces of Chinese folk religion that only hint about the doings of the post-worldly life. When people die and then become the earthly devas that are all around us they have to go through several weeks of orientation (ex. 49 up to 100 days) during which time they learn many things such as how to master the capabilities of their new spirit body. An individual who becomes an Earth Immortal while living, thus becoming a Daoist master, must go through a training and orientation process as well.

When you hear knocking on your wall from an unexplained source that is sometimes a deva demonstrating the power of *garima* by condensing his etheric form so that through density it can hit the matter of our material world. When you hear music being replayed in your head it is because a spiritual master and his students have shrunk themselves down to a tiny size through the power of *anima* (thus the Daoist stories of being able to turn one's body into the size of an insect), entered your brain and started activating the neuronal memories of the music. Science knows that you can use electricity to activate memories in the brain but spiritual beings use their Qi energy to do this because your body and consciousness run on Qi energy, but it takes training to do this with expertise.

When you see a martial artist like Sun Lutang (d. 1933) or a Buddhist monk or Hindu master such as Bhagavan Nityananda (d. 1961) walk so incredibly fast that you cannot catch up to them it means they are demonstrating the *laghima* lightness *siddhi* in the human world although the deva body can travel quicker, and this is the basis of the Daoist stories of magical footwear (also found in other spiritual traditions) that can let you travel great distances incredibly fast. Most all spiritual traditions talk about the fact that devas, angels, *jinn* (who are *asuras*, misbehaving devas or devas acting as if they were misbehaving) and so forth can travel incredible distances in the blink of an eye.

Any deva can also read your thoughts and memories stored in your neurons (after training) so spiritual masters love to astound students by telling them what they did in the past at such and such a time and place, which is from using one of their higher bodies to read your neurons. I once visited a Daoist temple in northern Taiwan where people would wait in line to hear a woman, who was possessed by the local guardian deity, to tell them what they had been doing wrong in their life. This always entailed revealing secrets no one could possibly know by checking people's memories rather than from reading an etheric "akashic record."

Or, like the Saint Padre Pio (d. 1968), sometimes spiritual masters intervene in human affairs using their higher bodies and later jostle those who benefited by reminding them of the help they had secretly received. Daoist masters are known to do this too but I'm using lots of examples from other spiritual cultivation traditions to stress the non-denominational characteristic of the path and also because there aren't too many stories available from modern Daoism.

Padre Pio even had a student, Sister Rita of the Holy Spirit (Cristina Montella), who would go with him in bilocation missions all over the world.[2] At one time Sister Rita (d. 1992) demonstrated how she could make her higher spiritual body materialize so that it became visible to Abbess Matilda of her convent, and then show how it could disperse instantly to disappear. The internet has stories about how she could appear and disappear at will while her ordinary body remained in her room, and how she could use it to travel to different places where it would behave just like an ordinary human body.

[2] "Christina Montella - Sister Rita of the Holy Spirit: 'The Little Girl of Padre Pio',"" Accessed February 5, 2024, https://luisapiccarreta.com/other-category/cristina-montella-sister-rita-of-the-holy-spirit-the-little-girl-of-padre-pio/.

Once you attain the highest two spiritual bodies you can readily emanate *nirmanakaya* projections, meaning that you can materialize a gross material body (*yang-shen*) at will and become visible to personalities that live on the gross material plane. For example, you can materialize in front of people, talk to them, shake hands with them and be of assistance in some way as would Padre Pio. There are, as an example, hundreds of recorded cases of the Carmelite nun Saint Therese of Lisieux (d. 1897) materializing on the battlefields of WWI in miraculous interventions to help French soldiers who invoked her name and prayed to her for intercession (see *Stronger Than Steel* by Les Poilus). She would materialize herself to heal horrific wounds, save people's lives, or simply offer comforting words of serenity to those who were about to die.

Now, devas and their masters masquerading as ghosts, demons, devils, spirits, deities, entities, aliens etcetera love arousing tremendous fear, anxiety or trepidation in people to stimulate their Yin Qi. Sleep paralysis is on rare occasions something they are responsible for doing. When you are on a drug trip and experience "alien entities" this too *is always the local devas and their teachers* masquerading as beings from another dimension or some other such nonsense. Devas, by nature, are always tricksters when dealing with people but love it because of the fun they get from a sense of superiority. Masters and their students will even show up at witchcraft events or occult rituals to mess with participants and stimulate their energies which, unfortunately, makes people mistakenly believe in the effectiveness of such evil rituals to everyone's detriment. Just because you have higher bodies doesn't mean you have common sense or higher ethics. Masters also love showing their students their power at taking over someone's mind and projecting thoughts, images or imaginary experiences such as out-of-body trips that are purely imaginative fantasies, and often make judgmental mistakes when doing this.

Enlightened beings in this world are basically humans who achieved the higher bodies and thereafter many love showing off their *nirmanakaya* energy skills for doing this or that such as controlling lower bodies, so they look for opportunities to do this. Where else are you going to use your powers? They love being tricksters such as by giving dreams to individuals (sometimes to help people, sometimes to trick people, or sometimes to frighten them with nightmares in order to temporarily raise their Yin Qi for health reasons). Devas love talking to people in useless conversations where they communicate absolutely useless nonsense in roundabout conversations that lead nowhere and prove nothing, and this communication happens by possessing our brain stem. Everyone at the deva stage can do this so it is no special power at all.

Because the astral subtle body of an Earth Immortal is the same as the etheric spirit body of ordinary people after they die (with the main difference being that it is *more purified* due to all the energy work that went into its attainment and thus it is equivalent to a Sakadagamin instead of Srotapanna Arhat), the subtle body is earth-bound and cannot reach more transcendental Pure Lands even though all the devas know they exist. Once you "get to heaven" all the secrets like this are revealed because you can see what's truly going on in the world in the lives of human beings.

When people die people they then learn that (1) reincarnation is real (because they actually see how the process occurs), (2) spiritual masters have multiple spiritual bodies that exist on various planes of existence, and we are capable of attaining the same bodies through spiritual cultivation, (3) those beings in the higher realms of existence are the ones who answer our prayers and are capable of ordinary powers in those realms that produce the "miracles" within our realm of existence, (4) intelligent life exists on other planets and in other different realms where many of those species are much more advanced than our own and some visit us frequently.

They also learn (5) that many spiritual doctrines taken as truths in their religion are wrong, and of course that (6) many things they believed about world events were false deceptions of propaganda promoted by various governments. History is not what people were lead to believe according to their religions, culture and governments.

Most of all they learn the truth that (7) man is basically just another internal part or process of the universe, Nature, without a beingness of his own (devoid of anything homogenous and self-arisen that constitutes a permanent self-core) and merged with the universe without mediation rather than an intrinsic, inherent independent, real sentient self. Humans arise in dependence on conditions so have no being (beingness) of their own and their existence flows with the waves or happenings of the universe. We simply hold onto the wrong notion that we are something different than the universe and that there is a difference between "me" and "experience," which means the I-self, physical body and the environment. (8) As a process or component of the universe we have within us an attribute called consciousness, mind, or Knowledge that is itself the product of the intersection of countless mental processes, and it is not an I-self ego entity but just a point of view. Knowledge is automatically being generated in a "sentient being" and this body of Knowledge is doing everything, such as thinking thoughts, processing perceptions, coming to conclusions and guiding the activities of the body within which it occurs. Knowledge is always just producing itself; there is no independent being, entity, soul or *atman* involved in producing Knowledge for it is the process of Knowledge itself that is producing Knowledge without an inherent soul being involved. Knowledge makes and experiences Knowledge so a Knowledge-making and understanding process is what experiences Knowledge in a self-contained feedback-process, and we call this sentience. A Knowledge-generating machine, process or object is experiencing

Knowledge by, in effect, talking to itself. No one is there, and yet there is understanding. Knowledge is talking to itself in a delusory circular fashion when there is comprehension because it takes itself as an entity, soul, I-self or knower in its self-talk.

One of the attributes to the processes of consciousness (8) is also the function to create an "imaginary" perceptual picture of the world from our physical senses. It is both incomplete in terms of dimensions and faulted with abbreviation (rounding) errors so that one can never experience the true nature of manifest reality as it truly is. Our sense perceptions and consciousness do not apprehend reality fully or correctly, but only in an abbreviated fashion that we can process, so they only produce false objective knowledge. In other words, what you perceive of the world is just a mind-only representation. It is an *imaginary picture* or similitude of the world that the brain concocts for you as a representation. The world really doesn't exist in the way it appears to us, and we only observe the universe in a certain way, rather than the way it really is, due to our existence stage of physical aggregation that has limitations to its sensory perceptions and capability for mental formations. We can never know for certain how it actually appears. Our views of the external world are merely illusory appearances created by our mind for that is what consciousness creates, as a process of sentient beings, in order to make the phenomena of living beings able to survive. To explain, (9) some animals have different sense organs than us or different effective ranges for their senses and perceive the world differently while some humans have more or less depth to their own perceptions (ex. color blindness) or even have synaesthesia such as seeing shapes when hearing music. Essentially, animals and human beings experience the world differently from one another and *there is no way to say which way is the correct way.* There is even (10) a time lag in mental processing so you never see the world as it is now but only some version of it is represented in your mind from milliseconds in the past because that's how long it takes for your brain to create an image. Furthermore, (11) our thinking processes of Knowledge-making are not just slow but often illogical in making conclusions, prone to shortcomings and faults (such as when you make a math error or misinterpret an optical illusion), and easily biased or distorted due to the influence of emotions, incorrect assumptions and false perspectives. So during the operations of consciousness it is Knowledge itself, rather than an I-self, that is experiencing thoughts (knowledge) and perceptions and producing a biased point of view that is often errant and certainly subjective rather than universal truth. Knowledge produces Knowledge, and the experiencer of the Knowledge is Knowledge as well without any true being, soul, spirit, personality, *atman* or *jiva* being involved.

Again, (12) we erroneously conclude that we are an inherent self-contained self, but our view of being an intrinsic self is a delusional (imaginary) set of thoughts automatically created as the basis of consciousness where this delusory perspective is built up during the infant-child stage of automatic conscious actions in order to make higher thinking possible. This I-thought gives you the sense that "you" are thinking "your" thoughts when in fact nothing of the kind is happening. Knowledge is just talking to itself without an intrinsic self being involved. You are just a process seamlessly connected to the universe without mediation and operating/functioning as your process is designed to do according to your anatomy and needs. The whole universe is getting into the act of composing you and having you think in a certain way, so the whole universe is the doer of you rather than an I-self you that you take yourself to be. During the process of thinking it is essentially the thought processes of consciousness itself that are doing the thinking rather than a separate, stable, eternal "I" or self that is an independent, inherent *atman*, soul, *jiva* or sentient being, and that process derives from your construction, upbringing, etc. with the whole universe getting into the act. Nevertheless that I-thought of being a self must be there for consciousness to operate while an inner subtle body needs to be there for there to be life but the thinking process itself, Knowledge, is automatically doing all the thinking and understanding without any real individual, self-entity, I, soul, self, *jiva* or *atman* being involved. It's just another process of the universe going on that is connected to and influenced by everything else but it "mistakenly" thinks it is something separate from the universe (Nature) and different from what it actually is. The self-concept is a fiction or falsity, a *Maya*, an illusion, a delusion. In Buddhism the self-sense or I-thought is the outcome of a complicated set of mental algorithms called the seventh consciousness while perceptual processing is performed by individual algorithms ("sense consciousnesses") for each sense organ, the sixth consciousness constitutes the mental algorithms for *thinking* and pulling the sensory outputs together into a single picture of the world, and the alaya consciousness includes our memories and all sorts of other mental forms (archetypes), mental algorithms, mental processes and interrelationships. The processes of consciousness, Knowledge, give rise to an assumed, apparent I-self that thinks it is the doer when that very I-self is just a mental product of myriad conditions that produce it within the processes of consciousness as a consequential result. Knowledge is the doer, not an I-self, and Knowledge itself is ultimately a product of the universe, Nature, which is the ultimate actual doer. Knowledge, when it provides understanding to itself, is just a process of Knowledge producing more Knowledge that also includes an illusion of understanding. There is conceptualization and intellectualization going on, but no being who is actually doing the thinking and producing the conceptions. Knowledge is doing the thinking and the understanding. Doing and thinking exist but there is no real doer or thinker within those processes, yet there is still doing, thinking, understanding and experiencing. In other words, Knowledge is experiencing Knowledge without there being an intrinsically real person in the process. There is understanding, but there is no being experiencing the understanding. *Knowledge is experiencing the understanding*, and so understanding is there for that Knowledge without there actually being a sentient doer within the process. There is just Knowledge doing everything. There is just Knowledge operating on its own without any inherent self being involved. Knowledge is not an I-self ego entity. Knowledge is just Knowledge – a point of view – a construction of a large set of self-referential mental operations and memories that constitute Knowledge. There is an apparent self involved in this process, a false self involved in Knowledge-making (that is itself just Knowledge) to make the processes of consciousness operate but there is no intrinsic permanent self or permanent process of knowing actually involved in all this. There is just a conditional process of knowing operating according to the rules of the process. Knowledge is knowing Knowledge without an intrinsic independent living being involved in that process, and yet understanding is there. It's the universe that is there. The self thinks it is calling the shots of thinking and doing the understanding when there is no true self-being behind those thoughts, and the assumed self cannot even control its mental realm as it wants. Knowledge without a self is doing all the doing. Knowledge is the doer of deeds, which also means that your attributes are not fixed. Furthermore, because this is what you are you have no reason to cling to any forms of suffering.

(13) Thus man, as a fluctuating energy process with a special attribute called consciousness (that other forms of inanimate Nature lack), acts as a channel of energy that shapes events through the ideas he holds. He is strongly influenced not just by his genes that produce his anatomy, his education, upbringing and training, local circumstances, his pondering and experiences etc. that fill his consciousness with thought patterns but also by universal forces such as those encapsulated in astrology (keyed to your birth time) and *feng-shui* (keyed to your location) or climate and so on. One way of looking at this is that you are controlled by the universe in so far as you constitute its body. You can read about all these factors and more in *Arhat Yoga*. However, (14) through practices such as visualization (see *Sport Visualization* or *Visualization Power*) you can fully imagine yourself using all five senses in the situations you want, and then persistently work to create a new future aimed at your goals through

your conduct and daily activities. You can actually create a new fortune other than what is already set to occur because of your current parameters of personality, psyche and behavioral conduct. *Liao Fan's Four Lessons, The Autobiography of Benjamin Franklin, How I Raised Myself From Failure to Success in Selling* (Bettger), *Quick Fast Done* (Bodri) and *Positivity* (Phil Hellmuth) tell you how to do this, which is why I always recommend them.

What you learn after your enlightenment as a Daoist is the same thing you learn after your enlightenment as a Confucian, Buddhist, Hindu, Jew, Moslem, Shinto, Christian, and so on, namely (1) your existence as having an independent, intrinsic, non-composite selfhood is a conceptual illusion, a false imagination, an errant belief, (2) all phenomena arise in dependence on other conditions so they also have no being (beingness) of their own. As conditions or forms that arise based on conditions they have no beingness on their own since they are dependent constructions whose existence depends on other factors (rather than them being self-so). Thus they are devoid (empty) of any core permanent self that stands/exists on its own. As it actually stands, all things are co-existent simultaneous arisings dependent on all other things for their existence. They appear or manifest because each is infinitely connected to all others with entanglement, and the whole is one single fabric that constitutes manifest reality. Individual phenomena are not only interdependent simultaneously arisings based on the existence or influences of everything else but interpenetrating, interfusing, mutually inclusive and all-pervasive within each other. This is because all points of the universe are entangled with every other point to make one whole. You consist of all things and they also consist of you (where one is in all and all are in one) because reality is one manifest unity of presentation within one single fabric substrate. (3) Therefore all phenomena are impermanent, non-homogenous, conditional constructions incessantly vibrating in a state of indeterminacy, all connected to one another through entanglement, and thus always changing while lacking anything permanent as an innate own-nature (permanent core) that can be grasped while you incorrectly see them as distinctly differentiated individual phenomena because of perceptual mistakes made by your mind. (4) You cannot ever correctly, objectively perceive the external world of dependent reality around you to know what it truly is (the ground of the world, or things in themselves) because there are limits to your sense organs and mental processing abilities, which are imperfect and inadequate. Hence all you can perceive is an apparitional, provisional mental reality (Mind-only) that is an illusion made by your mind. It is a similitude approximation or representation, yet that false *Maya* mental fabrication (together with other personal subjective biases) enables you to survive. You are an imperfect and inadequate mechanism that creates your own reality through patterns in your mind - thoughts. The ideas you choose to hold create your own reality. You are not designed for full spectrum facticity but for a level of fitness that temporarily enables your survival in the world for a period of time. (5) Besides your (false) sensory image of the world that you build up in your head (due to the consciousness algorithms for processing each type of sensory input) even your conceptual, "objective" *thinking operations* of consciousness (called the "sixth consciousness" in Buddhism) are fraught with logical errors, prejudicial biases and other imperfections so you can never create the one true perspective. This is why we must always observe our thoughts with clear mindfulness so that we can subject them to self-correction. (6) You're definitely imperfect, and you don't always function in the way you want to function as regards your thinking and behavior. You often get caught up in false stories your mind concocts (false perspectives) or ways of doing things that you cannot escape from. Sometimes you cannot control your behavior, or your mind, and in particular have troubles with transforming your emotions, eliminating mental afflictions, ending habits and maintaining perseverance and concentration (due to the algorithms of your alaya consciousness that rules memory and the structure and operation of countless mental operations and algorithms). You also create a *false image and identity* for yourself (due to the mental processes/algorithms that create your I-sense which Buddhism calls your "seventh consciousness") as well as false *limiting beliefs* that become difficult to unlearn even though they are untrue. Most important of all, (7) you cannot even mentally fathom or perceive the singular pure fundamental substratum of the universe that is the ground state of all being – what you truly are – and thus you can never know your real self, your true self-nature, your True Self. You can never perceive it through your senses (or any type of senses) or through any other way. No such thing as actual emptiness, nothingness, unmanifestness or qualitylessness can be experientially realized as Knowledge since thoughts are the antithesis of emptiness. You can make an image of the fundamental Self, the absolute substrate of everything, but then that would not be It or accurately represent It because any image has turned It into a phenomenon when it is a phenomena-less state. This is why Laozi said, "The Tao that can be named is not the eternal Tao."

You can read more about what the enlightened man or woman discovers in my books *Arhat Yoga* and *Correcting Zen* which, although it says "Zen" is actually the best guide available today for setting up Daoist practice routines.

In Buddhism the attainment of this independent subtle body - when you become an Earth Immortal - is called the "Stage of Attaining the Tao" or "crossing the stream." After you attain this independent spirit body, which is becoming a Srotapanna-Sakadagamin Arhat according to Buddhism, then and only then do you embark upon the "Stage of True Cultivation Practice" where you continue cultivating to attain the yet higher spiritual bodies of Arhatship until you finally reach the Great Golden Arhat, Immanence body or Tathagata body of Complete and Perfect Enlightenment.

This initial stage of becoming an Earth Immortal, which is attaining the subtle deva body composed of Qi energies while you are alive so that it is tethered to your living physical body, constitutes the initial stage of spiritual enlightenment or liberation. Its attainment is also called "crossing the shore," "ascending into Heaven," "the winged transformation," "liberation from the corpse," "becoming twice born," the "fruit of internal alchemy, "crossing the stream" or "entering the stream." It only constitutes the initial stage of the ranks of higher spiritual attainments.

The Spirit Immortal (*shenxian*) is the next spiritual stage of attainment after the stage of becoming an Earth Immortal. In Christian terms the Earth Immortal stage (of Qi) is like becoming an angel while the stage of becoming a Spirit Immortal (composed of Shen) is like becoming an Archangel. The Spirit Immortal's body arises out of the matrix of the Earth Immortal's spirit body just as the deva body, composed of Qi, arises out of the human shell when we die or succeed at spiritual cultivation. However, the body of the Spirit Immortal is composed of Shen energy that is one step transcendentally higher than Qi. This body is equivalent to the Causal body of Hinduism or Anagamin stage of Arhatship and is also known as the Mental body, Wisdom body, Mantra body, body of vibrations, *pranava deha*, man's spirit, Grace body, or purified illusory body in other traditions. All traditions have a name for it since it is a non-denominational achievement; regardless of your spiritual path we all cultivate to attain the very same spiritual bodies to progress out of the realm of matter forever.

The Spirit Immortal stage is also equivalent to the third and fourth Bodhisattva *bhumis* within Buddhism. It is also referred to as the conception skandha in Buddhism and *manomaya* ("mind-stuff") *kosha* in Hinduism, and is the stage of an Anagamin Arhat. When the Thai Buddhist monk Ajahn Mun (d. 1849) announced that he had become an Anagami at age 43 it meant that he had reached the stage of becoming a Spirit Immortal.

In Sikhism the rank of becoming a Spirit Immortal is the third level of development or sphere of spiritual attainment that corresponds to the *Saram Khand* "Realm of Spiritual Efforts." It is hard to pass through this level to attain the next higher Supra-Causal, Clear Light body, Dharma body, Rainbow body, or Wisdom Light Body of Buddhahood, which is the stage of the full Arhat or Daoist Celestial Immortal where one's new transcendental body is essentially entirely free of the lower realms of matter. That is why Buddhism says it belongs to the Formless Realm. When you achieve this body you become free of the lower realms forever.

The Celestial Immortal (*tianxian*) in Daoism is that exact same spiritual body achievement and is thus equivalent to a Buddhist Arhat. Buddhism, Daoism and Hinduism explain that those who attain this body become officials overseeing the human realm and administer various management affairs. As stated, the Supra-Causal body is also known as the Clear Light body, Wisdom Light body, *jnana deha*, Dharma body, Rainbow body, Buddha body, Arhat body, and so on. It is composed of what Daoism calls Later Heavenly Energy (Qi). It is "one with the universal life" comprising the lower levels of energy, meaning that it can sense the happenings in all the lower energy realms of Nature because its energy realm interpenetrates them at a very high stage of refinement. Hence it can be a "witness of the universe" able to freely hear and comprehend the minds of lower sentient beings (whose thoughts are composed of lower energies readily accessible to this body's more transcendental level), and able to access their knowledge and wisdom.

When you recite a mantra or prayer asking for help your plea is heard by Buddhas at this and the next higher level of being.

When someone attains this body we say "their wisdom opens up" because they no longer need to enter into someone and read their neurons to know their thoughts (as is necessary for subtle-bodied devas and Causal-bodied individuals, whose attainment stages are orthodoxly called the second and third dhyana in Buddhism or Earth and Spirit Immortals in Daoism). Rather, they can sense thoughts in the environment as they happen, or they can use *nirmanakaya* emanations to access the brains of individuals in order to know their memories and thinking, or to send them energy or give them thoughts or sensations. Krishna, for instance, at one time caused Durvasa Muni and all his men who were visiting the Pandavas to feel satisfied of their hunger through such *nirmanakaya* emanations.

The Celestial Immortals and higher can even do this for animals such as snakes, parrots, dogs, cats, horses, tigers, elephants, etcetera which is why enlightened sages can communicate with animals. The Hindu sage Ramana Maharshi (d. 1950), for instance, is famous for being able to communicate with animals and in China I once heard of a Daoist master who was always communicating with rabbits. With training, all of the higher sages can do this by emanating *nirmanakaya* to enter into and give animals thoughts and feelings, which is why they can tame them. You can even do this to deceive people and make it seem that an animal (like a mule) can talk, which is just the *nirmanakaya* talking rather than an actual animal speaking. Masters use such tricks all the time to convert people using miracles.

You can emanate *nirmanakaya* projections to make people see non-existent things by giving them imaginary visions. For instance, they might perceive someone floating in the air when that vision is only inside their consciousness that has this false picture then overlapping on top of the images constructed of an outer world. Basically you can make people see things that are not there. I've visited many Daoist temples in China where I would see etheric forms in the environment that were simply fake *Mara* projections in my consciousness because a local spiritual master wanted to try out his skills of projection by overlaying his powers of visualization on top of the workings of my consciousness. Whenever you see any type of vision it is due to an enlightened person putting those images in your mind, which is usually done by also giving you attendant thoughts that interpret them along the way he/she wants but you cannot tell that this interpretation is not yours either.

Shakyamuni Buddha spoke about ten large classes of *Mara* delusion and deception that spiritual masters project into people's minds within the *Mara* Demon section of the *Surangama Sutra*, which you should read. You might see a dragon in the environment, or a flying celestial maiden, or gigantic Buddha in the sky, an ancient ghost in a graveyard, or troll underneath the ground and all sorts of images that someone wants to conjure up as a joke, or sometimes to help you. You might see the stars of the Daoist Big Dipper practice in someone's chest, or an Immortal with a fan-furnace within his *dantian*, or a human master's body or face might even seem to somehow change in shape (as an etheric superimposition) when you view it.

You should laugh when you hear people say that they saw someone's face etherically change for a moment into that of a lizard, thus making that person believe they must be shape-shifting reptiles. Everyone with powers wants to practice on humans so they play tricks by overlaying images on whatever you are already seeing with your visual consciousness whereas these superimpositions are really just *mara* (delusion) projections in your brain being overlaid on top of whatever you are normally seeing. There is a tendency for ordinary, non-enlightened devas to just want to display their powers to their friends as a joke and decide to use you; none of them care a stich about you which is why many strange visions and events typically happen at hotels where there is a constant flow of guests that come and go without belonging to the local population. The enlightened ancient native American Indian masters love projecting *nirmanakaya* of scary humanoid creatures (skinwalkers, werewolves, pale crawlers, wendingos, black-eyed children, jinn, etc.) that instantly appear and then disappear, thus demonstrating their shape-shifting skills to deva students while greatly frightening onlookers who need Yin Qi stimulation (such as soldiers or hunters who cultivate too much Yang Qi or people who are sick and need a spike in their Yin Qi).

You can also project a *nirmanakaya* into someone and take control of their body so that they are frozen and cannot move, such as in night paralysis. Of course, you can even do this to someone who is standing and engaged in some type of physical movement. The Hindu Bhagavan Nityananda once froze in the air the arms of a thief who was assaulting him, and the Greek Orthodox Saint Arsenios the Cappadocian (d. 1924), who was the spiritual father of Paisios of Athos, was often known to freeze the movements of Turkish soldiers about to do the Greeks harm. This was done by emanating *nirmanakaya* to go into them to freeze their movements. By inserting thoughts within them through *nirmanakaya* emanations many saints have also brought thieves to their senses.

Many people suffer paralysis in bed at night and it is often the work of the local enlightened beings who are teaching lessons to deva students. During those times people suffer great fright, which is a way of raising their Yin Qi so it can be refreshed, and *nirmanakaya* emanations are also commonly used to arouse joy, courage or confidence for people who pray for it in need or any other emotion that the originating master has practiced to develop. Sometimes they "put words into your mouth" where you know the one speaking is not you so that those words can help others.

"Wisdom" means "understanding," and because you can know the minds of others and understand their thoughts automatically when you attain the highest bodies your wisdom will increase by leaps and bounds as you learn new things due to these spiritual body attainments. The Supra-Causal or Wisdom body is referenced as the volition *skandha* in Buddhism, *vijnanamaya* ("wisdom") *kosha* in Hinduism, and it corresponds to the *Karam Khand* "Realm of Grace" of Sikhism. It is the full Arhat stage that can finally project *nirmanakaya* emanations that are energy copies of that body. When a master can perform bilocation and be seen by others it is because he has attained this stage of achievement.

This is what a master normally uses to give thoughts to individuals, such as the urge to give to charity or even the urge to have sex with one's spouse so that an individual who is ready can reincarnate as their baby. In the Chinese classic *Journey to the West*, which was supposedly written by a Daoist, there is a section where a magic Six Eared Macaque impersonates Sun Wukong and no one can tell the two apart except for Buddha. The meaning is that when a *nirmanakaya* possesses your consciousness then your thinking will seem like it is yours but actually belongs to the *nirmanakaya* emanation of an enlightened spiritual being yet you won't be able to tell the difference.

For instance, the Hindu sage Neem Karoli Baba (d. 1973) was commonly known for being seen in several places simultaneously, which means he achieved this stage at the minimum. When you can carry things from one place to another it is even higher than the stage of just being seen as a tangible entity, which Daoism calls a *yang-shen*, and there are Daoist stories to this effect where a master and his students were challenged to go to a faraway location, pick a fruit and return with it. In this story you should ignore the mention of spirit animals since they are fictitious. Only the highest bodies can take an item from one location to another while the lower spiritual bodies cannot do so:

> The Tang Emperor Xuanzong counted several famous Taoists among his closest advisors. They were Zhang Guolao – one of the Eight Immortals – Ye Fashan, and Luo Gongyuan.
> One time the emperor wanted to test the spiritual and

magical skills of these three men. He invited them to his court and said, "I have heard that fruits are ripening in the southern province of Jiannan. I wonder if the three of you could go there and bring back some delicious fruit for me." Xuanzong deliberately devised this task to test the Taoists' ability to travel in spirit, for Jiannan was several thousand miles away from the capital.

The three men bowed and took up the challenge. The next day they gathered in the hall of the imperial Taoist shrine. Zhang Guolao said to the emperor, "By evening I will have the fruits here for you." Ye Fashan said, "Your Majesty, I can get them to you by midafternoon." Luo Gongyuan said nothing. He simply sat down on the ground, took off his shoes, and smiled. Incense was lit, and the three men went into a trance. The emperor reclined on his chair and waited.

The noon hour passes. Then it was midafternoon. Ye Fashan failed to produce the fruits as promised. The day went on. By evening Zhang Guolao had come out of his trance empty-handed. Then as the last light of the day disappeared, Luo Gongyuan opened his eyes and clapped his hands. A bowl of fruits from Jiannan materialized in his hands.

Surprised that he had come up empty-handed, Ye Fashan asked Gongyuan, "I was first to arrive at the orchards. How did you manage to get the fruits when I could not?"

"You must have used your magic to obstruct us," said Zhang Guolao jokingly.

"Yes, tell us what your trick was," added the emperor.

Luo Gongyuan replied, "It was no trick, Your Majesty. You see, we were all in the orchards of Jinnan. Fashan projected his spirit out of his body and went to the orchard in his mind. That's why he was the first to arrive. However, while he was able to pick the fruits in spirit, he could not return with them corporeally (this is the stage of an Earth or Spirit Immortal). Guolao, on the other hand, was able to send a double of his corporeal body to the orchard on his magical donkey (this is a Celestial Immortal). However, the fruits were lost when he mounted his spirit animal to return. I was able to procure the fruits because I not only went in my corporeal body but returned without the aid of a spirit animal."[3]

---

[3] *Tales of the Dancing Dragon*, Eva Wong, (Shambhala Publications, Boston, 2007), pp. 119-120.

Sometimes a *tudigong* (local protect god, which is basically a deva who attained enlightenment), *cheng huang ye* (city protect god), *sheji* (state protect god), or spiritual master who attained enlightenment will even generate a *nirmanakaya* emanation, appear to people and offer physical help of some type for their situation, or deliver some type of message or a warning to help prevent catastrophe. People normally cannot recognize their status as celestial and universal masters but afterwards think about the situation and consider this an encounter with an angel. If the individual is their spiritual master then they know it is just one of his or her *nirmanakaya* emanations but often other masters will project emanations that pretend to be deities or spiritual greats of the past. No one ever wonders how they knew it was a famous personage they never met, but it's because they projected thoughts of recognition inside you as well.

Since I mentioned the *tudigong, sheji* and *cheng huang ye,* which do exist for every locale, I want to bring up a disturbing development at temples due to the invention of electricity and electronics. That trend is the constant blaring of recorded music at a temple or place of worship, which is more of an obnoxious advertisement than an act of respect or reverence for those who might help us. If you were a deity would you want loud music to be continuously blaring at your "holy spot" all the time with blinking lights that are an eyesore? The practice is disrespectful and shows that people do not truly believe that spirits or deities attend those locations, but they do. The practice of blaring loud spiritual music at temples and flashing lights should cease. A temple should be a place of tranquility rather than an advertisement for commerce or donations.

In Buddhism the Celestial Immortal stage of Daoism is equivalent to the fourth dhyana attainment, 7th and 8th Bodhisattva bhumi, and is recognized as the stage of a full Arhat. This spiritual body achievement that resides on a very high plane of existence (which of course we cannot measure) is the classical meaning of "becoming enlightened" even though attaining the Earth Immortal achievement is technically enlightenment too, but just junior enlightenment. The everlasting and imperishable (long-lived) body of the Celestial Immortal is the attainment that people normally think of when they hear the word "enlightenment" or "immortality" or "escaping the lower realms of incarnation," yet the attainment of this transcendental body (which is free of all coarser levels of matter and energy so that it consequently exhibits a tremendous flexibility of shape) is still considered "*nirvana* with a remainder." That's because it is capable of "formlessness" due to shape-shifting yet imperfect since there is one remaining body attainment left that is a yet higher level of physical purification.

People always think that becoming enlightened is to experience some mystical mental state of purity, but *it actually means the attainment of these higher spiritual bodies* where your mind becomes more clear with each new body because the anatomical basis is closer to pure energy. For various reasons, the masters of most traditions, except for Daoism, have chosen to continuously misdirect people into thinking that enlightenment is simply a mental attainment of some type of special consciousness. I don't like deceptive misdirection so I'm spilling the beans so that your Daoist practice won't go astray. You can meditate all you want and will never generate a spiritual body. Try mentally projecting one and it won't happen either. You must do inner energy work, and then the process has to be taken over by countless spiritual beings that will continue working on you around the clock for twelve or more years of purifying transformations.

Tibetan Buddhism tells you clearly that emptiness meditation won't win you enlightenment even if you do it for ten eons, inner energy work won't get you there either, and so you must do both. You must meditate AND perform inner *nei-gong* exercises to attain the Tao.

The Buddhist sutras record that at one time Shakyamuni Buddha told a man that there is no God, and at another time he told a different man that there is a God. He explained to his students that each was told what he needed to hear to help him move forward. Furthermore, the Buddhist *Lotus Sutra* tells us a story about lying to children in order to save them from a burning house from which they must escape, and that compassionate motivation is the reason for the deception. Well, the same reasoning applies for presenting enlightenment as some type of mental realization which leads to people practicing hours of "emptiness meditation" or "mental watching." These are the easiest times for spiritual beings to help transform your Qi since they are not then fighting your Qi currents that instantly respond to your thoughts. If you are "empty" or "detached" then there are less errant Qi currents to fight against when devas use their own powers to move your Qi to help you.

You will certainly pass through many mental experiences when cultivating the spiritual path of Daoism or any other tradition, but the only true enlightenment is when you attain a higher spiritual body. In many stories where a master is "sitting in samadhi" without moving it is simply that his higher spiritual bodies are traveling around and we call that "deep meditation" to mislead people. The masters of Sufism directly tell people that. For instance, Sufi Sheikh Muhammed Hisham Kabbani stated clearly in *The Hierarchy of Saints* that the enlightened often travel from their locations, leaving behind their bodies, to help people who need help and their bodies remain motionless during their absence so you should not disturb them.

Incidentally, Sufism says that we have a gross body, subtle body, Mental body, Universal body and Shiva-atma or Paramatma body which accord with the stages of Daoism. Similarly, according to Sufi theology you must engage in an "unveiling" or "tearing off of veils" to see God's face and experience unity with Allah, which refers to casting off lower body shells/sheaths to attain the most primal form of man (the *atman*, Immanence body, or stage of the Great Golden

Arhat or Universal Immortal that is the highest core of humans). If people commonly knew that a master had spiritual bodies that travel around and can know things they would ask for this and that and put him under all sorts of burdens so everyone keeps this capability secret, and the fact that they are enlightened is kept secret too.

Now the body of the Celestial Immortal resides at the level of the "Formless Realm" mentioned in Buddhism since it is free of all lower forms of dense matter in the "Form" and "Desire Realms." Some schools call it a Wisdom light body or Rainbow body to denote the fact that its compositional essence is like light that can be split into many parts just as a rainbow appears from white light that passes through a prism. This body can twist and turn in all sorts of shapes without restriction, which enables it to create all sorts of energy movements and effects within any human body it enters including vibrations and sensations of various types.

In particular to the processes of spiritual cultivation, masters also learn how to control its Yin or Yang aspects so that they can supply people with the feelings of kundalini energy that can be hot or cold. The strange currents of hot and cold energy that people feel inside themselves during cultivation practices are typically due to a Celestial Immortal (Buddha) or higher beings helping them move their energies with his own. The phenomenon of *shaktipat* (where a guru "sends you his energy") is exactly this – a *nirmanakaya* emanation sent inside you to move your Qi/Prana by moving its own energy within yours and then affecting yours through the friction of contact. Some masters tap you on the shoulder when doing this, or point at you, wave a fan, shout a word, or perform all sorts of other non-essential movements to indicate, "Hey, I caused this in you." You can read about various masters from other traditions using different techniques to do this but they are all doing the same thing in disguise.

When you perform Daoist practices and feel energies moving inside you this is rarely due to the activation of *your* energy. It is usually an Immortal's energy moving inside you who in kindness has decided to help you by using one of his many body doubles (*nirmanakaya* emanations) to enter your body to help you purify your Qi. Daoists prepare you for understanding and accepting this fact, rather than have you recoil in fear when you encounter this, through fake stories about all sorts of deities living within your body so you get used to the fact that other beings will enter inside you. However, no one lives in your body, but various masters do enter your body temporarily to give deva students lessons on how the brain forms thoughts, how your internal organs operate, and for helping you rotate your inner Qi so that the friction of rotation will eventually purify the vital energy that is the material stuff of your inner spiritual body.

Your spirit body of Qi leaves your corpse upon death, but those individuals who have sufficiently cultivated during their life time have increased its purity to some extent and thus live longer in heaven than ordinary human beings, thus giving them valuable time to cultivate in the earthly heavenly realm. The Supra-Causal body of which we are speaking lives such a long life that this is where the term "Immortal" originally comes from.

This Supra-Causal, Celestial Immortal, Arhat, Universal body or Buddha body can generate energy copies of itself, called *nirmanakaya* emanations, just as light can be split apart by a prism and they can be projected as independent entities in the world to perform specific deeds. When you can physically see them as *tangible manifestations* rather than just invisible energy manifestations the Chinese call them *yang-shen* emanations or *fen-shen* body-doubles. A large portion of the Buddhist *Ksitigarbha (Earth Store) Bodhisattva Sutra* is about how Ksitigarbha Bodhisattva continuously sends countless emanations of himself out to help all sentient beings in all sorts of ways. The most common way of using *nirmanakaya* is by giving people thoughts and warnings but most people tend to ignore these emanations within our minds.

When you finally are able to attain the Celestial Immortal's body by cultivating the internal energies of your Causal body's existence you will live as a body vehicle whose structure doesn't deteriorate quickly because of the long-lived nature of its compositional elements (referred to as "light" or Later Heavenly Energy). Therefore it is said you will live practically forever as an "immortal," which just means *extremely* long-lived with the further connotation of escaping the lower realms of suffering forever. When it must die this etheric body is so high that it can carry strong memories of its life into a new incarnation, which even happens to some extent when lower level Arhats are reborn, thus *ensuring a type of continuity, unbroken continuum or immortality* from an entirely different aspect of deathlessness. With the attainment of the Supra-Causal body, or Celestial Immortal achievement, you escape further incarnations in the lower realms because of your transcendental physical composition that is absent of unpurified matter that transcends the lower realms.

Being free from the lower planes of existence because your energetic existence transcends all matter and energy within those realms, and now understanding oneself as belonging to the comprehensive unity of all things in the one soup of manifest reality (an attainee realizes that there is no such thing as a separate independent existence because the universe is one thing and you are It!), at this stage one recognizes that the universe of parts is actually a single fabric and they are like a tiny colored splot (portion) within it that is merged with everything else. One becomes free of ignorance, delusions, and misunderstandings as regards the origins and evolution of life because they can see events of the far past and events due to happen in the future since those events have an etheric pattern already existing in the higher planes of the universe. Thus one becomes emancipated from *Maya* (delusions and ignorance) *because one understands*. One becomes emancipated from the lower realms *because one's body composition transcends.* Devoid of ignorance and emancipated from the lower realms that one can still view, a sage realizes his eternal existence in the infinite ocean of Shakti as Shakti itself. You are the universe, and at the stage of personhood you are just a vibrating process within a single universe of vibrating fields and energies.

There is yet a higher stage of Immortals corresponding to the Great Golden Arhat, Immanence body or Tathagata's Stage of Perfect and Complete Enlightenment that is *nirvana without remainder.* Daoism says that this highest possible body, which is the true man of Daoism or *atman-jiva* of Hinduism within the hierarchy of bodily sheaths, is composed of Primordial Heavenly Energy. This attainment, which corresponds to the 9th and 10th bhumi stages of the Tathagata or Immanence body, is considered Complete and Perfect Enlightenment, which is the stage of becoming a Great Golden Arhat. In Islam it corresponds to the *insan al-kamil* or perfect, universal man. This is the Shiva-atma or Paramatma body of Sufism too. In Daoism this is the stage of the Universal Immortal.

This spiritual body arises out of the Celestial Immortal body after sufficient cultivation and is composed of Primordial Heavenly Energy – a term for the highest energy level we can reach to compose a body of existence. This highest body attainment is comprised of the most fundamental energies of the universe where a body formation is still possible because linkages can still exist between its rarified components. At this stage it is said that one does not hear, smell or see but becomes sight, sound and smell simultaneously (because through the mind of this level of energetic beingness one can instantly know what goes on *within the lower vibratory realms,* thus one is said to be all-pervading). Buddhism calls this the interchangeability of the sense consciousnesses.

This body is referred to as the consciousness skandha in Buddhism, the *anandamaya* ("bliss") *kosha* in Hinduism, the Stage of No More Learning (No More Training or Non-Practice) in Tibetan Buddhism, the stage of God consciousness in Kashmir Saivism, the 10th Bodhisattva *bhumi* or Stage of Complete and Perfect Enlightenment in Buddhism, the *Sach Khand* "Realm of Truth" attainment in Sikhism and the stage of "*nirvana* without remainder" because it is said that no higher body vehicles are possible. The truest human being, released from all its shell, *skandhas* or veils, now stands alone. This is the *real man* of Daoism, *perfect man* of Islam, and *true man* of Zen lore.

Hence you can see that the Daoist stages for Immortals correspond to the Arhat stages of Buddhism and the five eyes (of five bodies) mentioned in the *Diamond Sutra* of Buddhism (human, deva, wisdom, dharma, Buddha eyes). If all this information is truly real then it MUST BE the case that we have these correspondences in our world's genuine religions:

Human body = Human Immortal
Deva body = Earth Immortal = Srotapanna & Sakadagami Arhat =
    Angel
Wisdom body = Spirit Immortal = Anagamin Arhat = Causal body =
    Archangel
Dharma body = Celestial Immortal = Arhat = Supra-Causal body
Buddha body = Universal Immortal = Tathagata = Great Golden
    Arhat = Immanence body

The attainment of any new body is called breaking through a *skandha* in Buddhism, purifying a *kosha* in Hinduism, and dropping a veil in Sufism. Each new body is a new stage of Arhatship. In Hinduism the Daoist Immortal corresponds to individuals who have attained their subtle, Causal, Supra-Causal and Immanence bodies, which means individuals who have purified and cultivated all their *koshas* or bodies and finally reached the highest and purest body core possible for our existence. They also, as stated, correspond to the Arhats of Buddhism known as "*lohan*" in Chinese whereas Immortals are called "*xian*." The ranks of the Daoist Immortals correspond to stages of spiritual ascension across the world's religions precisely because they are all non-denominational ranks attained by the practitioners of *all religions*. When you think about it, for this to be real it *has* to be the case.

Now, it has already been explained that you enter the Stage of True Cultivation Practice after you become an Earth Immortal. Upon this accomplishment you then start cultivating the energy of this subtle body, which becomes your new center of life, to attain the next higher Causal body – the stage of the Spirit Immortal – that is composed of an even more transcendental form of energy that Daoism calls Shen, or spirit. You should think of Shen as the life force of bodies made of Qi just as you think of Qi as the life force of human earth bodies.

The process of working as an Earth Immortal to become a Spirit Immortal is called "refining Qi to attain Shen." It means working to attain the Causal body stage of the Anagamin Arhat, which is the stage of the Spirit Immortal, and afterwards you start working on refining/cultivating the energy of that body to achieve the Dharma body, Supra-Causal body, Rainbow body or Clear Light body of the Celestial Immortal that is the stage of the full Arhat. Daoism calls this process "refining Spirit (Shen) to attain *Emptiness* (the Supra-Casual body of the Celestial Immortal)." The "Emptiness" name for the Supra-Causal body means that it is free of all vestiges of coarse matter from the lower realms of existence whereas the Anagamin "Spiritual Immortal" body still had some impure energy-matter elements even though known as the "pure illusory body" in Tibetan Buddhism. These lower bodies of the Terrestrial (Earth) and Spiritual Immortal are still considered "illusory bodies" because they are not the highest core of the human being that Daoism calls the *real man*.

Finally, the vital energy of this Supra-Casual Buddha body, or

Celestial Immortal body, is cultivated to attain the Immanence body, or highest real man of existence that is his ultimate core. This final attainment constitutes the Stage of Complete and Perfect Enlightenment, the tenth Bodhisattva *bhumi*, the Stage of No More Learning, or final spiritual liberation.

The entire spiritual path of higher spiritual attainments is exactly this. You might also consider it a path of accumulating merit in this life through good deeds and a purification of your mind and behavior. If you are not a virtuous human being you will not obtain the help of hundreds of higher beings working on purifying your body by producing continuous microcosmic-macrocosmic circulations inside you so that you can achieve the next stage of attainment. They also will not give power to someone who is evil or an asshole. Therefore you must always be working on elevating your personality, mental patterns, habit energy, conduct and skills so that you become a better human being and deserve enlightenment. You want to create the habit of helping others and improving the world so that you create a better foundation and fortune for yourself in a subsequent life to achieve the enlightenment of becoming a Daoist Immortal.

People thus endlessly go round and round the cycles of reincarnation, which is administered by sages, Immortals or Buddhas (however you want to word enlightened humans) so that people's etheric bodies do not disintegrate, until individuals are finally virtuous enough and attain the purified subtle body so that they can then start working to cultivate the nearly immortal, indestructible highest spiritual body.

Daoism has a set of phrases that summarize the cultivation steps required for attaining the various bodies, thus illustrating what has been explained. According to traditional Daoist beliefs the practice of spiritual cultivation can be divided into five steps:

Transforming grain (food) into Jing,

Transforming Jing into Qi *(Lian Jing Hua Qi)*,
Transforming Qi into spirit *(Lian Qi Hua Shen)*,
Returning spirit to emptiness *(Lian Shen Huan Xu)*, and
Combining emptiness with the Tao, *(Lian Xu He Dao)*.

A rough way of translating this is that you eat grain (food) to maintain your life (Jing), and then "Jing transforms into Qi, Qi transforms into Shen, Shen transforms into Emptiness (the Clear Light body of an Arhat empty of the lower realms of form-based existence), and you must go beyond this stage to attain a Tathagata's body that is oned with the primordial energies of the universe." That is when one "becomes universal," which is the stage of the Universal Immortal. This is someone who perceives the energies that form the universe and can sense that those energies penetrate their own body, thus realizing that everything is seamlessly interconnected inseparably with a single fabric of the manifest universe. Hence, a Daoist classic states, "Perfecting (refining) one's Jing results in perfecting (refining) one's Qi, and perfecting (refining) one's Qi results in perfecting one's Shen" although this only refers to the lower levels of achievement.

A sage often starts teaching upon his or her attainment of the Supra-Causal body, which is the fourth dhyana attainment of Buddhism equivalent to a full Arhat or Celestial Immortal. In India a student who achieves full Arhatship (which usually happens around forty years old or earlier) is then, upon that achievement, often asked to take over a tradition. Upon the attainment of the Tathagata body a sage typically says things to followers like "my presence is always here with you."

When Daoists say that "Jing (the physical body grown from semen) transforms into Qi (the deva body), Qi transforms into Shen (the Causal body), Shen transforms into Emptiness (the Supra-Causal body of the Formless Realm) and you must achieve a higher stage where the essence of an Emptiness (light) body unifies with the fundamental substratum of Nature," this basically means that one spiritual body arises out of another. You refine the energy of each body until it differentiates into higher and lower aspects, and after sufficient purification efforts the higher aspect breaks free of the lower shell to become an independent new life and the new center of your existence.

The attainment of the Tathagata's Immanence body is composed of what Daoism calls "Primordial Heavenly Energy," which is the highest stage of corporality we can reach where this body's composition is closest in purity or refinement to the ground state of the universe, namely its fundamental substratum. Of course it is not the stage of the fundamental stratum because then it wouldn't exist. It is the most primal form of man we can achieve, the real man encased within all these energy shells, and is considered his perfect, universal form that can be reached through the practices and process of spiritual cultivation. It is the true center of the self in the midst of conditions. If we could go higher than that would be our highest self.

Thus the subtle body of Qi ("impure illusory body") arises out of our physical body of matter to make one a Daoist Earth Immortal. While working on purifying the inner subtle body it is termed by Daoism the "holy embryo," "holy fetus," "golden embryo" or "embryo of sainthood." There is no small embryo inside you. It is just that the subtle energy matrix of your body is as yet unpurified, unrefined or undeveloped so the term "embryo" is used.

The two bodies, the human physical body and the subtle body, remain tethered to each other upon this initial stage of enlightenment and Buddhism calls the transitional place where the physical matter and higher Qi energy are tethered to each other *ching-se*, which means clear matter or pure matter. You can see pictures of these two bodies attached to one another in the *Xingming Guizhi* (*Principles of Balanced Cultivation of Inner Nature and Vital Force*).

Next, the Causal body of Shen energy ("purified illusory body") arises out of the etheric body of Qi to make one a Spiritual Immortal. Now three bodies are tethered to one another with the Spiritual Immortal body connected to the terrestrial Earth Immortal deva body that is connected to the human physical body. An organism now exists that has multiple bodies composed of different energies and frequencies tethered to one another where each resides on a different plane of existence.

Next the Supra-Causal body of Later Heavenly Prana arises out of the Causal body to make one a Celestial Immortal that is tethered to the Spirit Immortal body and so on. This body can generate *nirmanakaya*, and the next higher Immanence (Great Golden Arhat) body can generate *nirmanakaya* that can themselves generate *nirmanakaya* emanations. Wow! A picture of this is found in the famous Daoist classic, *The Secret of the Golden Flower*, while Tibetan Buddhism also has many illustrations on the way this works. In fact, each of the *nirmanakaya* emanation bodies of the Celestial Immortal or Supra-Causal body can be purified enough to attain the stage of the Universal Immortal too! When you are going through the twelve years of kundalini transformations to attain the first spiritual body attainment many masters will visit just so that their own higher *nirmanakaya* emanations are simultaneously worked on as well in order that those *nirmanakaya* can achieve a higher degree of purification.

On the spiritual path you cultivate the internal vital energy or life force energy of each body, that energy becomes purified in the sense that a higher, more refined energy becomes differentiated from and then separates from a "less pure" energy residue (which is just the lower body) due to frictional churning, and then with sufficient separation and purification it can arise out of the denser body as an independent spiritual life. Every time a new body arises it is still attached to the lower body out of which it arose and all the bodies linked together are called one's *sambhogakaya*. It basically makes you a sentient being with multiple bodies, of different energy compositions, and these bodies on different planes of existence are attached to one another making a single organism that is thus no longer really human because of your anatomy and because the highest body becomes the new "I" center of your existence.

After you become an Earth Immortal it requires about three years for each new higher body attainment. Thus after the attainment of the astral deva body - which takes about twelve to thirteen years of active around-the-clock kundalini transformations where your Qi is constantly rolling around within your body to purify its energies through frictional contact - it requires another three years to attain the Causal body (Spirit Immortal attainment), and then three years for the Supra-Causal (Celestial Immortal) attainment and so on.

Some masters go into secluded retreat during the first of these three-year periods so that they can leave their bodies and travel around without being disturbed, or so that they can avoid other individuals possessing it while away and inadvertently causing troubles. In their later years many enlightened masters die from cancer because their higher spiritual bodies spend too much time away from their physical body. Because of prolonged periods of insufficient Qi (due to that absence) and then not repairing themselves upon return cancer becomes a common possibility. However, daily deep breathing methods to clear their body's Qi, and ivermectin (with food) together with fenbendazole might be a possible remedy to help such masters, along with other alternative modalities (see *Super Cancer Fighters* for information on Essiac tea, low dose naltrexone, etc.).

Humans who attain the subtle body attainment reach the Srotapanna-Sakadagami Arhat stage ("stream-enterer") of enlightenment, thus becoming an angel (deva) or *Homo Deus*, while devas who start out at this level (such as those born in Heaven) and start cultivating their body to a higher stage of purity reach the more purified Sakadagami stage of the Arhats but still remain just devas. This is just a higher stage of subtle body purification (the third and fourth Bodhisattva *bhumis*) whose attainment means that upon death the deva will, due to his purification, definitely be reborn in the realm of devas (Heaven) rather than the human realm, which to most of them is a great relief. If you were a virtuous person during your human life and cultivated spiritual practices then your Qi will be somewhat purified. Therefore virtuous humans in the afterlife will have a greater chance to be reborn in Heaven instead of returning to the material world.

When a human dies they become a subtle-bodied spirit or deva, and we can think of this as becoming an angel. Some humans with improper habit energies, bad minds and the tendencies for evil deeds are termed *asuras* and they always have to be reborn as humans again. The Koran contains many sections on *jinn* that are basically devas, such as *asuras*, and even higher enlightened human beings who use their superpowers to mess with physical human beings.

Devas are tricksters and play mind and energy games all the time on humans. If you were invisible to everyone with an etheric body that could travel anywhere quickly, could know everyone's secret activities and hidden thoughts, and saw all the stupid things people do you would look down on them with condescension and be tempted to use your powers to mess with them because it would be fun. That's a *jinn, asura* or deva that is basically just fucking with people for entertainment purposes, although sometimes it is for good reasons.

As a Daoist, you should throughout your life be working on cultivating the purification of your inner Qi through cultivation exercises. You should be cultivating to purify your inner energy through frictional Qi churning work. Then, even if you don't succeed in attaining enlightenment during this life then after death you will be far ahead of everyone else who didn't cultivate because you will have purified the Qi (Prana) energy of your subtle body to some degree. All devas within our earthly plane are cultivating their minds and bodies to reach a more purified stage of existence during their lifetime to assure for themselves, at the minimum, a rebirth in Heaven again when that life is over rather than rebirth as a human. Devas run around from master to master hoping that their teacher will use his/her *nirmanakaya* to purify their own Qi, and so when you are selected to go through the process of becoming an Earth Immortal and receive all that attention you will then be surrounded by countless devas all the time who hope to also receive work on their own bodies during that long period. They'll also be using your body for various types of training purposes.

A general Daoist rule states that you need to accumulate 3,000 great good deeds and 800 minor good deeds in order to deserve enlightenment and become an Immortal, which means you must be a kind, virtuous and charitable human being. In *Liaofan's Four Lessons*, Yuan Liaofan (d. 1606) vowed to change his personality and behavior and pledged 3,000 good deeds if Heaven would help him start changing his fate, which is what indeed happened from all his work at changing his personality and behavior. This is a book you should read. A similar book I always recommend is Eva Wong's *Lao-Tzu's Treatise on the Response of the Tao* but *Liaofan's Four Lessons* is far more important. It is a book you can get for free on the internet and has lessons you should introduce to your children.

Performing "good deeds" is one of the three vehicles of Daoism where saving a single life is not just a good deed but a "great good deed" because some deeds are more valuable than others. The Daoist adept Ge Hong said that you need to accumulate 300 good deeds to become an Earth Immortal (Srotapanna) and 1,200 to become a Celestial Immortal (Anagamin). Ge Hong's numbers simply tell us to perform acts of merit to be worthy of the stages of enlightenment.

Daoism states that the key to immortality, namely enlightenment, is that "you cannot exist for yourself," which means you must develop the mind and behavior of compassionately aiding others like a Buddhist Bodhisattva. This is what we discussed in Chapter 1.

When we read the stories of the Eight Daoist Immortals we can see them traveling everywhere doing good deeds. A similar example from the ancient Hellenistic world is the "divine man" Appolonius of Tyana (d. 97) who certainly attained enlightenment and then traveled around as a wonder-worker performing miraculous deeds to help people. Plenty of Christian, Moslem and Hindu saints became "wonder workers" by traveling around and publicly performing miraculous good deeds to help people after their enlightenment but most just perform them without anyone knowing that they were responsible. If you search the internet for "wonder worker" Christian saints who performed miracles you will find dozens with that name tag, most of whom had become enlightened.

The use of non-Daoist masters to teach you about Daoism should not alarm you or offend you since the stages of the cultivation are non-denominational. Because stories of modern Daoist masters who become enlightened are very lacking we must turn to masters from other traditions like this (such as taking examples from Hinduism, Christianity, Buddhism and so on) in order to derive some extra lessons that would be missing. For instance, in the stories of two Hindu masters – Bhagavan Nityanada and Neem Karoli Baba – you can see lives like those of the Eight Immortals of Daoism where countless superpowers and miracles are performed to help people. You can pick up a copy of *Nityananda: In Divine Presence, Bhagawan Nityananda of Ganeshpuri*, and *Miracle of Love* to investigate these two masters if you are interested. It's fun reading and you'll learn how some masters behave when using superpowers.

The kami of Japan (although spirits) are also just humans who have ascended and invisibly help people as are the orisha of Africa. Similarly, the saints of Christianity with their work as "advocates" and protectors, and the Bodhisattvas of Buddhism who fulfill their vows of compassion, are all examples of humans who have ascended as Immortals, Arhats, sages, saints and so on and take care of us. The stages of Daoist attainment are non-denominational so we are simply calling them by different names from different traditions. We all share the same ladder of spiritual progress or "spiritual ascension."

The basic idea is that to qualify for becoming an Immortal – which means to "become enlightened," "ascend," or become "liberated" – you need to be a good person who works for the benefit of others. *Liao Fan's Four Lessons*, which has a Confucian, Buddhist and Daoist flavor, and *Lao Tzu's Treatise on the Response of the Tao* can guide you along these lines.

For Daoists, your minimum target in life should be to follow Daoist ways to become healthy and prosperous, which is cultivating the pathway of Human Immortals who are different from everyone else eating junk food and following bad habits that affect their health, peace of mind and prosperity. Becoming a Human Immortal simply means becoming a better human being by cultivating your health, longevity, prosperity, mind (through meditation) and internal energy along with maintaining the right Daoist mindset for handling life. You want to live a long time, without disease or disability, with a happy mind, and remain youthful with sharp faculties. Health is not just an absence of disease or infirmity but a state of physical, mental, emotional and social well-being that Daoism can help you attain.

Now, if you cultivate the inner *nei-gong* Path of Tao you can also work on attaining the spiritual ascension stage of an Earth Immortal once you cultivate the basics of becoming a healthy human being, which is what Daoism calls a Human Immortal as compared to ignorant people who don't practice health or well-being with any particular practices at all. Luckily for us, Daoism offers many ways for us to improve our ordinary lives and meditation practice is always part of that prescription.

The reason we went into all these details is to break the big mistaken notion that enlightenment is just some mental state of realization, after which suddenly your mind has the ability to perform all sorts of superpowers such as create copies of your body that can appear everywhere to help people. All these body correspondences show that the true meaning of enlightenment is to attain transcendental spiritual bodies and the other genuine spiritual schools all recognize this because they have also given all these bodies names. The ranks of the Daoist Immortals absolutely match with these ranks of other religions. This *must be the case* if spiritual progress is a non-denominational process, and it is so the ranks match.

However, while many schools in some way name these bodies to denote their capabilities, only Daoism calls its sages "Immortals." This denotes the fact that spiritual progress is basically a body attainment and that even if you don't attain enlightenment in this life you should still be cultivating your health, longevity and prosperity. If you do attain any of these higher bodies you will live for a longer period of time than an ordinary human life. And, every time you attain a new body it will become the new center of your life and it will possess new powers and capabilities on its plane of existence.

In that realm your mind will be the ordinary mind you have now. It is the attendant consciousness that comes with that new body but is a lot more clear since your body has become more energy-like in composition, so everything runs better. Hence, there is no special mental state that you try to cultivate through spiritual practices to become enlightened although we do practice certain mental skills (such as calming, concentration, visualization, emotional control, control of one's Qi energy, and so on) through meditation. The idea of cultivating mental emptiness (empty mind or detachment) is so that your Qi flows better and so that junior devas have a chance to enter into you to purify your Qi while theirs is also simultaneously being worked on (when they are within you) by a *nirmanakaya* emanation due to their service. Therefore you cultivate periods of emptiness meditation where you are just watching your thoughts but more importantly you must also cultivate *internal energy exercises* that arouse your Qi in order to eventually generate the subtle energy body to become an Immortal.

This raises the interesting point that the *real you* after you become a Daoist Immortal (become enlightened) is not the physical body that everyone else sees when they look at your human body. Let's say that you attain the Supra-Causal Celestial Immortal body and generate a *nirmanakaya* body double that is then accused of a crime in the material world. People would then arrest your physical body because it looks like the *nirmanakaya* body-double that committed the crime. Well, the physical human individual did not commit the crime. The human body is just the home base for all the higher transcendental bodies upstairs; it is a shell they can withdraw into or appendage they can use. It is just the home of the higher guys so what you are seeing there is not the real man. It is just a living physical shell that the real man is indifferent to discarding so think of it as just an ornament.

The person in front of you did <u>not</u> project a *nirmanakaya*. The Supra-Causal individual, who has an entirely different birth time and different personality and resides on a different plane of reality than that of the human body from which he arose is the one who did something. You cannot arrest him because he's living on an entirely different plane of existence. He isn't the person you're seeing in front of you. The human in front of you did nothing! He did not generate that body double projection. The *transcendental guy living on a higher plane did* and you cannot touch him or hurt him in any way. You cannot bribe him, threaten him (or his wealth or relatives), blackmail him or cajole him into doing something for you in any way because he's living in another realm where your affairs don't touch him. He looks upon this world as a dream that he can cut off at any moment so whatever you do has no sway over him but is your own karma you are creating. In fact, many people on the higher planes where he resides can project *nirmanakaya* that look just like him too so how do you even know who actually did anything? It could be someone else just as countless different enlightened masters project tangible or visionary *nirmanakaya* in this world looking like (their version of) Jesus to believers in order to fulfill the demand and none of those images or figures come from Jesus. Millions of Buddhas are continuously intervening in human affairs across the world like this and everyone is oblivious to this fact. The very old Buddhas practice giving people "thin" (very fine) inkling warning thoughts about the future (so that we might have the chance to change our karma) but those are the thoughts we usually ignore due to their thinness.

Sci-fi movies always make the following mistake. They assume that an ordinary person can generate a body double to go and do things but no human body can do that. Only a Supra-Causal or Immanence body can generate an energy body duplicate capable of bilocation and other feats, and such individuals don't exist on this earthly plane. *They are individuals who reside on a higher plane of existence. Those are the guys who do it.* Because they reside on a higher plane of existence they only generate and project *nirmanakaya* in order to interact with us on this plane of existence. As Meher Baba explains in *God Speaks*, they typically just give people thoughts or invigorate them with their *nirmanakaya* emanations.

Everyone might think that a spiritual master's material body is the individual at fault if a *nirmanakaya* committed some type of infraction whereas it is an entirely different individual from the upper realms that would be responsible for a crime. The Supra-Causal body is an independent person and the physical body we see is like an empty sleeve or shell. In fact, from one of the sections of the *Surangama Sutra* one can infer that anyone who achieves any stage of Arhatship, which means to become a spiritual Immortal, is no longer even a member of the human species anymore due to their higher anatomy.

The third reason I went into these details is so that you could see some of the powers available to each of these spiritual bodies. In *God Speaks*, the Sufi Meher Baba (d. 1969) explains further details of the miraculous abilities available to each spiritual body such as being able to make flowers blossom out of season, being able to give life to small animals, being able to generate fire, give you thoughts and so forth. The reason that enlightened beings can give you thoughts is because through *nirmanakaya* emanations they can possess your brain stem, which in Daoism is called the "muddy pellet" and the part of the brain responsible for thinking and thus consciousness. All they have to do – and this has happened to YOU countless times during your life without you knowing it – is emanate a *nirmanakaya* body, possess someone and use it to think of something and then that individual will have those thoughts. The energy of a higher body can always override the energy of lower bodies, which is why it is always said that a master at a higher stage can shut off the superpowers of someone at a lower stage of attainment. Basically, the thoughts of the *nirmanakaya* projection will override your thinking. This can be done for emotions as well.

In Hinduism people worship an erect Shiva linga because it represents the brain stem and thus consciousness, which is the great miracle of existence. They also worship the wish-fulfilling cow *kamdhenu* whose Egyptian equivalent is the Sphinx because it represents the brain and thus consciousness. They worship the wish-fulfilling tree *Kalpavriksha*, which also represents the Qi channels of the spine and brain and consciousness once again. To some the erect Shiva linga represents the vitality of life, but it is actually worshipped because it represents the great miracle of the universe and our own greatest treasure, which is consciousness – the ability to be aware and have cognizance within a great sea of insentience composed of inert matter. Again: the Shiva linga represents the brain stem and thus consciousness.

One thing I almost forgot to mention is that when the Supra-causal body (Celestial Immortal) or Great Golden Arhat generate *nirmanakaya* to do things in the world they typically look very similar to their core body, but with training a master can generate a *nirmanakaya* that looks very different from his regular body such as by being taller, much younger or have a different appearance altogether. In fact, with many years of practice you can train to generate *nirmanakaya* that don't look like you at all! If you want to generate one that looks like Jesus or some other spiritual great then after years of practice you can do so. In general, however, a *nirmanakaya* will usually look very similar to the individual who generates it, complete in all details, because a body double is what naturally comes out of an energy duplicate.

This is also the case with reincarnations. When you reincarnate your appearance is affected by the genes of your new parents but you will still resemble your past life appearance to some extent because your subtle body, or soul, was inserted into the fetus for reincarnation, and its shape was morphed as it unfolded in growth.

If you investigate the story of James Leininger (*Soul Survivor: The Reincarnation of a World War II Fighter Pilot*) you will find that he looks very similar to the man he believes he was in his past life due to his retained memories, which was WWII pilot James Huston Jr. It is easy to find pictures on the internet to verify the resemblance. As another example there is the case of Carl Edon who believes he is the reincarnation of German WWII pilot Heinrich Richter whom he also strongly resembles. Richter lost his leg in a plane crash during his life and Edon was reborn with a large birthmark on his groin at the top of his right leg as a carryover of the accident. When you suffer a wound in a past life a scar or mark often appears in your present incarnation if you had not cultivated hard enough to purify your inner subtle body during that lifetime. This is another reason you want to be cultivating spiritual practice during this life. Yet another WWII reincarnation case where there is a strong facial resemblance is that of Martin Heald from Manchester who had strong recollections of his past life as a Sergeant Richard Seymour who flew as an RAF fighter pilot before being gunned down.

A *nirmanakaya* that is broken off from an enlightened spiritual master to reincarnate again will therefore resemble the originating master. This is a fact that settles the dispute between the two individuals claiming to be the 17th Tibetan Gyalwang Karmapa, who is supposedly the reincarnation of Ranjung Rigpe Dorje (d. 1981). If you just look at the two claimants to the Karmapa throne you will see who resembles the 16th Karmapa most, and if you then add any evidence of miraculous superpowers into the mix then you will find the right claimant.

Most of the assumed reincarnations in Tibet are entirely different individuals than those whom people say they are. They are usually just students who are simply being "sponsored" by the previously enlightened master so that they receive instant gravitas and good training, and the truly enlightened masters all know this but just go along with the charade. The enlightened master whose name is being used is not emanating a *nirmanakaya* for rebirth but simply wants to keep his *tulku* lineage alive so the masters appoint someone to assume his name.

It is very easy to cheat people into believing that a *tulku* is the reincarnation of some famous lama of the past. Sometimes they are, but you must remember what the Tibetan lamas would do in the past. If the Buddhist leaders ever discovered a talented youth they would quickly name him a *tulku* and make him a monk so that the government could not swipe him up and employ him for his skills. If the enlightened lamas found a talented youth suitable for training they would simply call him a *tulku* reincarnation and then the original *tulku* enlightened master would sponsor the youth and project a *nirmanakaya* emanation into him over the years to help him periodically. He would also take over his mind and body during the Tibetan testing process used to verify who he is so that the youth correctly chooses whatever items belonged to the master previously.

A *nirmanakaya* emanation can also be used to give people dreams or thoughts that in a past life they were someone great or did some wrong deed that accounts for their present misfortunate karma of some type, which is a fun trick often played by those who are enlightened in order to push people in certain directions. When you see visions this is due to some enlightened being projecting an emanation into you as well. Unfortunately, so much of what masters do misleads people that a lot of misdirection happens in the world.

No one, I repeat NO ONE who attains the Arhat enlightenment stage of a Celestial Immortal (Supra-Causal body) or Universal Immortal (Immanence body) will reincarnate using that body and thus lose all their skills and knowledge! Rather, they will project a *nirmanakaya* emanation for the purposes of reincarnation to fulfill their vows if they choose to do so.

For instance, once a couple asked the Sufi saint Sai Baba of Shirdi (d. 1918) for a child and he helped them conceive. Normally a spiritual master will simply arrange for another soul to be born into the womb but in this case he told the mother that he separated off a piece of himself to make the baby possible, which means that he used his own *nirmanakaya* to become her baby. The capability of "creating life" falls into the realm of the Supra-Causal and Immanence bodies (Arhats and Great Golden Arhats) who reside in the formless realm and this is what it means. When Shakyamuni was asked about the origin of life he would not trace it origins past the Formless Realm, which is their domicile of residence, and said that he would not speak about it.

As another example of miraculous abilities, when an enlightened Daoist master makes food appear he is not manifesting it out of nothingness but using a higher spiritual body to take it from somewhere else. He's basically *stealing it from elsewhere* (speedily taking it from one place to another using a higher spiritual body) rather than manifesting it out of nothingness. There are many stories in Daoism where a master gives apples or plums to the public and then local merchants find that their own stocks have dwindled the same amount. Using higher bodies the master simply takes them from one place to another. Hence, when Jesus "turned water into wine" during the wedding at Cana in response to his mother asking for help one very fair assumption is that he simply took it from another source such as King Herod's palace.

We could explain all sorts of miraculous abilities such as levitation, manifesting food, talking with animals, knowing people's hearts (minds) or future, bilocation, creating aromas, creating fire or rain, knowing the past and future and so forth but there is no reason for this discussion. If you attain a higher body you will have many abilities available to you and you just have to cultivate them like learning how to cook or go fly fishing.

The important point is to get started at becoming a Daoist Immortal, so the entire premise of this book is not on Daoist philosophy or such esoteric discussions but helping you to cultivate the Way and knowing what it entails. Daoists focus on the method of training, or the path, so we are discussing some very important points about the overall path that you will not find in print or hear from any master. This is meant to help guide you in Daoism.

CHAPTER 3:
THE PROCESS OF PURIFYING YOUR QI
TO BECOME AN ENLIGHTENED SAGE

It is no secret that ordinary people must devote a lot of time to cultivating a variety of spiritual exercises to become enlightened, which means to attain the higher spiritual bodies that make one a Daoist Immortal.

Some spiritual greats who become enlightened around twenty years old (such as Ramana Maharshi, Ramakrishna, Bhagavan Nityananda and Padre Pio) even report to us that strong energy sensations were continuously surging within their body starting from a young age. This is due to the fact that (due to help from higher beings) they were always experiencing automatic Qi flows along the microcosmic, macrocosmic and all sorts of other circulatory routes within their physical body where those rotations were slowly purifying its subtle energy. This happens to those destined to attain enlightenment early.

Unfortunately, we cannot have many discussions about Daoists who became enlightened at a very young age because those who accomplished this did not leave sufficient records. But because the stages of Daoist accomplishment are non-denominational we can turn to the sages of other religions who left sufficient records. We can do this because the stages of attainment are non-denominational, the transformation or transmutation process of purifying your Qi to attain the first of these bodies is common as well, and everyone goes through the same physical transformations to become enlightened. Therefore it does not matter which tradition we use when we want to make points about some non-denominational aspect of the process. I just feel bad that we cannot use as many Daoist examples as I would like and that is simply because the records are lacking.

The Hindu sage Ramana Maharshi said that as a young man he had strong burning (hot Prana) sensations in his body coursing through him all the time until he hugged the lingam at the Tiruvannamalai temple in Arunachala. The Christian saint Padre Pio, because of the energies coursing inside him, ran fevers at temperatures so high that they would normally cause fatality in humans, and it is recorded that those temperatures would even burst thermometers. The Hindu saint Ramakrishna would not only experience ecstasies like these two other enlightened sages but continuously felt tremendous energies coursing inside him as well when he was young.

These men were all going through the "internal alchemy" transformation process reported by generations of Daoist masters. During this process the microcosmic and macrocosmic circulations of your body become activated and the energies start rolling around within your body *continuously for years*. If the process is not continuous at 18-21 hours per day for years then you are not undergoing the true inner alchemy transformation process described by Daoism and the other spiritual paths.

This rotation of energy over time gradually purifies an individual's inner subtle body made of Qi so that it can eventually separate from the lower physical nature as an independent life on its own. It is only by igniting this automatic process of internal alchemy, which India calls a "kundalini transformation," that these men could attain the first of the independent spiritual bodies to become an Earth Immortal at a young age. After you attain this first independent deva body you start working on attaining the yet higher spiritual bodies and commence the path of ascending the ranks of the Immortals.

We cannot reference Daoists like this in detail because they did not leave sufficient records yet we know that several Daoist greats in ancient China did indeed become enlightened at a young age too. What we can easily find, however, are descriptions of strange events that will occur during the process of cultivation such as feeling sensations of lightness, heaviness, itching, roughness, smoothness, hot and cold, … and seeing strange visions such as golden lights, flying snow and falling flowers during the process such as reported in Lu Kuan Yu's *Daoist Yoga: Alchemy and Immortality*.

In the cultivation school of Swami Muktananda (d. 1982) people will often see a little blue floating sparkle in front of their eyes, and in other schools the masters project a different trademark vision to practitioners. These are all fake phenomena, namely illusions, where higher beings are practicing their powers of visualization within your brain. In other words, they are not naturally generated such that all people see them, and it is not that you will definitely see them or regularly see them when you perform the same practices. They are simply due to spiritual masters playing with the powers of projection in people's minds that are available due to the fact that they have higher energy bodies. Everyone wants chances to use their powers so even the ancient masters of various traditions cannot resist projecting things into people's minds using *nirmanakaya* emanations, such as happens with Marian apparitions (of Mother Mary) only seen by a few individuals. Masters often project special *nirmanakaya* visions to close students to notify them of their death as well.

This is why Shakyamuni Buddha gave a special lesson in the *Surangama Sutra* called the "50 *Mara* States of Delusion" caused by heavenly beings when you are cultivating the Way, and warned practitioners that these things will not only deceive you but can cause you to commit self-harm. You can find a translation within *Meditation Case Studies* although some of the explanations should be corrected.

In the *Surangama Sutra* Shakyamuni Buddha spoke about ten common types of delusion experienced by ordinary people during their cultivation such as feeling that their body is empty, experiencing unusual internal energy currents whose initiation is not of their own doing, having visions of things inside their body, seeing the bodies of enlightened spiritual masters seem to etherically change their form or shape in some way, hearing voices in the sky or within their head, seeing light surround or come off objects or other living beings, seeing amazing objects appear in space, seeing visions of spiritual lands and deities (which of course are fake like all the other things), being able to see in the dark, seeing events happening in the distance far away, and so forth.

For instance, there is a famous story of the Buddhist monk Han Shan (d. 1623) suddenly being able to see events in the far off distance. The Greek Orthodox monk, Saint Porphyrios the Kafsokalyvite (d. 1991), reported the same event to his spiritual master when he was just a junior monk going through the process of attaining enlightenment. At one time he could see his elders returning from a far-away journey. He saw them at a great distance far away although they were not within human sight. As a gift he was sometimes able to "see" the depths of the earth (oil deposits, subterranean springs, etc.) and the far reaches of space. His master told him to keep quiet about such occurrences, yet these instance also tell us why masters can tell where to dig water wells because the high stage adepts can see deeply into the ground to find the water.

These abilities (and even seeing in the dark) can be explained through a story involving Bhagavan Nityananda and a widowed mother who visited him with her blind child. The child said to Nityananda, "I would like to see my mother once," and it happened later that day that the child could see after the two left, but the joy of the child lasted only minutes before the blindness returned. Nityananda had generated a *nirmanakaya* projection of his body and used it to enter into the child and project what it was seeing into the child's mind so that she could see her mother. He also gave the child the thought of recognizing her mother. When individuals have visions of spiritual greats they never wonder how they know it is that special person since they have never seen them, but that is because those thoughts are being projected to you at the same time as well.

This same "superpower" of seeing events in the distance happened for the two spiritual greats, Han Shan and Saint Porphyrios, but everyone mistakenly thinks that they temporarily have superpowers or a heavenly gift when this happens. If you cannot control such abilities at will then they are not your capability. Someone else is doing it for you.

Basically these and the many other events reported in the first ten *Mara* states of the *Surangama Sutra* are all events where devas and their enlightened teachers enter your brain to project visions or sounds to play tricks on you. The images and sounds are just *mara*, which means fakery, delusions or illusions. This happens to students in Daoism and *all religions* so just beware. The *jinn* of Islam (misbehaving devas) are famous for doing this sort of thing. Once again, the reason that we can use the examples from other religions like this is because everyone goes through the same processes of attainment and reaches the same stages of attainment.

In the Zen school a student might visit a master who says something to him and then travels hundreds of miles to return home to be shocked when his own teacher repeats the very same words. This is because the master can shrink one of his transcendental bodies, go into the student's brain to read his neuron memories, and then speak of what happened in the past. All devas train to do this and to give people thoughts so they will often bother people this way because they are either practicing their skills or demonstrating them for their teacher.

Many masters, such as the Christian Saint Porphyrios, Saint Padre Pio and Saint Paisios, would even demonstrate the ability of listening to you speak in another language, respond in their own language, and you would mysteriously understand them. As an example, the Greek Saint Porphyrios had a dialogue with a German doctor who did not know Greek while Porphyrios never learned German, and though each only spoke their own language they understood one another without need of an interpreter. The saint had simply projected a *nirmanakaya* to enter into the doctor in order to understand his thoughts (of what he was saying) as well as to provide an interpretation to him of his own Greek words, which is why the doctor could understand him. Padre Pio would do this as well during confessions. I have had several experiences of thought reading like this as well, which is also how enlightened spiritual masters communicate with animals.

There is one story of Saint Paisios of Mount Athos (d. 1994), which can illustrate many related lessons in one go. A Greek man was having troubles and consulted a mage who gave him a bottle of certain substance with the advice to bathe in it and not bathe again for three months. From the moment he returned home all sorts of strange things started happening to his home. The doors in his home would open by themselves, the television would turn on and off on its own, and he would feel energies entering his nose and ears ("fairy brushing") bothering him to no end. This always happens to people going through the twelve years of internal alchemy kundalini transformation to become a Daoist sage at the later stages of the process, and they will suffer from lots of "fairy brushing" where spiritual entities will lightly brush your face with their Qi to demonstrate their skills to those testing them. This will irritate you tremendously. You can wear a balaclava face mask when going through the process to counteract the attacks by deadening the sensations, and you can put vibrators on certain body parts when they are attacked with pain or irritation, which especially happens on purpose to body parts you cannot easily reach. In particular you will be attacked on your face, in your nose and ears, at the nerves under the teeth, in and around your asshole, *on the right side of your body* and on the muscles running along the right knee. The kundalini transformation process is a very abusive process, which is why no one wants to speak about it.

At the end of the day spiritual practice all comes down to body attainments, and training one's higher spiritual bodies to emanate and use multiple *nirmanakaya* simultaneously. The Arhats and Great Golden Arhats of certain traditions, which includes the ex-serfdom (slavery) Tibetan culture, practice using their bodies all the time by inflicting painful abuse on lesser-bodied beings during the kundalini transformations. Incredible to believe!

In any case, this man and his friends decided to pay a visit to Father Paisios to tell him about these troubles. When they reached his hut they found seventy other pilgrims waiting outside so they thought they would not get a chance to meet him. Suddenly Father Paisios emerged from his enclave, looked at the men and called each of them by their names even though he did not know them. He then began to analyze the situation of each of the four individuals without anyone even informing him of their matters. He told one man that he had a problem with his arm that started on the day he went out with another man for a drink. He told the second man that he had started to take drugs and would die from this if he did not stop.

To the man who had visited a mage he told him he was facing serious problems because someone had performed witchcraft on him. He said that when he got home he was to look for a square stone in front of his house, lift it, and remove a small bag from beneath it and then burn it. Afterwards he should dedicate ten minutes of each and every day to worship, and go to church more regularly.

I've actually been told many stories of witchcraft in western China where people bury objects in another's lawn to hurt or steal their fortunes. When the locals visit Daoist masters asking for help to change their bad luck the masters usually tell them that it has been due to witchcraft and that they should dig up buried objects that are then found. A Taiwanese friend even told me the case of how her father was bewitched through Daoist magic by a maid, who planted hidden objects underneath the four corners of his bed that a Daoist master accurately revealed. It is actually enlightened beings that help local priests do their jobs when they have no stage of attainment.

Saint Paisios was able to identify the men by name since he was able to use his spirit bodies to check the memories of each one stored in his brain's neurons although the Church calls this the spiritual ability of "knowing a man's heart." As I have explained in many books, such as *Arhat Yoga*, all spiritual beings learn how to do this. Saint Paisios could tell what happened to them by doing this as well, and because he was a sage he could also see their future. He also gave instructions for each man so that they could change their fortunes, which is what compassionate sages do.

Later while Father Paisios was very ill and being taken care of at the Monastery of Souroti, two buses of people from the town of Veria decided to visit him but he was too ill to see them. However, several people reported that they saw Father Paisios hanging mid-air in the sky above the monastery giving them his blessing. This was actually just an illusory visionary experience he projected inside their brain using *nirmanakaya* emanations once again. That's why only a few people saw it. For instance, when Ramana Maharshi died some people reported that they saw a meteorite race across the sky whereas no such thing happened. It was just an illusory vision he gave certain individuals. Having visited many Daoist temples in China I have experienced many such illusory phenomena that are just the projections of the local enlightened beings playing around.

It has been reported in many accounts that aliens from other planets who arrive in our world via UFOs sometimes communicate with humans through telepathy. However, they are using the very same tricks because they, too, attain the higher spiritual bodies since they are non-denominational achievements for sentient beings. That is why Shakyamuni Buddha said that everyone has the "seed of Buddhahood," which means the potential to attain the highest spiritual bodies ... by unleashing them from within the physical body that represents a matrix of condensed energies. As soon as you ardently start cultivating your internal energy you will encounter many strange experiences because many beings will visit to try and help you.

Daoism, by the way, firmly believes in different heavenly planes of existence and foreign worlds, as does Buddhism (such as in the *Avatamsaka Sutra* where many different worlds are described) and Hinduism, but you can only reach them when you become a Spirit Immortal. A deva is called an "Earth" Immortal because it cannot leave the earthly plane. It is bound to the earthly plane of existence. Only at the Spirit Immortal stage of attainment, which is equivalent to an Anagamin Arhat, can you finally travel to Pure Lands of existence rather than remain bound to the earthly heavenly plane.

UFOlogist Dr. Roger Leir reported that he once interviewed a doctor in Varginha, Brazil who had treated an injured extraterrestrial at a hospital after it had been captured because of a crash, and during the procedure the alien seemed to automatically control the movement of the doctor's hands. It communicated telepathically with the doctors present saying, "I feel sorry for human beings. You can do everything we can do but you don't know how to do it because you are totally detached from your spiritual selves. You have no idea of the potential of who you really are." Presumably he was referring to the fact that few people, except for adepts, know that we have the potential to attain higher spiritual bodies if we just cultivate correctly. He was certainly using one of his own to control the doctor's hands and communicate with those present within their minds. Everyone calls this telepathy but it is basically using a *nirmanakaya* emanation or simply one of that being's higher spiritual bodies.

Nirmanakaya energy projections can appear in many different places to many beings simultaneously. They can move anywhere independent of the body they originate from, leaving behind the originating body that is its dwelling place, and appear to be distinct entities that are a mirror image of their originator although with training they can assume different forms.

Strange, supernatural or miraculous events happen to everyone on the spiritual path, especially those who surround a spiritual master for teachings because his heavenly students want to prove their abilities to their teacher by playing tricks on you using their powers. Visiting masters like to show off their skills, too. They especially start to occur when you embark upon the Third Vehicle of Daoism, which includes the practices of internal alchemy to transform your body and mind.

This is the stage of "refining your Qi," "refining your Jing (essence) and transforming it into Qi," "harmonizing your breath (Qi)" or "refining the form (body)" since you have to cultivate both your physical body and the circulation of its internal Qi energy to do this. This path of application is a stage of intensified yoga practices where you practice the "arts of the Way." This is where we cultivate the Qi of our body so that through a gradual process of refinement our inner subtle body of Qi becomes purified, strong and finally independent of your physical nature. The big secret is that it cannot be done successfully without the aid of higher beings lending their energies to your own to help you. You need to depend upon them for this process.

The *Surangama sutra* talks about ten methods for cultivating and becoming a *xian* Immortal by ingesting certain foods, minerals or herbs; physical exercises (like martial arts); (pranayama and *qi-gong*) breathing practices; *nei-gong* internal Qi circulation exercises; mantra recitation; sexual intercourse; by matching with the astrological, *feng-shui* and other transformative forces of Nature; and meditation. I have dealt with most of these and many other longevity methods, including those from other cultivation schools, in *Look Younger, Live Longer*. You might consider *Look Younger, Live Longer* particularly about Daoist longevity because of the heavy Daoist emphasis.

Now, this book you have right now is not the one to teach you Daoist practice methods. I have already done so in *Neijia Yoga* where I extensively go over the inner energy techniques in detail. In *Arhat Yoga* I explained countless other cultivation techniques and the overall pathway and philosophy of cultivation. In *Correcting Zen* I told you how to set up a practice schedule using the basic techniques used everywhere including Daoism including meditating without concepts where nothing is to brought to the mind. Although the title of the book says "Zen" it is actually written for any school of cultivation, especially for monastics. Hence, all of the most important methods you can practice to cultivate your internal energy are revealed in *Neijia Yoga*, *Arhat Yoga* and *Correcting Zen*. You could toss in *Buddha Yoga* and *Nyasa Yoga* for additional non-denominational details and techniques. These books give you enough teachings to guide your own personal practice or guide an entire spiritual tradition! Therefore there is no need to go over them again here. You will also find very good books on amazon such as those by Eva Wong that can introduce various forms of Daoist cultivation exercises too.

As a Daoist you should particularly study *Neijia Yoga*. Chapter 7 of *Neijia Yoga* is devoted to various ways you can spin the Qi energy within the various sections of your body no matter whether you section your body by the *dantian* (elixir fields) or by appendages. In Chapter 8 you are taught how to cultivate your Qi at specific *bindus* or points on your body. In Chapter 9 you learn how to lead your Qi through body circuits (*pratyahara*) according to a specific sequence. This is also done in the Nyasa Yoga technique of Hinduism so I wrote an entire book on these sequences and how to combine the rotation of your Qi through body circuits with various emotions or visualizations that you are a deity or supreme being in order to attract heavenly help for your efforts. Chapter 10 of *Neijia Yoga* is quite similar because it is about leading your Qi through meridian circuits to open up those passageways. Chapter 6 reveals specific breath training and pranayama exercises that will allow you to use your breathing to move your Qi throughout your body to wash its tissues. This is classically known as *anapana* in Buddhism.

Boundless, by Ben Greenfield, provides an excellent short summary of the *best-of-the-best* other breathing methods you can learn for various purposes such as "Box breathing" for quieting your mind during extreme stress (close your mouth and inhale slowly through your nostrils for 4 seconds, hold your breath for 4 seconds, exhale for 4 seconds, and then hold your breath for 4 seconds), or the "4-7-8 breathing method" for reducing anxiety (inhale for 4 seconds, hold your breath for 7 seconds, exhale for 8 seconds).

As a short summary, here is an excerpt from a forthcoming book I'm writing entitled *Self-Creation* (*The Superhuman Protocol* or some such title) that explains various cultivation techniques and why they work on purifying your Qi as well as how they prepare you to achieve the initial spiritual stage of an Earth Immortal:

> All the various spiritual exercises you find across the world
> attack the problem of Qi purification from different angles, but

they are essentially aimed at Qi purification nonetheless. This is the only way to attain enlightenment, namely the higher spiritual bodies of the spiritual path that gain you liberation.

Anapana uses breathing to push your Qi around within your body, and thereby washes your inner subtle body with your own vital energy by using the connection between your breathing and Qi. As your breathing goes in and out you can push your Qi to various areas of your body such as above and below, to the left side or right side of your body, to the arms and legs and so on to wash them with energy.

It is especially easy to push the Qi of your body upwards or downwards into your upper or lower torso and limbs according to your breathing. As is usual, the frictional rubbing of Qi over itself causes an abrasive (frictional) cleansing of its nature where the pure or more refined energy eventually separates from that which is less pure and of lower vibration due to the presence of impurities. The more refined or purified Qi is what escapes as your spiritual body of enlightenment. It is more purified than the angelic deva body that ordinary mortals obtain when they die and leave their physical shell.

The white skeleton visualization technique uses your mental powers of concentration to mass Qi within your body around your bones, and thereby wash your inner subtle body around the vicinity of the skeleton. It uses mental concentration on internal sections of your body to send the Qi there because of the principle that wherever you put your mind within your body your Qi energy will follow and mass at that region.

While anapana uses breathing, Mantrayana uses sound energy to stimulate your Qi and move it around within your body to thereby wash its tissues in order to purify your inner subtle body. You can also use singing to do this, or you can arouse strong emotions within yourself to change the tonality of your Qi by listening to music. By listening to music of various types – energizing, defiant, triumphant or heroic, amusing, calming or relaxing, dreamy, annoying, nostalgic, happy, inspiring, joyful or cheerful, scary/fearful or tense, sad or depressing, etc. – you can create internal energy sensations that wash your Qi.

The Four Immeasurables practice of Buddhism uses the arousal of great emotions and dominant attitudes to energize and thus wash the Qi of your body as well. Through large emotions you evoke sensations that arouse and color your Qi that helps to wash the quality of your energy. What contributes most to your energy vibrations at any given moment is your attitude so you can practice this technique using many types of attitudes and emotions and to help in washing your Qi and developing new personality traits.

Nyasa Yoga, and the *pratyahara* method of leading your Qi around within your body, teach you to guide your Qi movements using your thoughts and will. Using your mind you rotate your Qi around your bones, organs, body regions and appendages. Your thoughts and willpower allow you to move your Qi/Prana around inside yourself so that you can wash your inner subtle body with rubbings of your own vital energy. Through frictional churning (and other energy movements) you eventually purify the Qi of your subtle body for its emergence as an independent spiritual body on its own. As with concentration practice, this technique relies on the principle that your Qi energy will follow your thoughts so you can guide it around your body to do what you want.

Kumbhaka pranayama uses breath retention to help force open the impediments or obstructions to the Qi flow within your body. When practiced correctly, pranayama will clear out the circulatory pathways of Qi flow within you and speed your attainment of the independent deva body. The one idea of pranayama is to learn how to control your breathing and the Qi within your body, because the two are linked, which is exactly how you cultivate your inner subtle body. Every part of your body can be filled with Qi or Prana, and when you are able to actually do this you can become able to control your entire body.

Yoga, the martial arts, natural bodyweight training exercises and exercise in general use the approach of stretching to eliminate any knots or obstructions that impede the free circulation of Qi flow within the tissues/muscles of your physical and subtle body. Then you practice to gain control of the Qi/Prana in every muscle of your body, which helps to quickly develop your independent spirit body. That which takes a long time to accomplish can thus be shortened by the practice of yoga, dance, the soft martial arts and any other exercises that teach you to master your inner Qi circulation.

Running and other cardiovascular sports that involve high states of coordinated movements, concentration, breathing, blood flow and Qi flow also transform your Qi very well when these systems become synchronized into a harmonious state of flow. When during sports your concentration, breathing, Qi flow and blood flow reach optimal peaks and synchronize into one then you will truly cultivate the Qi of your underlying subtle body as a unit and speed the attainment of the first dhyana. This is how you also cultivate "flow."

Basically, anapana uses your breathing to wash/purify your Qi where you change your emotions while breathing in order to wash your energy with different Qi tones.

The white skeleton visualization method uses mental concentration to mass your Qi around the bones and thus wash them and the surrounding tissues.

Mantrayana uses sound power to vibrate your Qi and breathing to push energized Qi around your body to wash its tissues.

The Four Immeasurables uses great emotions or large attitudes to alter your Qi and by radiating those energies everywhere you slowly wash your internal energy.

Kaula Tantra uses ecstatic visualizations, often with an arousing erotic content, to excite your Qi so that you can then more easily move it using your will to wash your channels and tissues via mental guidance.

B*oran kammatthana* has you arouse mental factors or emotions within (invoking the mental factors/emotions as if they were gods) and you "invite them" to transform your body and mind since sentiments stir-affect-vibrate your vital energies. In this manner you try to recreate yourself as an Arhat or Buddha by strongly emulating specific emotions inside you.

The Path of Heroes *Viramarga* method has you rest in a *bhava* absorption by fixing your self in a given attitude for a prolonged period of time where you feel the Qi energy of that attitude penetrating all throughout your body in order to wash your Qi with that the total penetration of that flavor.

Vajrayana deity yoga uses imagined unification with a *yidam* deity or Buddha (as in Buddha mindfulness) to invite enlightened Buddhas into your body so that the presence of their energetic *nirmanakaya* within you washes your Qi and thus purifies it.

Nyasa yoga and *pratyahara* use your thoughts and willpower to move your Qi internally through special circuits and thereby wash your tissues. *Nei-gong* uses this method of mental guidance as well.

Pranayama uses control of your breathing to move your Qi

and wash your inner energy.

Kumbhaka pranayama uses breath retention to force open up your Qi channels and improve inner Qi flow.

Yoga and martial arts use stretching, muscle control and Qi control (mastery of internal Qi movements guided by your will) to cultivate the Qi of your body.

Cardiovascular sports use the coordination of movement, breathing, blood flow and Qi flow at their optimum peaks to drive your Qi flow to an optimum state of harmony, and then use it to wash your body.

Wim Hof breathing uses hyperventilation to wash all the Qi of your body although the most important part of this pranayama exercise is the breath retention part.

Fasting forces your body to rely on its inner subtle energy body rather than material food (just as breath retention forces your body to rely upon its Prana/Qi for survival when breath is unavailable), thus strengthening the integrity and efficiency of your inner subtle body.

Countless exercises are used across the world to purify the Qi of your inner self, which is basically differentiating the purified high-grade energy of your body from the low grade unpurified energy. To do so successfully you must daily practice a set of different types of spiritual exercises, which all work at purifying your Qi via different principles, in order to start transforming your Qi for the first dhyana attainment. The general rule of cultivation progress is: the more practices of different types that you simultaneously practice with consistency the better and quicker will be your results.

Hence, these are just a few ways to start transforming the internal energy of your physical body. If you purify your physical energy then you will live healthier and longer. If you transform it profoundly then you can attain a stage of spiritual ascension, which entails cultivating an independent spirit body, or first dhyana attainment, while alive.

This achievement is technically the first but lowest rank of enlightenment, and yet to the human body this is the highest next physical achievement possible for its existence.

The basic idea in Daoist cultivation is that you progress from *wai-gong* (physical exercises such as martial arts, dancing, athletics and stretching) to *qi-gong* (breathing exercises similar to pranayama that affect your Qi at a superficial level) to *nei-gong* (internal energy exercises) to the accomplishment phase of *Tao-gong* where you achieve the first spiritual body and then start working on attaining the others by manipulating its own internal energy. Here is the traditional sequence of cultivation work within Daoism:

Wai-gong > *Qi-gong* > *Nei-gong* > *Tao-gong*.

By far the most important techniques are the inner energy exercises of *nei-gong* that involve rotating your Qi throughout your body to purify its nature, which is like rubbing the folds of dirty clothing against one another in a river in order to cleanse it. The frictional churning of your Qi against itself and *doing so while arousing very strong Yin or Yang emotions will eventually purify the quality of all the types of Qi within your body.*

This is a primary secret of higher order spiritual cultivation – you must arouse your emotions to change the tonality of your Qi when rotating it in order to wash and thus purify all of its various energies. Cultivation schools hide this information but they all use it, and of course Daoism does so as well as we will soon see. You want to strongly activate, excite, move, energize or arouse your Qi while also circulating it through various exercises.

When we look at the most popular inner energy (Qi) exercises across the world's spiritual traditions we will find this principle to employ emotional priming when arousing your Qi energy. The most powerful ones that lead to tremendous spiritual transformation use it because by arousing your emotions you will end up activating or exciting all the Qi of your body at once and then it becomes easier to be washed through friction and thus purified.

Here is a quick synopsis of various Qi internal energy exercises and the principles upon which they work at transforming your subtle body to a higher stage of purity:

Circulating Your Qi Internally Without Engaging Your Emotions (Emotionally Neutral)

- Pranayama
- *Qi-gong*
- *Anapana*
- *Nei-gong*
- *Pratyahara*
- Nyasa Yoga
- Stable concentration that focuses on a location in the body (e.g. abdomen, energy center, chakra, limb) that consequently brings Qi to the area; focusing on one part of the body and letting the breath flow through this point of concentration or bringing the flow of Qi through this point of focus
- Visualization of light or fire with warmth at different body parts and also visualization of water, ice or cold feelings at different body parts
- Accumulating energy in certain centers (e.g. abdomen) and channeling it through certain pathways (e.g. spine, microcosmic circulation), which is basically *pratyahara*
- Combining inhalation and exhalation and (the subsequent movement of energy within the body moved by your breathing) with visualizations of energy, light, color, heat/cold, etc., which is a form of *anapana*
- Listening to singing bowls or a gong and feeling the corresponding vibrations and Qi energy moving within the body. Singing while moving your internal energy in tune with sounds and rhythm is also a technique
- Humming or droning continuously or reciting *bija* sounds in synchrony with optimal hand movements
- Mantrayana where you mentally or vocally repeat certain words/sounds while connecting them to the rhythm of breathing or while leading the flow of your Qi within your body; mantra recitation in general, as well as repeating mantras while focusing on specific points within the body, different sections of the body or as if from within those sections)

- Yoga stretches where you also concentrate on feeling the Prana/Qi of your limbs

Moving Your Qi Internally While Engaging Your Emotions in order to Color the Qi of your Body with a different Flavor

- Kaula Tantra ecstatic visualization meditations
- White Skeleton Visualization where you arouse repugnance visualizing how a dead body slowly decays and decomposes, and joy at giving away your flesh while becoming a shining white skeleton
- Anapana where you push your Qi by moving your breathing while engaged in emotions of joy, bliss, confidence, triumph, pride, … Also, combining inhalation and exhalation with visualizations of energy, light, color, temperature changes, etc. along with dominant attitudes or emotions to arouse whole body Qi
- Nyasa Yoga methods of internally moving your Qi while imagining that you receive the help of a deity or become a deity
- *Boran Kammatthana*
- Chanting while feeling strong emotions, or singing religious songs or sutras or glories of a deity with strong emotions while using the sound energy to move the Qi inside your body
- Repeating an affirmation and feeling the corresponding Qi that is evoked throughout your body and along any particularly relevant Qi channels

Coloring Your Qi (With Qi Rotation Being Stationary) by Holding onto Large Yin or Yang Emotions

- Simply holding onto a dominant attitude (that overwhelmingly permeates and suffuses your Qi) or intent for a prolonged period of time
- The Four Immeasurables concentration practice (infinite joy, infinite compassionate, boundless equanimity, infinite loving kindness)

- Absorbing oneself in the color and five element *kasina* meditations of the *Visuddhimagga* to feel the texture of that Qi
- The four Buddhist formless absorptions of infinite space, boundless consciousness, infinite nothingness and neither thinking nor not-thinking that are basically "formless" meditations on being bodilessness, with detachment to the things within one's awareness, while engaging in a peaceful but expansive mental experience of emptiness and equanimity in some way
- *Viramarga* Path of Heroes
- Bhakti devotional yoga
- Self-cultivation in continuously emulating your highest ideals in their most perfect forms; creating ideals of perfection that continually inspire you to levels of ever more perfect realization

Cultivating Large Emotions While Imagining that One is an Active Deity

- Buddha Yoga
- Guru Yoga
- Deity Yoga
- Nyasa Yoga
- Daoist deity possession
- Shamanism
- Bhakti devotional yoga (Ex. a Fool for Christ, Krishna bhakti devotee ...)
- *Boran Kammatthana*
- *Viramarga* Path of Heroes

Movement Exercises Where Strenuous Stretching or Cardiovascular Activity, Sometimes Combined with Aroused Emotions, Can Circulate Your Body's Qi

- Martial Arts
- Tirumalai Krishnamacharya Viniyoga
- Dancing

- High cardio sports such as soccer, basketball, dancing, swimming, acrobatics, track and field, …
- Sexual Intercourse

What you cannot know from Daoist or any other type of literature is what happens when the microcosmic, macrocosmic and other circulations within your body start transpiring automatically without your doing as was the case for the Hindu sages previously cited, and as has been reported by of generations of Daoist sages. When this happens to Christian saints undergoing the process they lack sufficient teachings so simply think they are being blessed by the Holy Spirit, or "breath of God." Here is a short explanation as to what is going on.

Various schools, teachings or methods of Daoism talk about various types of spirits living within the human body. The Hindu Yoga traditions and Buddhist Vajrayana also show tantric pictures of deities visiting inside the human body. This is simply a trick to prepare you for the fact that the process of becoming an Immortal will require countless masters and their students going into your body and helping you create and sustain various internal Qi rotations. Once it starts happening you will encounter their voices so these teachings were meant to prepare you for this discovery.

No matter what your cultivation school – Christianity, Judaism, Islam, Buddhism, Hinduism, Sikhism, Shugendo, Jainism, Daoism and so forth – everyone goes through this exact same process. Often enlightened masters will masquerade as devils or demons in order to arouse your Yin Qi by provoking fear and anxiety, and other times they will give you sublime visions to arouse your Yang Qi. Yin and Yang Qi are the trigrams of *Kan* (Water) and *Li* (Fire) in Daoist alchemical literature that you are always instructed to cultivate. In Buddhist temples devoted to Bhaisajyaguru, the Medicine Buddha whose Daoist equivalent is Baosheng Dadi, he is always flanked by statues of Suryaprabha holding a sun and Candraprabha holding a moon to represent the fact that health requires us to cultivate and purify both our Yang Qi and Yin Qi. Unfortunately people do not know this fundamental spiritual principle.

When a master starts young because he is destined to attain the Tao that life he will often be given visions of demons and devils when a child, as continuously happened to Padre Pio, or might unceasingly dwell on thoughts of death or hell that frighten him, as happened to the Zen monk Han Shan. Some will be forced to wear women's clothing at a young age, as happened to Nan Huai-chin (as a Chinese traditional village way of protecting him as a child), and others will be exposed to extreme sorrows, remain very sick for prolonged periods of time, or suffer a difficult life of privation and forced obedience. These are all ways to strongly stimulate one's Yin Qi that are sometimes pushed upon those who achieve the Earth Immortal attainment in their early twenties, which is a very young age.

The entire process of the kundalini awakening of Daoist internal alchemy involves washing your Qi for over a decade while provoking various emotions that evoke from you different tonalities of your Yin Qi and Yang Qi, or they will impose them on you using their own abilities. When Daoism reports that you must wash your Qi it means that you must wash your Qi while arousing its different qualities through different Yin and Yang emotions, the unique feelings of the five elements, the imagined feel of planets or lunar mansions from Chinese astrology, the feelings of the seasons and by *other ways of stimulating various inner energy sensations different than the norm.*

If you are a man you want to practice sexual restraint (discipline) as much as possible so as to prevent yourself from carelessly losing your Jing (semen) and Qi while on this pathway. If you are a man and let the "elixir" (Jing or semen) leak through ejaculation then your Qi/Prana will be lost along with your semen, and then the force of that energy will not be available for opening up and purifying your body's Qi channels. That internal energy should not be lost because it is necessary for strengthening the integrity of your inner subtle body that is intrinsically inside your physical body until released. Your inner subtle body composed of Qi or Prana becomes your independent spirit body at death, and is the basis of your Earth Immortal body attainment that is composed of Qi.

The famous Monkey King Sun Wu-Kong (from *Journey to the West)* was taught by his teacher Subhuti the following cultivation principle:

> Know well this secret formula wondrous and true:
> Spare and nurse the vital forces, this and nothing else.
> All power resides in the semen, the breath, and the spirit (Jing, Qi and Shen);
> Guard these with care, securely, lest there be a leak.
> Lest there be a leak! Keep within the body!
> Hearken to my teaching and the Way itself will prosper.[4]

Sun Wu-Kong is known for keeping his staff in his ear. The staff represents his Qi because it is a weapon he can use at will (like Hanuman's mace, Hercules' club or Thor's hammer) whose size and movements respond to his thoughts, and sometimes it represents his (extendable) penis as a sign of Qi virility. It was kept in his ear because there is a connection between the kidneys, ears, and your vitality according to the meridians of Chinese acupuncture. Furthermore, the power from below must travel up your spine to your head, so Sun Wu-Kong was said to store his staff in his ear to represent his physical power and vitality. He had retrieved this staff from the *haidi* or "bottom of the ocean" which represents our body's perineum or *huiyin* DU-1 acupuncture point.

During cultivation you must learn to lead your Qi with your thoughts

---

[4] *The Journey to the West*, trans. by Anthony Yu, (The University of Chicago Press, Chicago, 1978).

just as Sun Wukong controls his staff. This is symbolized in Daoism through discussions about lead and mercury. Mercury is a very shiny metal that easily scatters but after it scatters it can clump together again. Mercury is like thoughts that can become concentrated or scattered. Daoism emphasizes that the metal lead is dark in color but after being cut it appears shiny. At the cut mark a shiny white color appears that we call its whiteness. Lead is therefore like our Qi that can become lively, bright (symbols for purification) through cultivation.

In Daoism mercury represents your thoughts and lead represents your Qi. Before you cultivate your Qi it seems heavy and hard to move just like lead but you can change that quality by performing all sorts of inner *nei-gong* exercises. Mercury, on the other hand, represents your thoughts because it can become scattered and flow everywhere but can also become concentrated and unified. When you put lead together with mercury the two combine into an amalgam where the mercury doesn't flow anymore. The idea in Daoist cultivation, therefore, is that you have to unite your Qi with your thoughts and then your Qi will become still. You combine the two and then lead your Qi around your body to purify its coarse nature.

In *Neijia Yoga* I reveal all sorts of important Daoist secrets like this such as the fact that our pelvic region is symbolized by a four-sided square to represent the root chakra of the body because the major muscles surrounding the perineum form a square. Seen from below there are two ischiocavernosus muscles that form a corner of the square, the diagonal is the superficial transverse perineal muscle, and the ileococcygeous muscle forms the rest of the square. In any case, the highest yoga and martial arts attainments depend upon the principle of not losing too much Jing, Qi or Shen.

In the *Anapanasati sutra* of Buddhism you are taught to sit in meditation practice where you breathe in and out while trying to feel the Qi energy that is thereby pulsed through your body by your breathing, or *feel mental joy while simultaneously feeling the Qi of your entire body and pushing it around using your breathing.* You should also use your breathing to push the feeling of energy around inside your body while holding onto Yin or Yang emotions. During *anapana* you arouse your Yang Qi (through the use of joy that is a Yang emotion) while washing the Qi of your physical nature, and you can use other emotions as well.

Whether you are trying to calm your body's Qi through relaxed rhythmical breathing, or push your Qi around inside your body by using your breathing to move it here or there inside you, or trying to feel great happiness to the extent of excitation everywhere inside your body while using your breathing to amplify matters and push the energy around, these are just some of many possible ways to help "rotate" or internally circulate your Qi through frictional washing in order to purify it, specifically your Yang Qi when you use positive emotions. Other methods, such a feeling humbleness or contrition or related Yin emotions when you do this will help to wash your Yin Qi.

In many cultivation exercises you are taught to arouse negative emotions (ex. sorrow for viewing the sufferings of the world, distaste for the dissatisfactions in life, fear of future negative events that might happen to you, disgust from imagining a decaying corpse, guilt or shame for remembering personal faults, contrition while remembering misdeeds, etc.) while mindfully breathing slowly and deeply in order to purify your Yin Qi.

To cultivate your Yin Qi you should hold onto negative emotions that flood your consciousness and greatly arouse sensations within your body connected to those emotions while breathing deliberately with intent in ways that move that energy inside you. Christian Orthodox monks are taught to cry in sorrow and sadness when cultivating their Yin Qi (and also told to practice humility, patience, obedience, self-discipline, thriftiness, forbearance, and endurance which are all Saturnian Yin activities), Jain monks are taught to be overly anxious and fearful they don't hurt anything (and at an advanced stage to suffer the embarrassment of nakedness until they get used to it), and Buddhist monks are taught to feel great humility in silence when walking on alms rounds begging for food. These are all just methods of cultivating and washing your Yin Qi.

To wash your inner subtle body you need to arouse a certain tonality of your Qi (usually by strong emotions) and then rotate it via your will, or through the pushing of your breathing, or by vibrating it through mantra sounds, or moving it along with the internal sounds of singing, or by using any other methods that will link with your Qi and move it. Like combining mercury and lead to form an amalgam, you can use your thoughts to link with your Qi and guide its movements inside your body.

You must first feel the Qi of your body inside you as a specific type of energy and then wash that Qi by rotating it everywhere inside your subtle body. This is how you purify your Qi, cause a differentiation between your Yin Qi and Yang Qi, and prepare your subtle body to emerge as an independent spirit, which is the stage of the Earth Immortal accomplishment.

To the uninitiated this type of emotional washing sounds like it is not Daoist cultivation at all since most people think Daoism only advocates being serene and calm, but the adherents of all traditions are put through this type of emotional roller coaster and in particular you must suffer through thousands and thousands of repetitions of this during the twelve-year kundalini transformation period.

Normally you are just taught to cultivate emptiness ("release the mind," "calm the mental formations," "observe mental cessation," "practice relinquishment," "be detached from," etc.) while feeling a comfortable Qi flow within your body that is moved by your breathing. Other neutral and practically useless exercises are to be mindful of the rise and fall of your abdomen while breathing, counting breaths, being mindful of the sensations arising in the nose during inhalation and exhalation, being mindful of the respiratory flow within your body, scanning your entire body, observing how bodily sensations arise without adhering to them, and going into a state of deep relaxation while being fully conscious. These exercises might help you relax and harmonize your feelings but *they are useless* for transforming your spiritual Qi! You need strong *neijia, nei-gong* work.

These are harmless practices given to most everyone to help them relax their minds, but they do little as regards to Qi purification and transformation for spiritual ascension. For that objective they are a waste of time and your life. Only the wise know that you are to (1) raise your Yang Qi (such as during sports, sexual intercourse or by arousing happy emotions) or (2) Yin Qi (such as during states of mourning, remorse, sadness, depression, worry, contrition, humility or obedience) while also (3) performing various activities that involve strong Qi circulations because then you will finally be washing your Qi in a certain way and thus building the strength and purity of your inner spirit body.

You must understand that certain emotions like anger, pride, victory, confidence, domination, authority, etcetera cause your Yang energy to arise and then it is especially felt in the upper part of your body. This is why Tibetan Buddhism teaches some students to arouse "divine anger" and "divine pride" in various practices, which is in order to temporarily raise their Yang Qi rather than to cultivate these attitudes as personality characteristics. Unfortunately the monks don't know the principle being employed so some fall prey to anger and pride as personality traits.

Tibetan lamaism even allows sex in some situations because during sexual intercourse the passion, bliss and joy of intercourse, along with the emotions of happiness and love, can envelop you completely and energize your full-body Qi, as also happens during sports, and then you can use the ability of sex to stir your emotions and energy during that physical exercising as an process for Qi cultivation. Daoism also uses sexual intercourse in its cultivation practices.

Negative emotions such as fear, disgust, contempt, sadness, depression, shame, jealousy and envy cause the body's Yang energy to contract and its Yin energy to be stimulated. Feelings like sadness and depression are strong Yin Qi evokers as are fear, trepidation, guilt, shame and anxiety. You will sometimes feel coldness in the body, especially within its lower extremities such as the legs and feet, when they are stimulated. Feelings of coldness within the body are typically a sign of Yin Qi which becomes prevalent when people are sick with the cold or flu. Those are good times to spin your Yin Qi during those unfortunate situations.

Daoism has some martial arts styles that help you cultivate your Yin Qi but people normally neglect Yin cultivation in Daoism and primarily focus on Yang cultivation instead. This is *incorrect* because both modalities of Qi must be purified on the spiritual trail, which is why masters will often force their students into Yin situations such as working in a mortuary, hospital and so forth. These are big secrets I am revealing so pay attention. This is why the Tibetan master Padampa Sangye (d. 1117) once advised, "Approach whatever you find repulsive. Anything you are attracted to let go of it. Visit cemeteries and places that scare you." If you visit and temporarily stay in such places to arouse your Yin Qi you can help purify its nature *as is necessary for attainment of the higher spiritual bodies.* This is one of the reasons that that Hindu god Shiva, who leads people to enlightenment, is said to hang out in charnel grounds surrounded by ghosts and ghouls.

Notable periods or events where your Yin Qi becomes predominant within your body include times when you are sick (such as having the flu) or experiencing pain (which makes this a good time to "spin" your Qi); crying due to sadness or feelings of unworthiness (which Orthodox Christian monks are taught to do); walking with humility to collect alms for food (which Buddhist monks do); being caught naked with embarrassment (which Jain monks and certain sadhus do); walking over a (scary) high altitude bridge; living in fear (with anxiety) for an extended period of time; remaining depressed or forlorn for an extended period of time; feeling grief due to the death of a loved one; imagining that you absorb cool lunar energy from the moon; performing inner water washing visualizations; standing under a cold waterfall; cultivating within a room of mirrors that makes you feel cool or coldish; visualizing or imagining that you undergo age regression; fantasizing that you transform into a young girl (femininity practices) or age regress into a powerless young boy; visiting limestone or other "cold" mineral formations or living in a cool cave; negative planetary aspects such as Saturn transits; working in a monastery's ossuary; doing sneaky or evil deeds such as stealing or killing; visiting a hospital filled with sick patients that makes you feel ill at ease; visiting a mental asylum that unnerves you; visiting a (sad) funeral or wake or cultivating in cemeteries or charnel grounds (where you are both afraid and disgusted); watching a horror movie that frightens you; eating cold minerals such as calcium; ingesting cooling herbs, Yin foods or Yin medicines (such as antibiotics); watching someone perform voodoo, sorcery or witchcraft practices; "seeing ghosts" or having scary visions; performing Hell being, hungry ghost, purgatory (*preta*) or death sadhanas while feeling sad for sentient beings; feeling guilty, humiliated or ashamed of doing something; etcetera.

These are all situations that arouse the Yin Qi of your body because at those times your Yin Qi is stimulated and temporarily dominates your physique. There are even times of the day when environmental

Yin Qi is strongest, which is why Immortal martial artists like Sun Lutang would try to absorb Yin energy at a specific time on a daily schedule. There are also times of the month when Yin energy is strongest, such as during the full moon. If you create a forecast of stock market movements using neural networks fed with astronomical lunar data (see TimingSolution.com software) then you can recognize that down movements will be when earth Yin Qi is strong and rising prices when Yang Qi is rising. This, too, can be used for the timing of specific cultivation exercises or ceremonies rather than just using the new moon date or 21-24th days of the lunar month when the full moon is declining.

Sometimes Daoist or other enlightened masters will put their students in these standard Yin situations or other difficult situations for an extended period of time in order to stimulate their Yin Qi for purification purposes yet the students who are suffering have no idea what is actually going on. Nevertheless, this is the actual process of spiritual cultivation to purify all of your Qi so that you can attain the first transcendental spirit body and thereby become an Earth Immortal or Srotapanna Arhat.

The basic purpose of most spiritual exercises is to circulate your ordinary Qi without any emotional involvement that changes its tonality through energization. Alternatively, they have you arouse Yin and Yang Qi through internal sensations provoked by strong emotions so that the new Qi sensations totally suffuse your body with full permeation. You then hold onto that energization with stability, soaking in it, or rotate your Qi at the same time.

An example is the use of visualization to stimulate certain types of inner Qi experience, which is common in Daoist practices. *Adding visualizations to a practice means using your imagination to arouse your Qi to have a certain quality, texture, modality or flavor.* Then you hold onto that new feeling to wash the Qi of your body, or rotate your Qi internally while experiencing those strong emotions and inner sensations. You can also mentally flood an area with bright light or change its color to transform the temperament, quality or tonality of its Qi, or visualize an image within specific body parts because those actions will bring Qi into the region and the coloring will add emotional content that changes the flavor of the Qi. *Visualization Power* discusses such techniques that are also found in the *Visuddhimagga (The Path of Purification)* by Buddhaghosa (5th century), but people don't really understand how to use his recommended exercises.

This is the big secret of *real* spiritual cultivation work; it is about cultivating all the tonalities of your Qi by exciting its different flavors through various emotions, activities, environments and so on and then circulating, strongly vibrating or simply suffusing your body with a grand permeation of that Qi feeling during those times. Therefore people arouse emotional fervor through specific prayers, songs, remembrances, arousals, provocations, deity invitations or meditations where you then hold onto the aroused Yin or Yang Qi respectively and through prolonged practice of this nature you over time gradually end up toning, purifying or "washing" the relevant Yin Qi or Yang Qi of your subtle body that must emerge in order for you to become enlightened. If you pray regularly with emotion this accomplishes the same thing!

These principles are revealed in the second set of *Mara* states mentioned in the *Surangama Sutra* of Buddhism, which provides clear examples of what cultivators will go through as they are trying to "break through the form skandha (physical body)" to attain the independent astral body, deva body or subtle body that makes you an Earth Immortal. Breaking through the form skandha refers to your deva body (made of Qi) becoming free by breaking through (leaving) the shell of your physical body. It means you become an Earth Immortal. This information is also transmitted to us in the story of the Ten Trials of Daoist master Lu Dongbin and hardships of

Naropa!

Remember that the teachings of cultivation are universal or non-denominational, and so we can borrow the teachings of other schools to use in our practice because we should be non-sectarian and always seek after good results. The principles of cultivation apply to everyone so we must use the most efficient practices to make progress. Daoism follows this principle and so should you. It takes hundreds of years for the teachings from one spiritual school to become absorbed by another but you don't have to wait this long since you now have books and the internet. Simply use whatever teaching methods and teachings are helpful, expedient, effective and true. I am explaining the secret basis behind them.

During the twelve years of the kundalini awakening process of *internal alchemy* where "your Qi rotates through all your meridians (your entire body)" the enlightened masters of your tradition, whatever it is, will put you through countless Yin or Yang emotional experiences to wash your Yin or Yang Qi respectively. The second set of *Mara* states described in the *Surangama Sutra* tell you that during the stages of internal alchemy (kundalini transformation) you will be put through various strong emotional experiences such as:

- Great sadness or pity (Yin)
- Excitement and boldness (Yang)
- Hopelessness and forlornness (Yin)
- Pride and arrogance (Yang)
- Dread, anxiety and distress (Yin)
- Purity, peace and joy (Yang)
- Intense self-satisfaction and feelings of superiority (Yang)
- Infinite lightness and purity (Yang)
- Fear of death or absolute extinction (Yin)
- Boundless love, desire or even lust (Yang)

Many emotions are aroused within you during the overall process of spiritual cultivation so this short list is only indicative. Enlightened masters, deities and devas do this in order to alter the temperament of your Qi during times when you are washing your Qi. If you are lucky, your teacher will put you in different Yin environments or have you perform different Yin activities so that appropriate situations arise to arouse and wash your Yin Qi.

The Aghoris of India, for instance, send their students to a cemetery, at midnight, during the darkness of the New moon, to perform a ceremony involving a dead body. They tell the students that the ceremony will invite ghosts, demons or some other Yin beings while enlightened masters in their spirit bodies try to frighten the shit out of them in order to arouse and wash their Yin Qi. Shugendo students are hung upside down off of cliffs in order to arouse their fright and thereby stimulate their Yin Qi.

As for Yang environments and activities, such as attending a sporting game or watching an exciting action movie, they are easy to find.

An important lesson on this topic comes from the popular Finnish heatmap pictures, readily available on the internet, which indicate where various emotions are typically felt within the human body. Each human emotion excites your Qi in a different sort of way thus changing it quality, temperament or flavor. That excitation is felt strongly in different areas of the body for different types of emotions. One such study of these thermal heatmaps is called "Bodily Maps of Emotions" by Lauri Nummenmaa, Enrico Glerean, Riitta Hari and Jari Hietanen.

You should study these pictures of "emotion-induced bodily sensations" because this knowledge is the *secret basis* of many Daoist, Tibetan, Hindu, Yoga, Sufi, Shugenda, Shingon, Christian and Buddhist cultivation techniques meant to stimulate your emotions or arouse "dominant attitudes" of either Yin or Yang Qi.

From these valuable maps you will see that Yin emotions and Yang emotions cause different energy responses within your physical body. Positive Yang emotions like friendship, happiness or love are felt throughout your entire body while some emotions are felt strongly in specific locations. Your internal energy feels different when you experience different emotions, and this is the principle that is used to wash your Qi to prepare your spiritual body for emergence.

As previously noted, certain emotions like anger, pride, etcetera cause your energy to arise in the upper part of your body, and they also provoke your Yang Qi into rising within you. This is why Tibetan Buddhism employs great arousals of "divine anger" and "divine pride" in various practices, which is in order to temporarily raise the Yang Qi of practitioners rather than to cultivate these attitudes as personality characteristics. During sexual intercourse the happiness, excitement, joy and pleasurable feelings of sex can envelop you completely and then you can also use sexual intercourse's ability to stir your internal energy as an activity for Qi cultivation too.

Feelings of anger, pride, courage, triumph, heroics, victory, domination, confidence, euphoria, exhilaration, enthusiasm, joy, cheerfulness, awe, optimism, sexual excitement, love, amusement, strength, willpower, mirth, brightness, aliveness, attending weddings or other happy ceremonies or festivals, active exercise, fighting, masculinity practices, sunshine visualizations, pranayama cultivation, positive planetary aspects etcetera are all situations that raise or "stimulate" the Yang Qi of your body. The basic cultivation method of all spiritual schools is to enter into an emotional state that accordingly arouses sensations inside your body that will, in turn, stimulate or arouse your Yang Qi.

An example is whipping up devotional emotions for a deity to enter into an ecstatic state of Yang Qi. You can also *pervade your entire body with positive mental states or attitudes* that will stimulate your Yang Qi so that those resultant Qi energies will pervade and thus wash your subtle body. Sometimes you should do this because you want to develop those characteristics as personality traits, and in those cases you must break the comfort zone barriers you've established for normally experiencing that emotion so that at this time it overwhelms your normal limits and truly energizes your Qi to an uncontainable degree that is beyond the standards of your normal personality. Don't worry that you will become wild with that energy as a personality trait because you will slide back to your steady state of normal mental routines for holding yourself unless you are actively cultivating a new trait constantly.

When you perform meditation practices that hold onto feelings of infinite joy, universal loving-kindness, boundless compassion and so forth this is just another form of this technique where you try to strongly and energetically stimulate all the Qi inside your body using emotions as a prompt (where because an emotion is "infinite" or "boundless" so that you go beyond yourself with limitless energization and fully become that emotion).

When your methodology is so good that your emotions stir you inside and the energy totally infuses you then the practice is not just a mental phenomenon but becomes a physical phenomenon too, and that's what you want. You want to be stirring up or shaking the Qi of your body in an excited fashion when you use these techniques. In Daoist cultivation you are supposed to arouse the feeling of those mental-emotional states within your body in order to stimulate and thus activate/purify its Yang Qi.

From these thermal images you will also see that negative emotions such as fear, disgust, shame, anxiety, nervousness, guilt, inferiority, embarrassment, contempt, sadness, depression, shame, jealousy and envy will cause your body's Yin energy to be stimulated. When cultivating you will sometimes feel coldness in the body or a coolness like vapor surrounding you and rising into the sky (sort of like the feeling of light air conditioning) which is a blessing from higher spiritual beings trying to help you transform your Yin Qi. Other than Daoism, you will not find much information on Yin blessings and washings other than in the European Michael Maier's (d. 1622) hermetic classic *Atalanta Fugiens*, an alchemical emblems book.

Another blessing of Yin Qi purification is a temporary chill state within your body so cold that you must wrap yourself in blankets while your teeth actually chatter and your body shivers. It is not a sickness because it will last no more than a few minutes and then suddenly depart. Feelings of coldness within the body are typically a sign of Yin Qi, and sometimes during cultivation, as stated, you will suddenly feel so cold that your teeth will chatter, which is another type of blessing scenario that only lasts for about 15-30 minutes or so.

Also, it is common at the initial stages of cultivation for your salvia to become very sweet like a thick sweet wine for intermittent periods of time, and then the phenomena will disappear for many years but return in the very final stages of the process where you might experience a fuller, lighter and more profuse type of sweetness while at the same time all food might become tasteless (you will feel like you have lost your sense of taste).

This tastelessness is not due to a zinc deficiency, so perhaps it is due to the taste nerves being played with by devas at the end of the twelve-year kundalini purification process. Buddhist sutras say that the first dhyana involves having no taste, which is nonsense, so I do not think this is a tie-in explanation. I can only point out that the transformation process is abusive in ways too numerous to mention (although this depends upon your spiritual tradition) where to demonstrate their skills attending devas will often momentarily rob your ankles of strength, hit you here or there with pain, flash visions before your eyes, make you sneeze many times in a row, and make you go through all sorts of painful indignations. Tantric pictures aptly show deities standing on top of suffering human bodies. When the eyes are finally being transformed near the end of the process your vision can go blind or become inverted (you see the world upside down), which is a temporary event for just a few days, so perhaps the mention of having no taste was also referring to a temporary stage of body purification and transformation that was mentioned so as not to worry practitioners going through the process.

Daoist practitioners are typically not told about any of these things. The usual descriptions of cultivation *gong-fu* they experience (caused by masters performing Qi energizations within their bodies) fall along the following lines from this famous Daoist text:

> When [Jing transforming into Qi] is produced the practiser will feel as if the top of his head is raised; the dragon's hum and tiger's roar are heard in his ears; his body floats on the clouds and itches all over; he rises in space and rides on the wind, with an accompanying sense of boundless bliss. He will then feel as if a spider's web covers his face or tickling ants swarm over it from his forehead to the bridge of the nose, eye sockets, cheeks, jaws, teeth and mouth causing continual secretion of saliva which cannot all be swallowed (in one gulp). He is now disinclined to open his mouth or move his body, thus falling into a state of indistinctness in which nothing seems to exist, even his own body cannot be found, his breathing (appears to) stop and his pulses (to) cease beating. Vitality is fully developed and nurtures the immortal seed. Hence it is said; 'Fullness of vitality makes the practiser forget all about eating.'
>
> At this stage if he continues waiting, the negative principle will remain and the positive principle will not be genuine and will arouse his appetite. As a result the immortal seed cannot form because of deficient vitality.
>
> The practiser should train until he achieves stillness and radiance of his spirit which, when full, will make him forget about sleeping. When his vitality is fully developed and enables

him to dispense with eating, he reaches the stage of constant stillness and radiance in which breathing (appears to) cease and a massive golden light manifests while all discriminations stop arising, prior to this realisation of perfect serenity. This achievement is revealed by the moonlight appearing in the forehead which will remain constantly there if he is firmly determined to hold on to the original cavity of spirit (between and behind the eyes) while sparks appear between the eyebrows; both manifestations announce the full growth of the immortal seed.

Henceforth the practiser should guard against the drain of vitality in order to hold it in the body for nurturing and developing the immortal seed. During the latter's growth he should avoid the ten following excesses: 1, excessive walking which adversely affects his nerves; 2, standing, his bones; 3, sitting, his blood; 4, sleeping, his blood vessels; 5, listening, his generative force; 6, looking (at things), his spirit; 7, pleasure, his life; and 10, eating, his heart. In short he should avoid all excesses which are very harmful.

While sitting in meditation the practiser should never: 1, give rise to thoughts which cause the (inner) fire to flare up; 2, relax his concentration to avoid cooling down the (inner) fire; 3, look at external objects, for there the spirit wanders thereby harming the incorporeal soul (hun); 4, listen to outer sounds, for this scatters the generative force and so harms the corporeal soul (p'o); 5, breathe quickly, for such breaths disperse easily and cannot be regulated; and 6, break his breath rhythm, for its abrupt stoppage will make it weak when resumed; and when he suddenly stops breathing he cools his (vital) breath and when he starts again suddenly he heats it thereby damaging the immortal seed. If he does not pay attention to all this he will achieve nothing.[5]

As stated, the emotions of fear, fright, shock, hurt, anxiety, sadness, worry, sullenness, disappointment, loneliness, isolation, hopelessness, helplessness, resignation, vulnerability, rejection, unimportance or inferiority, insignificance, feeling unwanted, feeling let down, feeling confused and lost, feeling on guard and uncomfortable, inner turmoil

---

[5] *Taoist Yoga*, Lu K'uan Yu, (Samuel Weiser, York Beach: Maine, 1984), pp. 116-117.

and travail, physical pain, intimidation, humility, yearning, hunger (fasting), depression, suicide, guilt, embarrassment, shame, humiliation, grief, apathy, disgust, revulsion, jealousy, treachery, sneakiness, greed, and chills or the flu all stimulate, vibrate, energize or raise your Yin Qi.

When trying to purify a practitioner's Yin Qi, enlightened masters put individuals through very painful emotional experiences like this and sometimes even use their own *nirmanakaya* energies to cause physical annoyances, irritation or pain within their student's bodies to arouse their Yin Qi, especially during the last years of the transformational period of internal alchemy rotations when one's feet become extremely cold due to the fact that their Yin Qi is being worked on. All of this is quite distressing to practitioners who don't know what is going on and the lack of understanding prompts many to consider suicide due to the excessiveness of the process. In Christianity the monks going through this are taught that it is the work of devils, which adds fear-based Yin Qi to the pain-based Yin Qi, but actually it is a Qi washing process that is going on. Being only human, unfortunately the specific devas overseeing the process sometimes get carried away and go astray.

All these principles are even taught to us in the Ten Trials of Lu Dongbin that parallel the second set of ten *Mara* states within the *Surangama Sutra*. The ten trials of the Daoist sage Lu Dongbin refer to the internal alchemy cleansing phase of the twelve-year internal alchemy transformation period (of kundalini awakening) where he also passed through various emotional states in order to wash his Qi:

In the first trial Lu Dongbin is caused to feel great sadness (Yin Qi was aroused) because he thought his family members were dying.

In the second trial he felt great anger (Yang Qi was aroused) because he was cheated of money in the marketplace for his goods.

In the third trial he responded with compassion (Yang Qi was aroused), and then indignation and irritation (Yin Qi was aroused) because he gave money to a beggar who kept asking for more and more endlessly.

In the fourth trial he felt great fear (Yin Qi was aroused) because he crossed paths with a hungry tiger.

In the fifth trial he resisted the pull of strong sexual desire that arose within him (Yang Qi was aroused) when a beautiful girl tried to seduce him. In the Aghori tradition of India the masters will ask an attractive enlightened heavenly maiden to produce a *yang-shen* emanation to attract a young adept's attention and provoke his sexual interest from afar.

In the sixth trial he felt dejected, depressed and at a loss (Yin Qi was aroused) because his entire estate had been completely burglarized.

In the seventh trial he experienced great astonishment and happiness (Yang Qi was aroused) in the face of greed (Yin Qi was aroused) when he discovered that some bronze utensils he bought were actually made of gold, so he returned them.

In the eighth trial he aroused fearlessness/courage (Yang Qi was aroused) by drinking a magic potion said to make one an Immortal.

In the ninth trial he experienced great worry and terror (Yin Qi was aroused) due to a flood, but then he composed himself.

The tenth trial is the most enlightening. Lu Dongbin was alone reading a book in his room when countless ghosts, demons and monsters suddenly came from every corner of the world to attack him (Yin Qi was aroused). This type of illusion often happened to

Padre Pio and the Tibetan adept Yeshe Tsogyel (c. 757), which you can read about in her autobiography. Despite the attacks, Lu Dongbin kept on doing his chores without paying the demons any attention, ignoring them entirely. That is the instruction for us even though our emotions are being unbalanced during these operations. One of the monsters yelled that Lu Dongbin had wronged him in a past life and now needed to sacrifice his life. Without any fear Lu said, "Go ahead and take my life since I took yours in a past life. This is fair."

Suddenly Lu heard the clapping of hands, a shout in the air, and then the sky turned blue and all the ghosts and devils vanished. Standing there was his master, Han Zhongli, who had been looking and laughing at him while all these events were happening. In other words, Han Zhongli (and other spiritual masters who were helping him) had been supervising the charade of illusions and emotional promptings (while his Qi was being worked on). That's what happens when you go through the advanced stages of internal alchemy for the twelve years it takes to purify your body's Qi so that an independent spirit body can arise out of it. The masters will provoke all sorts of strong Yin or Yang emotions to arise within you to wash your Qi and masquerade as devils or angels to do so.

Speaking frankly, the tail end of the process is extremely abusive because while you are going through it, which is being overseen by spiritual masters who are transforming your Qi through various manipulations of *nirmanakaya* emanations from their higher bodies, devas and lower level Immortals are all passing in and out of you because they are being worked on at the same time. They surround you daily because they all want purification work on their bodies. The big boys, or enlightened Celestial and Universal Immortals, also want work on their *nirmanakaya* so that those emanations also become purified through those blessings to gain an ascension that the master cannot himself produce through his own internal alchemy work on them. If the big masters are working on you they are working on enlightening many devas in your vicinity at the same time, and this includes teaching higher skills to the local *tudigong* protect gods.

Thousands of local devas around you want higher beings to work on transforming their Qi via their *nirmanakaya* emanations, and to dissuade this amount of wannabes from training sessions within you they make the process especially painful at times so that many leave. If you have to suffer incredible pain and anguish due to an abusive process at times then nobody complains, "Well, why does he or she get to go through it and not me?" No one is jealous when they see the pain and abuse you have to suffer.

Since you are the host within which most of the *nirmanakaya* Qi washing action happens locally and the local testing ground to see the skills of the devas striving for the higher bodies, you are used as the arena for training the higher beings in your area how to do advanced energy manipulations to wash people's Qi. The fully enlightened masters do this on you while simultaneously performing the exact same energy washing techniques on worthy students who visit you in various training sessions, and you remain the one constant sufferer of the painful experiences, which can damage your body permanently if you are not careful during the process.

This is why enlightened masters rarely ever speak of what happens during the kundalini transformation process that Daoism calls "inner alchemy." It would scare everyone away. They typically only say, "I spent twelve years with my teacher," as you will see commonly mentioned in the stories of the 84 Mahasiddhas or in the biographies of various saints, but no one mentions much about this time. Even Shakyamuni only hinted about the details yet he gave some warnings about it since some people commit suicide when going through it due to unskillful management of the process.

The same basic principle that your Qi needs to become washed through experiences that arouse emotions that strongly stimulate your Yin or Yang Qi is illustrated in the Tibetan story of Naropa (circa 956-1040), who spent twelve years with his teacher Tilopa on the banks of the Bagmati river at the site of the Pashupatinath Temple before he attained *siddhi*, which people equate with enlightenment even though it only means the first stage of the Earth Immortal attainment. Whenever a story involves twelve years they are usually talking about the kundalini washing experience that takes place during which time your Qi is rotated and washed until you attain the independent subtle body.

The story of the "Twelve Minor Trials (Hardships) of Naropa" recounts various Yin and Yang Qi experience that Naropa went through before he could meet Tilopa, but few understand the secret meaning of this story. In this story the student Naropa goes looking to meet master Tilopa and encounters many shocking experiences during his journey. The idea being transmitted is that each of those experiences strongly stimulates his emotions and consequently the Yin or Yang Qi throughout his body. We must be given some leeway in interpreting which emotions were stimulated during the encounter of each experience, but it doesn't really matter because the story is only meant to teach you that *this emotional priming has to happen.*

For the first trial Naropa encountered a leper woman covered with wounds who could not move, which caused disgust and repulsion to arise within him (and thereby stimulated his Yin Qi). In the second trial he came upon a dog infested with lice and maggots that were eating its rotting flesh, and various emotions of compassion and repulsion thus arose (stimulating his Yin Qi and Yang Qi). For the third trial he encountered a man trying to play devious tricks on his parents who asked him to help. Refusing this man with criticism, indignation and detestation provoked his Yin and Yang Qi. Next in the fifth trial he met a man who was tearing up a corpse for its intestines, and naturally fear and abhorrence arose from seeing such a ghastly sight (arousing his Yin Qi). Next in the sixth trial he came upon a man having an open stomach wound that he was washing with water and who asked Naropa to help him wash the wound. Afraid and disgusted but also feeling compassion, his Yin and Yang Qi were strongly evoked. For the seventh trial he became interested in marrying the daughter of a king because his sexual desire was provoked strongly (thus stimulating his Yang Qi). For the eighth trial he came upon a hunter with his hounds, who asked him to join him on the hunt. This spurred his sense of excitement, fun and courage (thus arousing his Yang Qi) but Naropa refused and continued on his journey. Next in his ninth trial he encountered a couple by a lake who made him a non-vegetarian meal that he refused to eat, so the man said in indignation and anger that he would kill Naropa's parents. The unruly, unpredictable and vehement unreasonableness frightened him thus stimulating his Yin Qi. In the tenth trial he came upon the terrifying scene of a man who had impaled his father upon a stake and imprisoned his mother in a dungeon, both of whom asked him to free them from their murderous son. Fear, worry, anxiety and feelings of unjustness at the misery he viewed arose within him to wash his Qi. Next in the eleventh trial he came upon a hermitage where he was received with pomp because of his status, thus raising his pride (and Yang Qi). On the premises was a beggar named Tilopa cooking fish, so the residents started hitting him and Naropa became confused and perplexed with Tilopa's doings and teachings, thus arousing his Yin Qi once again. In the twelfth trial he came to a wide open plain populated by people with strange abnormalities, and the strange sights prompted disgust, fear and other Yin Qi emotions to arise.

Remember this principle: the only way you can achieve enlightenment is if your Qi becomes purified, and the only way this happens is if hundreds of masters lend their energies to the process of helping to purify your body's energies while raising your Yin Qi and Yang Qi, basically putting your Qi through all sorts of modalities so that all the energies of your physical body are washed. You need to depend upon others to attain enlightenment rather than just your own efforts alone. This is why you should do as much of this work *on your own* through your own personal *nei-gong* practices that employ the education you are receiving and your own wisdom. You cannot just cultivate Yang Qi but must cultivate Yin Qi as well. Remember what Padampa Sangye said: "Approach whatever you find repulsive. Anything you are attracted to let go of it. Visit cemeteries and places that scare you." This was advice for washing your Yin Qi, which people hardly ever do.

Any local deva in the vicinity of a purification session on you wants to be worked on as well and will come within you for some sessions if an enlightened master is working on you for purification purposes. Hence, if the process wasn't abusive involving lots of undeserved pain then thousands of unqualified individuals would clamor to be worked on within you as you are being helped daily during the twelve years of internal alchemy kundalini washing that wins you the stage of the Earth Immortal. When ordinary devas see and experience the incredible pains that you must suffer through the process (assaults that last hours to your ears, nose, head, face, teeth, asshole, right side, knees and so forth) then no one complains that they aren't being worked on. This is why I stress that you do a lot of purification efforts yourself, and develop the neural patterns for the various patterns of washing your Qi to speed the process which will often be neglected at times by spiritual masters overseeing it.

The ten trials of Lu Dongbin were given to us to let us know what to expect when going through the transformational experiences of internal alchemy that wash your Qi and produce the astral deva body that is the stage of the Earth Immortal. The twelve minor trials of Naropa are meant to teach the same lesson. Parts of Yeshe Tsogyal's autobiography refer to the same process. Shakyamuni Buddha also gave us explicit teachings in the *Surangama Sutra* on the fact that this was the process, and he also *gave us warnings not to let the devas lead you astray into doing things against common sense and the laws of society that will get you into trouble because they certainly will try to do so.*

This is the first time I have ever revealed all these secrets about the process, which is kept secret because (1) people wouldn't normally understand the process or believe these details to be true, and (2) it would dissuade people from the cultivation path to enlightenment. However, students from every religion go through this very same process without exception and need to know. For instance, this is the very same process that Christian monks go through where they are undergoing the physical Qi purifications necessary for the transfiguration of their subtle body so that they can begin a higher existence.

How did you think all these individuals in Christianity, Islam, Hinduism and so on became saints and developed superpowers? It is because they all undergo the exact same kundalini transformation process, or inner washings of internal alchemy that Christians call the blessings of the Holy Spirit out of ignorance. During the process, which Christianity calls called "spiritual warfare," they too are deceived into believing that they are fighting devils and demons as they are put through trials and temptations and emotions that wash the various tonalities of their Yin and Yang Qi. Afterwards they achieve the first of the higher spiritual bodies, the process is explained to them, and they start working on cultivating the rest. They achieve the initial stages of *Homo Deus* and then sometimes travel to a new location to attain the Causal body made of Shen, which is the stage of the Spirit Immortal or Anagamin, and then so on so as to give the local guys a break after working on them for so many years.

As an example from Christianity (which I am using a lot simply because we simply don't have sufficient recorded Daoist accounts), Saint Paisios the Anthonite said that he engaged in spiritual warfare with demons when in 1962 he visited Saint Catherine's Monastery in the Sinai to live as a hermit. Many Orthodox monks are sent there to go through a specific stage of transformation due to the expertise of the ancient enlightened masters in Egypt who still help people. Lu Dongbin and Yeshe Tsogyel reported going through similar challenges in fighting devils and demons that was an intercession by spiritual beings masquerading as such to stimulate their Yin Qi through fright for a specific period of time in order to help purify it through stimulation and rotational washing.

Saint Paisios reported that the devil himself materialized in front of him and battled with him in a great spiritual struggle, but of course this was really a *nirmanakaya* emanation from an enlightened master who made him think it was the devil but certainly was not. At one time Paisios went through a two-week period of seclusion in a small hermitage (*asketerion*) above Saint Catherine's Monastery where the trials and warfare with the devil were so severe that he later told monks: "What I experienced up there from the devil in those fifteen days cannot be expressed. It is impossible to imagine. I felt as if I was nailed to the Cross." In a Russian Youtube video with English subtitles (St. "Catherine's Monastery: St. Paisios at Sinai") he describes some of those spiritual struggles with what was essentially the *nirmanakaya* emanation of an enlightened master who was actually helping him by disguising himself as a devil.

The last thing you should know about purifying (transforming) your physical body's Qi corresponds to an earlier stage of cultivation and transformation, and pertains to the fact that it is difficult to seamlessly link and unify the Qi in the upper and lower halves of your body. I have dealt with this extensively in *Correcting Zen* and *Neijia Yoga*.

The two halves of your body, upper and lower, are separated by your pelvis where your hips divide the upper part of your body from the bottom part. There is actually a great temperature difference between the upper and lower halves of your body that is easily seen in thermal images. It occurs due to poor blood flow through the hips and pelvis because of the complicated anatomical structures within this region. The delineation border is the waist line just above the pelvis so this is where the region of transition begins.

This also makes psychological sense because for many lives we have been told to restrain the energy flow in our hips and have developed some psychological blockages due to disciplinary issues around shitting, pissing, farting and sex. We've been taught, "Don't do that. Hold your energy." Various stretching exercises are available from yoga and the martial arts, including leg splits, that can help people gradually open up their hip region so that your energy can more readily pass through this area, which will also help men decrease their tormenting problem of sexual desire.

I also recommend practicing the abdominal *nauli kriya* yoga exercise and *pawanmuktasana* because this will help with sexual control and help prevent hernias, which are an increasing problem for men. I do not recommend hanging weights from the scrotum or penis, as recommended in some Daoist texts, because a Taiwanese surgeon I once met said that he had performed countless surgical operations on Chinese men who had practiced this Daoist technique and torn the tendons in their groin. Rather, I recommend the standard Daoist exercises found in *Neijia Yoga*.

And incidentally, if a man is interested in sexual virility due to his advancing age I suggest the following article (which offers alternatives to Viagra for nitric oxide supplementation, focuses on ultrasonic treatments to help flagging erections, but fails to mention similar blood flow benefits from using nattokinase):

https://bengreenfieldlife.com/transcripts/transcript-best-sexual-biohacks/

As to the topic of flagging testosterone, while many tout *tribulus terrestris, tongkit ali,* fenugreek and D-aspartic acid to increase testosterone perhaps the best ingredient is *bulbine natalensis* from South Africa, which is found in "Mahler's Aggressive Strength Testosterone Booster." Some feel this is superior to testosterone replacement therapy since hormone usage has some drawbacks.

Basically, the complicated structure of bones, ligaments, tendons and muscles within your pelvis makes it hard for Qi to smoothly ascend, descend and circulate freely through this region. It is therefore hard to link your upper body with your lower body in the martial arts until you conquer this internally complicated transitioning zone whose structure makes it difficult to transmit power from your feet and hips to your striking. In the martial arts and yoga you need to learn to control your upper and lower body as one by linking their energy into a unified whole. You want to be able to achieve the level where a wave of energy can arise from your toes, move upwards through your legs to your pelvis/waist and then into your hands and fingertips for as the *Taiji Classic* says, "The energy is rooted in the feet, develops in the legs and is directed by the waist."

You want to become able to spiral energy from your lower body on through the muscles of the pelvis to your arms for striking motions in the martial arts but this only becomes possible if you stretch the muscles in your pelvis and open up the Qi channels within this region as well. This is something to work on during your life. The famous inventor of *baguazhang,* Dong Haichuan (d. 1882), had most certainly achieved enlightenment and is said to have been taught by master "Coiling Cloud." This might actually refer to a real individual or his method of training and transformation wherein he was always coiling, spiraling or rotating his inner Qi in various ways. Most individuals who train in *baguazhang* never realize that while their physical body is twisting and turning in the outward form of the practice they are also supposed to practice the same spiraling and coiling with their body's inner energy as well, which other schools term churning or washing.

Your Qi everywhere needs to be naturally connected as a single seamless unit of energy, which is what you must work towards during all your years of cultivation practice. Your entire body with all its joints and extremities should become threaded together without the slightest break. All the muscles, ligaments, bones, organs and appendages must be integrated into having one unified Qi. Don't remain in a broken and non-continuous state but refine your one Qi during life as you are really just a being of energy but don't know it. Unify that energy! Perform yoga *asanas* to stretch all the muscles of your pelvis (especially those within it), Ben Patrick "knees over toes" exercises to strengthen your leg muscles, the appropriate Z-Health exercises for your hips (and feet), martial arts horse standing postures and Qi exercises to lead your Qi through this region to totally free it of internal circulatory impediments.

Another fact that can be seen from heat images of the body is that our poorest blood circulation areas are localized in our hands and feet, *which are therefore bottlenecks preventing the smooth flow of Qi everywhere else within the body!* This is why those regions need special attention in our efforts at Qi cultivation. We should daily practice specific hand and foot exercises designed to open up their Qi channels and try to rotate the Qi within the hands, feet and pelvis every day.

For the fingers and hands I recommend the Z-Health finger-hand exercises, the finger exercises of isolated activated stretching, using an inexpensive rubber finger grip strength trainer (stretching exercise device), and Daoist finger-digit counting where you should try to feel, push or energize the Qi throughout your fingers when counting. The best method is to daily stretch the muscles of your fingers (such as through a grip strength trainer) and try to activate the Qi within your fingers and vibrate it with mantra sounds, emotions and visualizations. You want to practice stretching your finger muscles so that you can actually *feel them* and send Qi through them in an active state, which is how normal exercise becomes internal energy work on the fingers when done properly.

Tibetan Buddhism has specific finger exercises while Japanese Shingon practitioners recite various *bija* sounds when doing specific hand mudras, but most practitioners simply go through the motions of making the mudras and voicing the sounds without realizing that they are supposed to recite the sounds as if from inside their fingers to help vibrate the internal energy of those digits while performing the mudras. I have discussed such techniques within *Correcting Zen* and *Neijia Yoga*.

The warmest part of the body is the spine, which is the easiest Qi pathway to open via various exercises (such as microcosmic breathing or visualization practices), and the root of the spine is the sacrum in the pelvis. You can learn how to do spinal Qi exercises to open up the *ida, pingala* and *sushumna* channels within the spinal cord in *Buddha Yoga, Arhat Yoga, Neijia Yoga* and *Correcting Zen* once again. As Zen Master Nan Huai-chin commented on the initiating this microcosmic circulation in the spine so that it runs automatically, which means that spiritual masters are doing it for you:

> Very few can achieve genuine rotation of the river chariot (this circulation of Qi within your body) and circulate Qi among the eight extra meridians (of the body). Even fewer really understand the stage of separation and unification of body, mind and the origin of Nature (the generation of the deva body that makes one an Earth Immortal). Therefore, even if one sincerely wants to teach this, a student with the ability to receive this supreme instruction is rare. After this stage, a person goes beyond earthly things and enters into the metaphysical realm. Even if a teacher wished to describe this in detail, a student with the wisdom and

experience to receive these instructions beyond the realm of the human world would be exceptional."[6]

This is not a book on instructions, as stated, because such information is readily provided elsewhere and deserves books of their own. This book has the task of revealing the information you don't know about Daoism so that your own practice effort blossoms and that at the minimum you attain greater health, longevity and prosperity. I sincerely hope this information improves your practice and makes many things clear so that you don't make mistakes.

---

[6] *Tao and Longevity: Mind-Body Transformation,* Nan Huai-Chin, trans. by Wen Kuan Chu (Samuel Weiser, York Beach: Maine, 1991), p. 79.

CHAPTER 4:
WHAT DOES THE HUMAN BEING DESIRE OUT OF LIFE?
SOME POSSIBLE ADDENDUMS TO UPDATE DAOIST
PHILOSOPHY

Daoism emphasizes the principles of wisdom and inner peace, softness and humility as virtues, gentleness as a way of doing things, resilience while staying centered in life, effortless acting (*wu-wei*), and living modestly and cohesively in harmony with nature.

When people think of Daoism various images often come to mind. This includes living with utter simplicity in harmony with nature, practicing the martial arts, eating natural foods, abiding in quiet peacefulness, using Chinese herbal medicine, reading *Zhuangzi* and *Laozi*, listening to Chinese flute music and being spontaneous, free and in tune with nature so that you flow along with the currents of life by aligning yourself with methods of least resistance.

There are countless books and movies about Daoist philosophy which portray a certain romance in living as a Daoist. A main principle is not using force when there are simpler natural ways to accomplish the same objective. One should instead adopt the practice of living modestly in harmony with nature and one's fate rather than acting counterproductively against forces larger than oneself.

Since so much free information is available to you about Daoism there is no reason to write extensively about the Daoist philosophy sources already available. Those sources commonly render advice like the following: "You should be like a fallen leaf moving along a stream. If you allow the stream to carry you (rather than fighting against it) then its strength becomes yours. You then become one with nature, moving without attachment so that you are always unbound, and by always leaving the past behind you can guarantee yourself to always be fully present in the living moment." Also, "Don't differentiate yourself as apart from the world because it is all you. The universe is just you. You are a simply a part within it with an imaginary consciousness rather than an independent standalone identity."

One of the practical aspects of Daoism is gaining a correct understanding of how the universe works so that we can approach life more intelligently with our actions. We want to be living life with less friction by going along with the flow of phenomena. The Daoist guiding principle for life is to develop wisdom, which means a knowledge of the reliable patterns of cause and effect that characterize existence, and thereby use sophistication rather than force to accomplish things. It is not that the Daoist eschews modernity and innovation like the Amish but that he strives to learn the easiest and best ways to do things that tend to be naturalistic solutions.

The Daoist ideal is to develop wisdom (understanding) as to how the world works so that we can actually improve how we act and behave, which will in turn lead to better outcomes in life. What this actually means is aligning or partnering ourselves and our actions with the forces of nature using optimal, skillful methods of least resistance. We want our actions to be intelligent, skillful efforts rather than just applications of brute force to situations. Being attuned with optimality is a key feature of Daoism.

Another aspect of Daoism is working to achieve the state of flow or effortless action illustrated in the famous story of the effortless butcher (Cook Ding) found in the *Zhuangzi*.

In the flow state you enter into a zone where you seem to be acting without striving and everything seems to flow. You seem to actually become the act you are doing because of a very special mental involvement. You start performing actions with full concentration and engagement (deep involvement such as becoming one with music you hear) along while experiencing a sense of presence with pristine clear awareness.

This is a state of clear mindfulness and focused attention absent of mental afflictions or distractions. You become so immersed in the immediate task at hand that you forget about the future and just live in the present moment. You basically enjoy a state of pure beingness during your doing. You focus on the present and "forget results," which means that you don't worry about the past or future in whatever you are doing but simply perform your actions with as great a skill as possible due to having focused concentration. As the Daoist butcher in the *Zhungzi* said, "perception and understanding come to a stop and spirit moves where it wants."

Daoism states that you are completely in the present when you let go of concerns such as freeing your mind from the regrets or burdens of the past. It tells us to leave each day behind like flowing water, and at every moment to free yourself from the anxieties of the future. Dwelling in the past can prevent you from truly living in the present because you should be naturally making the most out of the present moment without occupying it with past engagements. Water flows in the present moment always reaching its future destination, so similarly you should always be enjoying the present moment absent of any other concerns.

Daoism teaches that if we can keep our mind in the present moment focused on the task at hand and let go of clinging to (anticipating) future results we can act more effortlessly and just live in the act itself. This is akin to achieving the state of flow. By being fully present with awareness we can live life to more fullness because awareness then opens to the wonders of the living moment rather than remains shackled by being encased in images of something else. This is why we should quiet our minds by freeing them of distractions. Why? Because the open, quiet mind allows us to take in the present moment instead of preoccupying it with something else.

It is indeed important to work for a more beneficial future, which is working on achieving progress or development, but we must avoid letting our expectations for the future take over the present moment in our minds. We must focus on the task or circumstances at hand and then we are truly living life even when in difficulties.

The state of flow and how to achieve it is something I've explained extensively in *Neijia Yoga*, which is all about Daoist practice for martial arts and the appropriate inner *nei-gong* exercises that take one to becoming a Daoist Immortal. I am not going to cover specific Daoist cultivation techniques because I've extensively taught them elsewhere in *Nyasa Yoga, Buddha Yoga, Arhat Yoga* and *Correcting Zen*. Therefore I am also not going to talk much about Daoist mind cultivation either, such as how to live consciously by bringing awareness to everyday activities such as when making tea or sweeping the floor. Nonetheless you can find some Daoist exercises in the appendices.

As to Daoist philosophy, it has developed over the centuries by absorbing influences from many streams of thought, especially Buddhism, Confucianism and the cultivation schools of India. Buddhism had a big impact on Daoism and society at large and both schools influenced each other. Zen was especially influenced by

Daoism and Daoism by Zen to the extent that Daoism eventually developed its own tradition of communal monastic practice and living. Organized forms of Daoism only developed after hundreds of years of its existence.

As a proper course of development, it should now absorb the civilizing influences of science as well as anything else that is good that will elevate its adherents. People have a tendency to oversimplify Daoism and concentrate only on the earliest Daoist texts like *Laozi* and *Zhuangzi* without focusing on later Daoist developments that focus on more complicated schools of thought. This exclusive focus on what they believe is "pure Daoism" is a mistake, as you should be concentrating on mastering the greater bodies of Daoist knowledge and how they can help your life or teach you to cultivate to attain the Tao.

Although the following is not recognized as Daoism per se, my vision of a more developed Daoism that transmits a fuller and more proper perspective on life would incorporate the following elements including the psychological findings of modern man:

MORALITY AND ETHICAL PRINCIPLES

First, people must understand that the basis of Daoist practice should always be an ethical foundation of behavior. Most everyone knows the common ethical rules of behavior include not killing, stealing, lying, sexual improprieties and the Golden Rule that we should treat every person as we would want to be treated, meaning that we should do for them what we would want done for us but should not to do to others what we wouldn't want done to us.

Yes, Daoism certainly points out that the rules, ethics and values within society are all man-made inventions. There are no such things as rights, fairness, ethics, justice or proper conduct in biology or

Nature. These are imagined natural orders that don't truly exist in the universe. There is just Nature, and there is no book of ethics inscribed within it. However, from the sense of justice and fairness people create ethics, moral codes and rituals in order to benefit humanity with peaceful cooperation and a bonding social cohesion even though they form an artificial way of life.

So while it is true that our ethical rules and standards of behavior are man-made artificialities they benefit humanity even though they do not truly exist as ontological musts. We are basically animals that cannot live alone but must live in groups. Therefore we require cooperation with others in order to maintain our individual existences. Because we must live together with others we need such rules in order to curb our aggressive, anti-social behaviors in order to maintain neighborliness, friendliness, peace, harmony, fairness, cooperation and order in society.

There is also a personal advantage to such rules in terms of helping us be our true selves. The rules of ethics and morality help us make our intentions perfectly genuine so that we can be true to our authentic self. They allow us to demonstrate straightforwardness, honesty and sincerity in our thoughts and deeds so that they reflect who we truly are.

We should definitely be taught from youth on through to adulthood various moral principles such as the following: to love (treat) your neighbor as yourself; to guide your own actions according to the behavioral principles of *moderation, balance and the golden mean* rather than flying off to extremes because of arrogance, pride or *hubris*; to enrich all your actions with consummate skillfulness and good intentions (a principal awareness, dominant attitude or aspiration of special intent that elevates them through reframing or reinterpretation); to follow the rule of doing all the good you can, by all the means you can, in all the ways you can, in all the places you can, at all the times you can, to all the people you can, as long as you ever can (which means to be unremitting in the doing of good deeds by doing them with all your might and by every possible means); to strive to bring about good in all your actions and support goodness whenever you find it while cutting off evil whenever you encounter it; which means to always encourage unborn good to arise and always try to prevent unborn evil from arising (which means taking positive steps to *prevent* evil or harm from occurring); to avoid any evil deeds, foster all that is good and virtuous, and work on purifying (taming) your mind; to be natural in your ways but always *purifying your mind and behavior* to become the best version of yourself possible, which means "beautifying" (elevating) your mind and behavior; to always adhere to the principles that your actions must produce more good than harm, never increase a risk of harm to others, and if harm must be done then to minimize the harm you must do; to follow the principle of non-violence to take no actions that will harm life nor by inaction allow life to be harmed; to treat all people fairly, work for the benefit of those unfairly treated, and stand up for their rights and protect them when they need support or protection; to impose no unfair burdens on others, and always provide people with whatever they are owed or deserve; and lastly not to waste resources that could be used for good.

Like all human beings, Daoists should also pledge themselves to the fundamental principles of ethical behavior such as the cardinal ethical principles not to kill, lie, steal, engage in sexual misconduct, and so forth. They should respect people's autonomy (which means forbidding slavery, serfdom or the exploitation of others), not aggress upon their person or property, and be honest in their dealings with others.

They should cultivate the virtues of civilized man (filial piety, honesty, fairness, kindness, acceptance, reciprocity, generosity, etc.) and respect the obligations within the traditional relationships of parent-child, brother-sister, self-friends, student-teacher, employee-boss, citizen-society, man-environment, and other relationships as seen below. To help cultivate virtues the repetition of slogans, aphorisms or affirmations, such as is done in Stoicism, will be a great helpmate to Daoists. Repeating affirmations releases your inner will so that you can align yourself with a higher intention.

REFINING YOUR PERSONALITY, MIND AND BEHAVIOR (CONDUCT) - THE "CONVERSION OF MANNERS"

We are living beings with consciousness but still basically animals. To rise above the animal stage of existence to become truly human we must purify our minds and behavior, which also means beautifying or elevating our thoughts and conduct to become our best or highest self.

Most societies have rules of behavior designed to help us transcend the lower impulses of our animal nature so they basically help to raise us up. While Daoism is naturalistic, by no means does it espouse that we should not elevate our behavior to remain at the stage of animals that are not in control of their passions and impulses. Without the influences of education and the moral rules of society each one of us would simply be an animal that followed its own selfish personal interests. While Daoism paints an ideal picture of not following any fixed rules but going with the natural flow of Nature the majority of mankind needs ethical, moral and legal guidelines.

Confucius said that he *refined himself* by basing himself on virtue and by taking recreation in the arts, which in his day this was a set of self-mastery disciplines that included archery, charioteering, writing, ritual and music. This is how he *elevated himself* above being just a very healthy animal with great vitality. Today "refining ourselves" would go beyond social education and include activities like yoga, martial arts and athletics that cultivate/refine your physical nature and Qi; the active literacies (reading, writing, public speaking) that cultivate your intellect and give you the power of elegant, effective expression; repeated exercises in the forms of good manners and politeness; adherence to a personal code of standards; training in logic in making judgments and caution in reasoning to conclusions; and familiarity with the fine arts since they pacify emotions and help to refine/elevate your tastes and character. We need pursuits that raise us up and help us become the best versions of ourselves.

Hence, in life you must not just cultivate your virility, vitality or Qi health and physical strength (animals do this because females are attracted to the strongest "alpha" males for breeding) but must refine your personality, mental activity and behavior through training and by exposure to the highest examples of culture that are worthy ideals for emulation. Cultural refinement helps to "make noble the beast within us." Refinement or elevation of our intellect and behavior (through propriety, discipline, patience, wisdom, kindness, compassion and the other virtues) are what make us ascend instead of remaining just animals.

Therefore we must elevate society through the civilizing influences of education, religion, ethics and law to become human. We must all engage in the daily activity of policing ourselves through self-reflection to correct errors in our conduct, thinking and behavior. I have written my thoughts on this in *Color Me Confucius*, *Correcting Zen* and *Self-Creation* (*The Superhuman Protocol* or some such title) which all include teachings on cultivating your mind so that you can ignore distractions and eliminate afflictions to maintain your focus, concentration and attention in the present moment on whatever you are doing. Life depends upon our thoughts and desires which create harmony or disharmony in our lives, our family, our community and state so we must learn how to govern our mind and pacify disquieting thoughts. This is part of Daoist spiritual practice, which includes how to cultivate a quiet harmonious mind in the here and now, which means a continuousness of clearly knowing every present moment.

We should also strive to develop *all the various skills possible to consciousness* such as mentally rehearsing future scenarios, memory skills, excellent physical coordination, spatial reasoning, mental mathematics, musical creativity, scientific acumen, and all the other many capabilities of the mind. This means developing the countless *skills possible for consciousness.* We are beings of consciousness so it behooves us to develop all the capabilities of this miraculous attribute that we luckily have. This includes gaining control of its many automatic and deliberate functions, and especially its ability to shut off automatic intrusions (of emotions or wandering thoughts) that disturb or pollute its focus and concentration on the present activity in the here and now.

We can reach the apex of humanity only when we achieve the level of *consummate conduct*, which entails usage of our minds and behavior in proper skillfulness, and we become "spiritual" when we forget selfishness and direct our efforts to help others in ways we would want to be helped ourselves. It is only by cultivating virtue that one becomes a better human being and qualified for the help necessary in attaining the Tao, so this is essential to Daoist practice.

THE TWELVE RELATIONSHIPS

Confucius specified five major relationships of mankind, namely the relationships between parents & children and your relationships with your siblings; spouse; friends and authorities.

However, we should also include several other relationships: with your physical body; society (your community, city, state, country and culture); Nature and the environment (including your living conditions); living and non-living objects (the various phenomena of manifest reality); your personal character attributes such as your personality, psyche, mindset, attitudes, perspectives, ethics, wisdom, knowledge, strengths and skills; your natural conduct or behavior along with your deliberate activities, namely goals and vows that are noble directions and purposes for your life that give it meaning and significance. Lastly, the relationship with your life in general and life fortune (fate or destiny of conditions) which is determined by all these various attributes along with your circumstances.

There are specific principles and approaches we should use to cultivate these relationships and they should be incorporated into Daoist doctrine other than just "naturalism" as the answer to all things. A man could make a career at the pulpit simply by discussing this extended set of relationships that are greater than the standard Confucian five, our obligations within them, and how to optimally manage them in life. The Daoist philosophy of living in harmony with nature is just one of these relationships.

SAT (EXISTENCE), *CHIT* (CONSCIOUSNESS), *ANANDA* (BLISS), AND *DHARMA* (*IKIGAI* OR PURPOSE)

We should accept the Hindu principle that it is better to exist rather than not exist (*sat* = existence), and that we should also treasure having consciousness (*chit* = sentience, consciousness or awareness) rather than exist without it because existing without having a mind would make us insentient matter such as an automaton. Because we exist as a life process with consciousness we are always seeking bliss (*ananda*) during life. You can consider "bliss" as the absence of suffering (unsatisfactoriness), peacefulness, internal harmony, well-being or just having positive emotions like happiness. Christians, for instance, stress *makarios* (supreme happiness or supreme blessedness) as the ultimate aim of humans for their ideal of bliss. Bliss should also include healthy, comfortable physical states of being.

Basically, the idea of *ananda* bliss should be expanded to encompass both physical and mental-emotional bliss. It should not just include the passive state of mental peacefulness but also include a high level of health and energy and the positive *joie de vivre* emotions that celebrate the existence of our life. Routine and inattention, on the other hand, dull our perceptions and the sense of wonder and awe we term "bliss" where we can feel something deep in life about our existence and the world.

These ideas should be adopted into Daoism with the additional ideal of living for a purpose of significance (*ikigai*) that has personal meaning and personal agency rather than simply living like a plant or animal hedonistically chasing transient joys and pleasures. This is why relationships, the striving to help others within those relationships, and the desire to make the world a better place comes into play.

Purpose implies progress, development or growth. Most religions do not include progress in their theology but just focus on the alleviation of current suffering rather than steps that eliminate it forever. Even Daoism concentrates more on naturalism and cycles rather than progress, development, growth or *ikigai*. But this is a necessary principle that is missing since it is responsible for the development of new medicines, increased food production, education of the public and so on, all of which are properly Daoist objectives.

The Zen school is similar to Daoism in emphasizing that we cultivate clear presence, or pristine awareness, where your mind is quiet but quite open to experiences that then seem more vivid due to the silence of less wandering mental pollutions. We are just a process of consciousness operating through a body so this is the only thing we *can* cultivate – pristine clear awareness. This open clear awareness of one's thoughts, environment and beingness (presence), which is pristine clear mindfulness, is the *chit* (consciousness) aspect of our life experience that also includes Knowledge and understanding.

Some Daoists and Zen aficionados, however, incorrectly suggest that we should cultivate an unperturbed peacefulness of no-thought that is really equivalent to the insentience of nothingness or non-existence rather than liberation. This is wrong because no-thought is an absence of consciousness rather than the peaceful clear mind of Daoism that we should desire as *chit*. An *ananda* bliss that is an equanimity of no-thought or deep sleep peacefulness is not what we're after. We should seek a bliss of clear awareness and understanding that accompanies our mental flow.

Daoists should be cultivating the *ananda* of a peaceful, quiet mind such as exists in the flow state where there still are mental operations going on but you are so focused and absorbed in the activity at hand that you are not perturbed by mental distractions or afflictions that normally arise automatically within the workings of consciousness. This would include unwanted emotional pollutions that disturb your focus, attention and engagement. The state of bliss entails recognition of one's existence through the feedback of physical sensations, a recognition of objects (the environment and one's activities), a feeling of deep engagement (a depth of involvement) with life, and of course whatever thinking operations (thoughts) that are necessary within your mind. In the flow state your mind of awareness and involvement remains pristinely clear and not disturbed by afflictions that would deflect its attentional focus or engagement with the moment of life one is experiencing.

Our conscious beingness likes experiencing mental calmness and tranquility within a tableau of lucid clear concentration that is fluid and sharp/clear without any afflictive agitations. When the mind is quiet or still it is not just enjoyable (blissful) but we can get closer to perceiving reality as it really is (given the limitations of our algorithms of consciousness and sensory perceptions) just as you can see better through clear water rather than agitated water.

At the same time we want our physical body to be feel very pleasant, very blissful, or so comfortable that we can even forget the feeling that it is there. However, we don't want to totally forget the feeling of having a body because people who cannot feel their physical body can accidentally hurt their body without knowing it, such as happens with those who suffer the medical condition of CIPA (Congenital Insensitivity to Pain and Anhydrosis). Because they cannot feel pain and therefore don't react properly to protect themselves, people with CIPA typically suffer lots of accidents such as burns. Often they are discovered to be walking on fractures that heal badly. They are constantly hurting their bodies and then walking around with injuries without knowing it. Hence, you have to feel that you have a body but you want it to feel comfortable (pain-free) and permeated with vitality and vigor all the time, which happens after practicing sports training where you perform lots of stretching and cardio exercises. Yoga, dance, athletics and the martial arts fall into the category of activities that can help your health, physical comfort, energy levels and longevity. The ideal of physical bliss is that you feel *very alive* or *the most* alive. If you want "to feel alive" you should not be pursuing excitements and sensory arousals but pursue cultivation of the state of your physical body as Daoists recommend.

There are many types of physical bliss we can cultivate but this pursuit requires exercise, diet and lots of inner energy work. Today there is an entire field of "body hacks" which aims to do this in optimal ways.

While we all additionally want to be happy so that cheerfulness and joy always accompany our life, these excited mental states of bliss are considered disturbances or agitations compared to the refined state of "flow" that is internally peaceful, calm and tranquil. To be perennially sunny, "glow" or "shine" (beam with joy), or feel lightness or freshness, or simply to be cheerful allows one to maintain their zest without much less energy loss. Hence, while most positive emotions are enjoyable states we should seek higher bliss states that are more refined and peaceful as our baseline rather than lower states of joyous excitation, exuberance, euphoria or elation that continuously expend energy as a form of leakage.

From the vantage point of the higher types of refined bliss and joy, the lower states of thrilling happiness and extreme joyousness are a disquieting irritation or disturbance. Yes, we should regularly experience them and welcome them, but we should also seek to that the more refined states of equanimity, bliss, cheerfulness and shine become the basis of our personality. These produce a passive, full-body bliss experience for our naturally tranquil temperament.

PHYSICAL CULTIVATION

Daoists should know how to cultivate a healthy physical body from the time when a couple decides to produce a pregnancy, on through pregnancy, and then on through to childhood, adulthood, and then old age. This involves an appropriate diet, exercise and internal energy exercises so that one prepares a body in the best and fastest possible way to attain the Tao.

There exist optimum exercises for every type of sport or for specific areas of the body such as Z-Health for the joints, martial arts standing postures for the legs, Ben Patrick "knees over toes" exercises or "Bullet Proof Knees" exercises for the knees and lower body, abdominal yoga exercises for the belly that prevent inguinal hernias, and so on. Such specific optimum exercises, along with yoga, the martial arts and cardio exercises, are the foundational basis for cultivating your body's strength, flexibility, dexterity, adaptability, endurance, stamina, energy, agility, coordination, and speed.

In addition to cultivating our physical nature we must learn to cultivate various methods of breathing for different situations, for managing our Qi or internal energy, and then eventually for progress in attaining the higher spiritual bodies that are locked within the matrix of the physical shell. You achieve these higher bodies by cultivating your Qi (internal energy) through various purification exercises.

SKILLFUL BUT COMPASSIONATE ACTION

Daoists must learn the rules and patterns that order phenomena within each specific field of activity or body of knowledge that they engage in such as farming, cooking, medicine, governance and so on.

In the field of science these principles become the cause and effect rules of transformation. In the field of human affairs or human nature they typically become the principles of psychology such as the principles of governance or persuasion. In the various fields of human attainment these principles are to be studied and become skills that you can master. Learning these things helps you become effective and your future best self.

In Daoism the knowledge and understanding of reliable cause and effect patterns becomes "wisdom." Once a Daoist understands some area of knowledge or activity they must learn the most skillful ways for navigating that field to control its results. By learning and mastering such methods a Daoist can then "act with ease" and become his future best self. The true Daoist approach is to learn and master the best methods for accomplishing any activity, which is basically a *combination of the science of optimization and skills perfection*. They practice gaining expertise in skillful behavior.

Daoists devote themselves to using the patterns of the universe and humanity to cultivate themselves, accomplish goals in the most skillful ways possible, and help establish peace and prosperity for society. I've created several compact collections of such principles for various fields (such as for agriculture, medicine, politics, marketing and so on) in *Buddha Yoga*.

Basically, in Daoism you strive to master phenomena, which requires that you develop a deep understanding of phenomenal changes and the skills for successfully controlling them. Then you use your skills in helping people, which is compassion, service to others, Karma Yoga, or fulfilling Daoist vows and pledges.

THE SCIENCE OF HAPPINESS, THE THEORY OF WELLBEING AND FLOURISHING, MASLOW'S HIERARCHY OF NEEDS, THE BLUE ZONES RESEARCH, AND MINIMIZING YOUR LIFE REGRETS

Daoism was developed over the centuries based on literature such as the *Laozi* and *Zhuangzi* that contributed greatly to its naturalistic philosophy. Because our knowledge of human life has progressed over time Daoism should also incorporate more modern findings such as results from the Science of Happiness, the Theory of Wellness, Maslow's Pyramid on our Hierarchy of Needs, Blue Zones research, and our knowledge of what dying individuals most regret about their life when surveying their past.

The <u>Science of Happiness</u> is all about spiritual, physical, mental (intellectual), emotional and relational well-being. *Spiritual happiness* concerns finding meaning and purpose in work and life; *physical happiness* concerns health and a lack of stress; *intellectual happiness* concerns following your curiosity and becoming deeply engaged with skills, topics or materials; *relational happiness* concerns spending quality time with people we care about and who care about us; and *emotional happiness* comes from cultivating gratitude rather than pleasure. Researchers have found the activities that make people happiest by increasing positive emotions include *active leisure, eating, socializing, hobbies, sports, listening to music, meditation, charity work, and spiritual activities.* Hence, you can create happiness through your behavior. Happiness is also a mental choice. Rather than trying to avoid painful events that would make you unhappy a better strategy is to become anti-fragile, namely tougher and more resilient so that unfortunate circumstances do not affect you as much. Through various methods one can achieve happiness as a combination of frequent positive emotions, high satisfaction with life and infrequent negative affect. Strategies that help people relieve stress (that subdues happy states) are called restorers and include listening to music, solving puzzles, singing or dancing, drawing, painting or sculpting, and creative writing.

Martin Seligman, who is considered the "father" of positive psychology, states that we can cultivate three types of happiness or three different elements of happiness: positive emotions, engagement (deep involvement) and meaning. (1) A *Pleasant life* (of pleasures) is about pursuing positive emotions and feelings and cultivating skills for amplifying those emotions (of ebullience, contentment, warmth, joy, happiness, good cheer, etc.), (2) a *Good life* (engagement) is about experiencing *flow* (merging with or being one with an absorbing activity to the extent of losing self-consciousness while becoming oblivious to time) and can be cultivated by using your signature strengths to obtain abundant, authentic gratification and (3) a *Meaningful life* can be pursued by serving a significant end that is much larger than you are. Those seeking a life of pleasure to attain happiness tend to try to maximize their positive emotions and minimize negative emotions. Those seeking a life of engagement seek out activities that let them be in flow. Those who strive for a life of meaning, purpose, significance or doing (agency) try to find happiness and contentment by serving something bigger than themselves such as family, religion, community, country, a mission, ideal or other large entity.

Basically, you can raise your level of happiness by working on these three components to get more pleasure out of life by savoring experiences, becoming more engaged in whatever you do, and by involving yourself in paths that make your life feel more meaningful such as through service to others. Seligman believes that happiness is derived from your genetic predispositions (set point characteristics) plus the circumstances of your life and volitional activities under your voluntary control, which includes your mental state. His research showed that positive emotions *about the past* (such as contentment) are driven by thinking and interpretations that govern whatever emotions ensue and can be increased by cultivating gratitude, forgiveness and by freeing yourself of imprisoning ideologies. Optimism, hope, faith, trust and other positive emotions *about the future* can be increased by learning to recognize and defuse pessimistic thoughts that automatically arise within the mind. Happiness, joy, ecstasy, calm, zest, ebullience, pleasure (positive emotions) *in the present* can be increased through mindfulness, by breaking habituation and by savoring them. They can also be divided in two ways: (1) *momentary pleasures or delights* that come through the senses and stimulate our emotions with raw feels of thrills and pleasures like orgasm, rapture, bliss, euphoria, elation, ecstasy, delight, mirth, exuberance, comfort and excitement that all leave with little trace (wearing off shortly after being secured and also declining with habituation) but can be savored by indulging the senses, losing one's self in the wonder of the moment, expressing gratitude for the blessings being experienced, and by basking in praise and congratulations, while (2) more *abiding gratifications* tend to be hard won and characterized by absorption, engagement (deep involvement in creative or playful activities or with one's family, work, romance or hobbies) and flow but not necessarily accompanied by any raw feelings at all.

The Theory of Well-being pursues the ideal of increasing one's flourishing and has two competing philosophies. There is the six-factor model of human well-being, rather than "happiness," that believes it is based upon having a purpose in life, positive relations with others, environmental mastery, autonomy, personal growth and self-acceptance. There is also the Seligman theory of "flourishing" that a meaningful life, or good life, is *where you use your signature strengths every day to produce authentic happiness and abundant gratification*. The Seligman theory is that a good life entails having a significant meaning or greater purpose for one's existence, good relationships with others, accomplishments that indicate mastery and success, engagement in activities of one's interest (that often lead to flow or peak experiences), and many positive emotions that include more than just happiness, cheerfulness and joy. Seligman believes your wealth should be used in the service of your well-being. After all, you will have to depart one day leaving everything behind without gaining, in any sense, an iota from it all.

According to modern astrology, your life and fortune can be represented in twelve houses that are affected by the transits and progressions of the planets in the sky. The placement of planets in your natal birth chart reveals your personality characteristics and life path, including strength or weakness in what each of these twelve houses represents. In order to pursue well-being you need to learn how to moderate negative influences to each house when it becomes astronomically afflicted by applying appropriate remedial measures, and you must do this because your twelve houses indicate *the quality of your life*. By learning how to work with your chart to maintain a quality of living – rather than get emotionally tossed around by celestial influences that affect your psyche and mindset – you can better achieve a life of well-being and flourishing.

According to Abraham Maslow human needs are arranged in a multi-hierarchical model often depicted as tiers or levels of a pyramid. The lowest level at the base concerns immediate *physiological survival needs* (air, water, food, sleep, clothing, heat, shelter, reproduction) that must be met before higher needs can be fulfilled such as more creative and intellectually oriented "self-actualization" needs at the top. The second pyramid tier concerns *safety and security needs* of health, employment, property, family and social ability (basically health issues along with personal, emotional and financial security). The third tier concerns *love and social needs* for family, friendship, intimacy and a sense of connection and acceptance by others. *Self-esteem needs* are the next tier (the respect of others, confidence or self-esteem, status, recognition, freedom and autonomy), and *self-actualization needs* are at the top of the pyramid (the desire to grow in personal development to become the most one can be through creativity, morality, spontaneity, purpose, and inner potential).

An extended model of the pyramid added a level of *cognitive needs* above self-esteem needs to denote the that some individuals are intrinsically motivated to use their cognitive skills for creativity, foresight, curiosity, brainstorming and problem solving to become more educated people. An additional lawyer of *aesthetic needs* above cognitive needs was also added for individuals who are intrinsically motivated to beautify their life such as by beautifying themselves and making their environment pleasant to look and be around. Also, a top tier of *transcendence needs* was later added to denote spiritual needs to experience feelings of integrity, wholeness, unity and peak experiences in life.

The Blue Zones research found nine evidence-based commonalities, called the "Power-9," among the people who live longest in the world. What they have in common is that they (1) move naturally, (2) have a *ikigai, plan de vida* or sense of purpose in life for why they wake up in the morning, (3) like Daoists they meditate, pray and use other methods everyday to downshift their anxieties, worries and distress, (4) they follow the Daoist rule to stop eating when they are 80% full, (5) like Daoists their diets have a plant-based (vegetarian) slant to them, (6) like Daoists they drink alcohol moderately and regularly because of its benefits when used in moderation, (7) they belong to a faith-based community of some type, (8) they put their families and loved ones first instead of careers or other concerns, and (9) like

Daoists they belong to social circles, social connections or relationships that support healthy behaviors.

Nurse Bronnie Ware of Australia worked in a hospice for people living out the last three months of their lives and kept a record of the top regrets the dying reported for their lives: (1) *I was not true to myself* in following my dreams and being who I wanted to be, so *I didn't become the person I was capable of becoming* because of living in a way that met other peoples' expectations of what they wanted me to be. I lived a life other people expected of me, a life I was programmed for, instead of the life I wanted for myself that expressed the music in me. I didn't have the courage to be truly myself but suppressed myself in order to please others or be accepted by them, (2) *I worked too hard or spent too much time or was driven by something* to the detriment of spending time with my family and relationships (the people I love) or traveling and doing the things I enjoyed doing, (3) I was afraid to be authentic and lacked the courage to *express my true feelings, express my feelings more, express myself or speak my mind more* in order to please or keep peace with others. This regret of suppressing their emotions so that they would be accepted sometimes caused people to settle into a mediocre existence rather than a greater one they were capable of achieving. (4) I did not *stay in touch with friends to keep good friendships alive* (or for some reason wasn't able to touch more lives in ways they wanted) whereas life all comes down to your family, your relationships (your personal community) and love in the end, (5) *I did not make myself happy or let myself be happier* with more playfulness and joy. People chose not to live in the present moment, and sacrificed joy and play in their lives for success and all sorts of superficial, not important things. Many people on their deathbeds realized too late that happiness is a choice whereas they had voluntarily stayed in unhappy patterns of negative thinking or doing, and many wished that they had found their satisfying life purpose earlier in life.

Other individuals who have polled terminally ill patients have found that people had gained a healthier perspective on life. They wished they had *traveled more* instead of working so hard in their life, and wished they *had more sex* too. They also wished they had been a better spouse, had spent less time worrying about things that never happened, they wished that they had taken more risks, that they had quit their job and found something they really liked doing, spent more time pursuing their dreams, cared less about what other people thought about them (since it doesn't matter), paid less attention to other people's expectations, spent more time thinking about life's large questions (and done this earlier), wished they had spent less time chasing the wrong things, wished they had taken better care of themselves, and wished they had spent more time living life in the moment. It is especially a shame that women today are sold feminist tales that their career is more important than family and relationships. Many women who buy into feminism often wake up far too late realizing that they were sold a false bill of goods and then suffer the loneliness of a household empty of children or a spouse where their career that feminism promoted cannot provide them with fulfillment, fill up their loneliness or satisfy their sense of purpose.

To guide yourself through situations so that you focus on what is important in life, such as what is indicated here, never undervalue the usefulness of *affirmations, aphorisms and slogans* that you can repeat at decision points to make sure that you focus on thinking the wright way and experiencing or doing what is important rather than focusing on what is insignificant.

To help you create life goals I have put together some methods in *Quick, Fast, Done*. Its companion volume is *Move Forward* that reveals a big portion of my philosophy on life.

THE GOOD LIFE, PURPOSE, PEACE, JOY AND PLEASURE

Aristotle said that what separates man from the other animals is human reason, and therefore a "good life" of *eudaimonia* (human flourishing and prosperity, the highest and happiest state possible for humans) can only be achieved by people of exceptional character who have taken care to cultivate their rational faculties and virtue rather than be ruled by their animal nature. They are guided by the golden mean of moderation and refrain from succumbing to hubris. Greek philosophy believes that the proper goal of human life is to strive for *eudaimonia* to live a wise, good life of happiness and well-being, and this requires that we develop our reason and cultivate virtues as nourishing qualities. Thus we must also pursue personal *phronesis* (practical and moral wisdom), and *arête* (excellence or virtue) where you cultivate your individual prowess to live up to your full potential of excellence so that virtuous qualities and methods become your natural disposition rather than just a diluted light tendency.

In ancient Rome the *mos maiorum* set of Roman values involved promoting the common good of the people, which means that the Roman hero was someone who served the nation by self-sacrificing themselves or employing their wisdom or courage for the nation's benefit just as would a Bodhisattva hero. Christianity was born out of this grounding culture and espouses that we need to love one another (love thy neighbor as thyself) as its goal. The pathway of Christian perfectionism also prescribes that we unrelentingly perform good deeds for other people by every possible means while devoting ourselves to the perfection of our character and other forms of self-improvement.

Confucianism requires that we engage in self-cultivation, which is the activity of always improving ourselves in terms of thinking, developing skills and polishing virtues. Therefore during this life we should train to brighten our inherent virtues; love people and act in ways that beneficially help them and society (we service others by enriching the world with benevolent activities); and continuously pursue these endeavors until we reach and reside in the highest levels of excellence.

In Confucian education it is especially emphasized that you are to polish your virtues, learning and your abilities at self-correction and performance (achievement or skillfulness). You must be careful in your conceptions by becoming aware of your own thinking processes in order to assess yourself for self-correction. You must engage in proper conduct so as to live in a righteous way (propriety entails the way things should be done), and you should always treat others with a heart of benevolence, consideration, kindness, caring and compassion.

Hinduism says that during life we should pursue four goals called *Purusartha*. We are to pursue *Moksha* or spiritual liberation (the attainment of higher transcendental bodies and concomitant enlightened mental states). We are to pursue a proper means of *Artha* (wealth, career, prosperity, success, livelihood, etc.) to enjoy a virtuous livelihood and not be a burden to others for our existence; and pursue *Dharma* so that we can elevate our behavior and live harmoniously and cooperatively within society. To follow *Dharma* means to regulate our behavior so that we are in accord with ethical, moral, wise, compassionate, benevolent and virtuous ways, and the pathway of *Dharma* elevates our conduct and behavior so that we can harmoniously live together with others in families and society. We are also to pursue proper forms of *Kama* that constitutes joys, pleasures, amusements, and positive emotions during life.

The *Purusartha* also espouse that *Kama*, or pleasure, is one of the *fundamental* goals of human lives. In one sense you can consider this (1) the pursuit of Hinduism's mental/emotional and physical *ananda* (bliss), (2) a pursuit for the elimination of suffering and unsatisfactoriness with life as taught by Buddhism, (3) as a striving for peacefulness, equilibrium and tranquility as in Daoism, (4) the

Greek target of *eudaimonia* (happiness or welfare), and (5) *makarios* (being supremely blessed) as in Christianity, or related objectives.

In astrology pleasure is centered in the fifth natal house that represents singing, creativity and artistic expression (the creation of arts and culture such as through painting and drawing or music making), risk-taking excitement, sports, charity, pleasures, sexual pleasure with a partner (love affairs and romance), and fun play with children.

Daoists believes in not doing anything along the lines of pleasure-seeking that harm the body such as drinking too much, engaging in too much sex, eating too much and so forth. It offers rules of behavior that focus on maintaining a harmony of one's spirit through moderation and by avoiding certain activities or circumstances that might harm one's vitality. Humans typically obtain pleasure from excitement and sensual delights like alcohol, drugs, sex, food gambling, shopping, and so on since they provide a feeling of aliveness. However, as a general rule Daoists avoid excessiveness in smoking, alcohol intake, drugs, dangerous sports, overeating, sexual relations, pornography, gossiping, shopping, debt, gambling and speculation, fighting, and abusing others (using power to control others).

In one's desire to experience novelty and pleasure a Daoist does not have to follow an entirely non-eventful peaceful life but can certainly pursue adventurous exploration, the satisfaction of problem solving challenges or satisfying one's curiosity in various areas of pursuit. He can certainly follow promptings to engage in creative activities such as the arts, sports, and various other forms of self-expression.

In Daoism, the instructions for human society and for your life are represented in the symbolism of the Three Divine Teachers, or the "Three Pure Ones." The third of The Three Pure Ones, "The Universally Honored One of Tao and Virtues," is the one most appropriate to us in terms of guidance for our life because he represents an enlightened sage, which is your inherent potential if you cultivate spiritual practice. He holds a fan to indicate that he has mastered the internal life force Qi energy inside us that must be cultivated in order to attain the higher spiritual bodies of enlightenment although the fan also symbolizes mastery over the energies of the universe and human activities so that we can achieve happiness and well-being.

Because man is a living being with a mind (consciousness) that can form thoughts he can develop understanding (wisdom) that lets him gain control over phenomena. Therefore he can to some extent both achieve an end to suffering or unsatisfactoriness and achieve happiness or bliss, and this is the instruction for our lives. We are to grow by developing our consciousness and cognitive skills in various ways to gain control over nature (the environment), our circumstances, and ourselves … with the objective of making our lives better by reducing suffering and achieving peaceful tranquility, bliss, happiness and flow. This involves gaining control over ourselves by elevating our thinking and emotions and by pursuing noble behavior.

"PEAK STATE" EXPERIENCES AND THE STATE OF FLOW

We have the capability of cultivating states of pristine presence that are extremely bright or vibrant with an inner fire of subtle bliss, but most of all brilliant with vivid clarity. These are sometimes described as states of pristine awareness, egolessness, emptiness, clarity, detachment, or desirelessness but of course the mind is filled with mental activity and cognition when they occur. Perhaps you have experienced one of these moments in life. Rather than just peaceful mental stillness where the clarity of awareness seems pristinely pure and thought-free (but isn't because otherwise there would be no experience) and the mind seems very open and large (openness "as big as a cloudless sky"), Daoists should also treasure such active peak states of experience.

In life you want to experience suffering-free, affliction-free, distraction-free mental states by pursuing Daoist mindsets of calmness, detachment, desirelessness, dispassion, equanimity, naturalness, peace, harmony, etcetera but you should also want to experience an active *joie de vivre* during life that includes frequent pleasurable enjoyments and joyful self-expression. Otherwise what is life for? Life is not simply about existence. To say that life is only about a clear and peaceful awareness of your experience while emotions such as bliss, joy and other positive emotional states are missing would make it an entirely robotic undertaking that would hardly be worthwhile. However, you don't want to become entirely mindless like the world of natural phenomena either. You want to embrace the life you have, engage with it fully with affliction-free attention (awareness), and enjoy it and your beingness.

The rewarding emotional feelings of life give it meaning and make it worthwhile yet the highest mental states are those veering towards clear mental peace, presence, tranquility, lightness, equilibrium, equanimity and flow. Nonetheless there are tremendously rewarding peak experience states as well involving joy, shine, glow, happiness, a feeling of connected oneness with the universe, and other highly rewarding peak experiences too numerous to mention.

Basically, there are active peak mental-emotional-physical experiences that we can experience in life that complement the peaceful states primarily espoused by Daoism and other pacifist ideologies. Of course we value a peaceful life void of troubles or inner turmoil but life should certainly also be filled with fun and humor, a *joie de vivre* and a celebratory involvement that affirms its vital essence.

To have the ability of awareness, consciousness or illumination – which is rare in the universe – is to be liberated from inert matter and thus sentient life should involve a full enjoyment of *sat-chit-ananda-ikigai* where we participate in the bliss of living. We don't want to suppress "feeling alive" or turn aside from our potential for *joie de vivre* since they help give life its full meaning. You want to *embrace life with positive emotions* because it should be about more than just existence, and it certainly isn't about thought suppression (a deviant pursuit of empty mind or "emptiness") where you become mindless like Nature or pacified to the extent that you suppress thoughts rather than elevate them. You want to become skillful in how you handle the activities of your mind. The great learning in life is learning how to elevate and evolve yourself to become better than your base case of being just an animal.

Proper spiritual cultivation should entail cultivating and radiating an inexhaustible *joie de vivre* - a vitalizing energy from the joy of living that is fully engaged in activities. The goal is not an enforced (passive) equilibrium of suppressed emotions and thoughts or restricted behavior as you see in many monkhood traditions such as Hinayana Buddhism.

You must never lose the ability to enjoy simply being alive, but some spiritual traditions incorrectly try to squeeze this out of people through incorrect notions of discipline, detachment and what is proper. Isn't the invigorating joy we feel when surrounded by Springtime life energy (that makes us feel great inside) something we should want to experience despite any rules of religion? We can create such feelings inside ourselves on our own and should. In fact, on the path of purification that frees our inner subtle body we can only purify it by arousing all sorts of emotions inside us while simultaneously circulating our body's full Qi so as to frictionally wash and transform it.

We can cultivate *states of bliss* that are vibrantly engaging and fill our life with such energy that it seems as if all your cells are vitalized with energetic, pleasurable but subtle blissful feelings. Our potential for *peak experiences* include those that are deeply moving, exhilarating, or elevating such as exciting, intense, oceanic moments of highest happiness and fulfillment or flowing moments of intensely clear awareness. These are times when your mental realm expands beyond your normal limits and you physically experience vitality, virility, and advanced forms of perceiving reality with a focused clarity of mental concentration.

Such mental states are often triggered by the arts, listening to music, sports, creative work, sexual intercourse, the sublime beauty of nature, the joy of discovery, engagement in altruistic behavior, or religious worship and spirituality. In those moments reality is often perceived with emotions such as wonder, awe, humility, reverence and aesthetic feelings of goodness, beauty, truth, wholeness, uniqueness, self-sufficiency, perfection, completion, richness, effortlessness, playfulness and aliveness. Daoist philosophy is not written as to specifically cultivate this, although Daoism recognizes that you can experience such events when appreciating Nature, but this indeed belongs within Daoism.

Daoism espouses cultivating a "state of flow" that does not just refer to smooth, effortless behavior executed with ease but a mental realm that is pristinely clear and internally quiet due to their being no distractions. The mind becomes fully immersed in an activity and energized with focus while the experience feels intrinsically rewarding. While in the flow state you can find deep fulfillment in the present moment. It is as if your consciousness is unified so that self-notions are forgotten and you touch a supreme peace while being fully engaged with activities. One might say that flow *feels* like the meaning of life.

During the *flow state* you lose your sense of self (there is a reduction in reflective self-consciousness) while experiencing great focus and bliss (enjoyment) by being fully present with maximum freshness in attention to your activities. *This feast of lucidity is an optimal way to exist in life* as you go about doing whatever you need to do. Thus it is called *aliveness*, the state of presence, "flow state" or bliss. It involves an intense and focused concentration on the present moment where there is a merging of activity and awareness and yet there is an intrinsically rewarding heightened sense of personal control, agency, skillfulness, mastery or engagement over the situation or activity.

This *is* the meaning of existence, consciousness, bliss and *ikigai* (purpose). At times it might seem as if there are no thoughts during this state of *vivid presence* but there are always very fine thinking processes going on within your mind whenever you are conscious. Whenever there is awareness, cognizance or notice there is thinking going on as a function of consciousness no matter how pure, empty clear or quiet your mind may seem. There is also a subtle tinge of bliss originating from the vitality of your body sensations without which there would be no sense of presence. The sense of presence always includes a knowingness of sensory perceptions and the feeling of your body via a sort of feedback mechanism where they are constantly being fed to your mind to help you recognize that you have a bodily existence and self-identity. The sense of presence includes a subtle recognition of the familiar sensation of having a physical body that at this moment of time is extremely smooth and comfortable, or we can say that the feeling is blissful to denote a very subtle (almost unnoticeable) state that you can readily ignore.

The *flow state* can be triggered by scientific discovery or immersion in music (while playing your instrument), absorption in the arts, gaming, times when you experience the sublimity of nature, from creative work, during sex, during sports ("being in the zone" where you have fully internalized mastery of a sport such as the effortless Zen state of "mind without mind" that is the *wuxin* of martial arts), or during religious worship.

Some individuals can achieve a taste of "being in the zone" through yoga practice, and some can achieve a similar runner's high (a low octave of the flow state) due to great athletic conditioning and rhythmical breathing that synchronizes perfectly with their inner Qi and blood flow. Hence, you can train your body, breathing and mind to welcome this state of experience more often which often appears when you become completely absorbed, focused, and involved in your activities. As stated, being in shape health-wise, Qi-wise and breathing-wise can help you attain the state of flow, or simply attain states of advanced mental clarity and focus.

FATE, FORTUNE AND DESTINY, DOMINANCE HIERARCHIES, VOWS AND PLEDGES

All Daoists should know that there is such as thing as your (astrological) fate, fortune or destiny initiated at your birth time, which sages of the Celestial Immortal and higher stage can see, and should know how to change their fortune, fate and destiny by changing their personality, behavior and the activities and conditions of their life. I discuss how to do this in *Self-Creation* and for this specific topic *Liaofan's Four Lessons* is mandatory along with the other books I've mentioned.

Daoists should also work on determining a meaningful life purpose for their existence (*ikigai* or significant reason for being). Astrology or a living sage can tell you your fortune but you must figure out your own life purpose or calling yourself because you were created through universal interactions without any specific reason for your being, and you were not created for any special purpose. Once determined, a Daoist should start taking more direction of his life story as much as possible. The target should not just be to follow one's inner calling and the life purpose one chooses but to experience more of the positive emotions of peace, happiness, bliss, joy, amusement, love, compassion, gratitude, basic prosperity, well-beingness, the flow state and peak experiences possible from life.

We all need to learn how to think and behave so that we smile more, laugh more, dance more, create more, have less worries, and live for something bigger than ourselves. We can forget ourselves and our suffering by working to make the world a better place for others. We all derive deep satisfaction from working on fulfilling our life purpose, which is what is really significant in our life, and which usually involves charitable service to others that are acts of love or which further some cause we choose to support and advocate (to and help bring well-being to the world) despite significant challenges or adversity.

The idea of the solitary Daoist recluse is appealing, but if everyone did that then society would collapse. Therefore, the greater number of people must engage in doing something that will benefit their families and communities rather than just make themselves the "be all and end all" of their existence since this never provides any sort of deep meaning or life satisfaction for anyone. They must also try to make the world a better place for the next generation.

One can read the lament of King Solomon in the Bible (Ecclesiastes 2) who found that despite his great power, wealth, access to sex and status that transient joys could never please him or any other man: "I said to myself, 'Come now, I will test you with pleasure to find out what is good.' But that also proved to be meaningless. 'Laughter,' I said, 'is madness. And what does pleasure accomplish?' I tried cheering myself with wine, and embracing folly—my mind still guiding me with wisdom. I wanted to see what was good for people to do under the heavens during the few days of their lives. I undertook great projects: I built houses for myself and planted vineyards. I made gardens and parks and planted all kinds of fruit trees in them. I made reservoirs to water groves of flourishing trees. I bought male and female slaves and had other slaves who were born in my house. I also owned more herds and flocks than anyone in Jerusalem before me. I amassed silver and gold for myself, and the treasure of kings and provinces. I acquired male and female singers, and a harem as well—the delights of a man's heart. I became greater by far than anyone in Jerusalem before me. In all this my wisdom stayed with me. I denied myself nothing my eyes desired; I refused my heart no pleasure. My heart took delight in all my labor, and this was the reward for all my toil. Yet when I surveyed all that my hands had done and what I had toiled to achieve, everything was meaningless, a chasing after the wind; nothing was gained under the sun." Ecclesiastes 1.14 says, "all is vanity and chasing after wind."

In the sixth century, Anicius Manlius Severinus Boethius was born into an aristocratic Roman family, received the finest education, married well, lived a life of privilege, and accomplished the astounding feat of being made a Roman consul in his twenties. He was appointed chief of staff of Emperor Theodoric's court but was unjustly accused of treason, thrown into prison and wrote *The Consolation of Philosophy* on death's row. He, too, lamented that fortune comes and goes as it pleases and that you should never rely on it. Happiness, he concluded, was not high position, wealth, honors, public esteem and reputation, fame and the advantages of high birth because (like King Solomon) he had enjoyed all these things and found them lacking.

Lastly, the *Liezi (Lieh Tzu)* from Daoism, which is one of its three most important philosophical books, states, "Some people think they can find satisfaction in good food, fine clothes, lively music, and sexual pleasure. However, when they have all these things, they are not satisfied. They realize happiness is not simply having their material needs met. Thus, society has set up a system of rewards that go beyond material goods. These include titles, social recognition, status, and political power, all wrapped up in a package called self-fulfillment. Attracted by these prizes and goaded on by social pressure, people spend their short lives tiring body and mind to chase after these goals. Perhaps this gives them the feeling that they have achieved something in their lives, but in reality they have sacrificed a lot in life. They can no longer see, hear, act, feel, or think from their hearts. Everything they do is dictated by whether it can get them social gains. In the end, they've spent their lives following other people's demands and never lived a life of their own. How different is this from the life of a slave or a prisoner?

"The ancients understood that life is only a temporary sojourn in this world, and death is a temporary leave. In our short time here, we should listen to our own voices and follow our own hearts. Why not be free and live your own life? Why follow other people's rules and live to please others? When something enjoyable comes your way, you should enjoy it fully. Don't be imprisoned by name or title, for social conventions can lead you away from the natural order of things. It doesn't matter whether you will be remembered in generations ahead, because you will not be there to see it."[7]

The Daoist view is to strive for personal fulfillment by achieving freedom and autonomy. In the *Zhuangzi* is a story of independence where the Prince of Chu sent two officials asking Zhuang Zi to become an official in his administration. Zhuang Zi asked them, "I have heard that in the State of Chu there is a sacred tortoise that has been dead 3,000 years and which the prince honors in his ancestral shrine. Do you think that tortoise would rather be dead and have its remains thus honored, or be alive and wagging its tail in the mud?" When the officials answered that it would rather be alive with its tail wagging in the mud, Zhuang Zi answered, "So would I, and so I decline the offer."

---

[7] *Teachings of the Tao*, trans. by Eva Wong (Shambhala, Boston, 1997), pp. 49-50.

Daoism recognizes that people are seeking something out of life, but most people are not clear enough about what it is that they seek. Usually men are striving for excellence in some way. They usually try to climb the dominance hierarchies of their society for status such as the ranks of money and power, and pursue the development of high skills or talents within their trade, career or occupation. Some pursue excellence as a sports champion instead of just becoming someone very good at a skill who is so good you cannot ignore them.

Most human beings seek money because it can eliminate a great deal of misery in life. Money cannot buy happiness but it can eliminate many forms of misery. Some seek money, power and status so that they can find a suitable mate for their happiness but everyone also treasures health so that one can say people typically seek health, wealth, status and love for their well-being.

Hence, most typically pursue the four P's of life: *Profit (money), Power, Prestige and Pleasure.* Individuals tend to feel a need for personal achievement, affiliation with others (social relationships), and power in life. However, such pursuits, while attractive, seldom satisfy us for long as already noted by King Solomon, Boethius and the *Liezi.* You always hanker after hollow illusions and then leave the world empty-handed. People who find happiness in life tend to be healthy (disability lowers happiness), take care of their body and mind, enhance their positive virtues (such as coping skills and ethics) to bring happiness, cultivate optimism and search for a more profound meaning for their life rather than these other things.

At this point you might want to *retrieve a yellow marker and be ready to mark* the things which are most important to you in life so that you can work on putting more of them into your living.

The psychological components to inner happiness include the feelings of internal harmony and balance (inner peace, contentment, serenity; a positive relationship with oneself); positive emotions (cheerfulness, happiness, joy, merriness, lightness, glow, shine, freshness, feelings of comfort and moments of pleasure); a sense of overall well-being; feelings of achievement, fulfillment and satisfaction; an optimistic or sunny attitude/disposition; freedom and autonomy of the self; a feeling of being loved and accepted by others; an active engagement with life and association with meaning.

What people consider meaningful in their life as the greatest components of happiness and satisfaction includes family, work, interpersonal relationships, health, and personal growth.

The items of essential importance to happiness in your life are therefore said to be passion in your work, career or vocation; wealth (money or economic resources or standard of living); positive relationships with your family (parents and siblings), spouse, children, friends and the social connections of your community and society; your educational trajectory; the nobility of your personal conduct and success at self-improvement; how you protect yourself from temptation; meaningful goals, activities and achievements; taking care of yourself through attention to your mental and physical health; your personal interests or useful things you do when not working (free time activities); positive emotional experiences; your life balance; and your life purpose. This is all entirely aside from the state of flow or treasured feeling of being fully alive and fully engaged with the present moment through a lucid, pristine state of consciousness.

Your work, when it concerns happiness, can be either a (1) job, (2) career, or (3) a *calling* that energizes you because it is intrinsically fulfilling. When it is intrinsically rewarding you don't do it to achieve anything else, and then it can even become part of your life purpose because it gives you a connection to greater than yourself in life.

A larger list is that in life humans are seeking prosperity (natural abundance and lack of want); financial freedom and independence; a fulfilling, rewarding and passionate career that provides autonomy, enough income and where you are competent at what you do; a high level of health and energy; to be surrounded by order and beauty; involvement in activities that require deep engagement but which are personally expressive; the opportunity to be your true, authentic self; peace of mind; frequent positive states and peak experiences of mental delight and pleasure; high status and prestige within dominance hierarchies and the social chain; intimate loving relationships; good social interactions, high-quality friendships and affiliations that fulfill a need for belongingness and to feel connected with others; self-esteem from appreciation and acknowledgement by others (a deep human urge is to be important, be great and be praised or appreciated); to demonstrate virtuous behavior and consummate conduct; feelings of personal fulfillment (self-actualization), competence, mastery or achievement (from accomplishing success in one's endeavors, mastering certain dharmas or overcoming challenges etc.); worthy goals and ideals and worthwhile life purposes that provide you with meaning and deep satisfaction.

We should list this in a format where it becomes easier to see what human beings are most interested in obtaining during life:

- An engaging, meaningful, interesting, passionate and fulfilling work livelihood (career, vocation or occupation) that provides financial freedom while characterized by self-determination and autonomy where you feel authentic in what you are doing, in control of your destiny and where your contribution has positive significance (such as by leaving golden footprints everywhere)
- Prosperity and abundance (a high standard of living) that provides excellence in human living (an opulence of *Artha* that includes wealth, power, status, prestige, and education)
- A high level of physical health, physical capability (strength, flexibility, dexterity, adaptability, endurance, stamina, energy, agility, coordination, speed, etc.), energy and feelings of vitality
- Psychological well-being and peace of mind (internal harmony,

equilibrium, and balance free of stress or afflictions) along with a high degree of positive mental states (positive emotions), frequent *peak experiences* and enjoyment of states of mental *flow* where you become fully engaged with challenging activities requiring skills of competency, control and mastery that test your limits while you enjoy unbroken concentration without distraction

- Accomplishment in mastering skills where your competency provides you with internal feelings of mastery, strength, accomplishment, self-esteem and self-expression
- Feelings of self-esteem, fulfillment, competence, and accomplishment due to one's skills and personal achievements being recognized by others who provide acknowledgement, praise, appreciation, respect or status as well as general social acceptance and approval; feelings of status and respect for being recognized by others for climbing various types of dominance hierarchies (Note: John Dewey said that the deepest urge in human nature is the desire to be important, Freud believed that the chief human desire apart from sex was to be great, and Lincoln said that the greatest human desire was the craving to be appreciated)
- Close, affectionate, intimate, caring, loving family relationships (positive relationships where you feel loved, valued and supported by your spouse, family, children)
- Strong feelings of connection, companionship, loyalty, friendship, and belongingness with colleagues and friends
- Good social relationships, interactions, connections and acceptance by the community and greater society
- Ample leisure and free time for *Kama*, relaxation or play and frequent experiences of positive mental states of delight, pleasure and sensory or emotional gratification such as experiences of novelty, variety, creativity and imagination and other aspects of *Kama* (including creative activities such as the arts, sports, problem solving challenges and various forms of self-expression that may all lead to peak experiences)
- Personal growth (self-improvement) in "perfecting your soul," cultivating moral virtue and excellence, or "converting one's manners" by taking the virtuous actions that you admire in others (even if you don't feel like it) that make you admire

yourself because they embody your ideal self; substantial progress in achieving one's potential to become their highest and best self by pursuing virtue and ethics, consummate conduct, ideals by which to steer one's life, the right activities and by work at perfecting one's character, attitudes and perspectives, mental capabilities, signature skills, and achieving progress in self-actualization and self-expression

• Worthy ideals, goals, aims, aspirations, engagements and a sense of purpose in life or purposes for life that give it meaning, significance, and satisfaction or fulfillment (such as by serving something greater than oneself), or ideal guidance for daily activities, interpersonal relationships, and life events that produce a sense of meaning, belonging and identity

Many of these goals can be summarized under the three Greek ideals of what men are seeking in life:

• *Eudaimonia* – happiness, well-being, flourishing and prosperity, enjoyment of the state of highest human good
• *Arete* – pursuing excellence and living to one's full potential or highest effectiveness in using all of one's faculties in the process of living and to achieve results in the world
• *Phronesis* – practical wisdom, prudence and know-how regarding concrete actions that achieve good ends in life consistent with ethics, virtue and the overall aim of living well

This is the package of a fulfilling life that men and women pursue. It is an undeniable fact of life that many people pursue wealth, power, status, privilege and so forth for the goal of happiness. It is also true that most religions teach us that we should conduct ourselves in life in an ethical, virtuous, excellent manner because this is exactly what lets you move up the various dominance hierarchies pf society.

You can achieve and enjoy such things only as a consequential karmic reward of virtuous, ethical good behavior. It is the same for achieving enlightenment because all the Immortals, Arhats, spiritual masters and Buddhas who arrive to wash your Qi during the multi-year internal alchemy transformational process will not do so unless you are a virtuous individual.

We strive to manifest these conditions in our lives through our actions and activities, and their accomplishment requires specific types of doing. To achieve any of these goals we must train our thinking, feeling, ways of behaving and willpower. We must strive to master our minds to handle troubles, increase our resilience, and produce new circumstances that will reduce cases of mental, emotional and physical states of suffering for ourselves and others. In life we need to work to reduce the conditions causing us and others to suffer.

Alternatively, we can strive to cultivate our minds so that we can rise above most of these desires that ordinary people hanker after yet must still always pursue the cultivation of virtuous behavior because it is the right thing to do while pursuing the Tao.

Lastly, most people never consider what they would be doing if they did attain the higher spiritual bodies of enlightenment. How would you occupy yourself during a very long life?

The answer is the ideal of the Bodhisattva vows that pledge one's efforts for purposes of significance and an ideal of saving or taking care of sentient beings in some way. For instance, in Buddhism the "Medicine Buddha" Bhaishajyaguru has vowed, "If people are sick I will save them, if deformed I will fix them, if they are not pretty I will help them become more beautiful, if they are embarrassed I will protect them, if hungry I will feed them, if they don't have any clothes or housing or shelter then I will supply them, if they want education I will arrange for them to be taught, if they want children I'll help them conceive, if they want to change genders then I'll help them do so for their next life, if their sense organs are defective then I will help restore them." Krishna said, "For the protection of the righteous, for the destruction of the wicked, and for the establishment of Dharma (right moral conduct) I will be born in each millennium." Please read *Buddha Yoga* for many other vow examples.

Daoism encourages us to make vows like this too, but most people don't recognize this directive even though Daoists take a crucial step in their training which Buddhism unfortunately does not encourage in its monastic system, which is that Daoists start training in all sorts of various skills and excellences so that they can perform meritorious deeds in the world now and have those capabilities ready for after their enlightenment. You want to learn a variety of skills, capabilities and excellences in life so that you can *use your knowledge and experience to benefit others* rather than simply remain an ignorant monk who studies scriptures and parrots back their words to others. The difference between a Daoist who achieves enlightenment and a Buddhist monk who achieves enlightenment is that one of them usually breaks free from the physical realm with a set of worldly skills that can be used to help people while the other does not develop any special talents, and then has to rely on helping people primarily through energy manipulations of his or her *nirmanakaya* emanations.

One of the cores of Daoism is to become master of many bodies of knowledge and skills, including mastering one's internal energies, so that one might be free and autonomous but also capable of performing great compassionate deeds on behalf of the people. Unfortunately, most people do not recognize this objective.

As stated, Lu Dongbin and the Eight Immortals of Daoism, represent the third of The Three Pure Ones (Taishang Laojun or Daode Tianzun). They represent the Bodhisattva vow that we find in Buddhism – someone who achieves the Tao and then works for the welfare of others. Li Tiguei is an expert at medicine who heals the sick and helps the needy. Han Xiangzi, a flute artist, is the patron saint of musicians and someone to call upon when you want to change your mood to happiness. Cao Guoji helps government officials or people trying to deal with the government. Lan Caihe helps gardeners and florists, but also farmers with their crop decisions. Han Zhongli is the patron of the military and longevity and the equivalent of a wealth god who helps people with business, careers and making money. Lu Dongbin, the leader of the eight, is called on for many activities and especially when you are trying to defeat evil to establish justice in the world.

I strongly, strongly recommend that you read *Buddha Yoga* to see how to come up with your own Daoist pledges or vows to become a certain way or devote yourself to certain commitments, objectives or callings and then start developing skills in those directions so that when you do become enlightened you are not like most useless monks. Everyone expects care and beneficial influences from us because we have a mind.

As I explained in *Correcting Zen,* which is written for Daoists too since its practice techniques are non-denominational, you might create a mini-ceremony each evening where you light an incense stick and report all your day's deeds (including infractions) to Heaven, repent before the deities for behavioral lapses and for not achieving as much as you would like in terms of living up to your vows and life purpose, and ask for heavenly assistance to become better, avoid the same errors, achieve what you want and become the being you want to be.

You should take that time to look back as to whether you remained totally clear and mindful of your thoughts and actions during the day, whether you were honest with yourself as to your motivations and intentions, whether you were useful to others and acted with a heart of compassion, whether you made the best of every moment, whether you make progress in self-perfection and your goals, and whether you had truly lived.

Each morning as a daily Daoist routine you should also light an incense stick and pause to first *shape your motivation* for the day and remind yourself of exactly whatever it is you will be doing. Using the To Do list created the previous night, you can mentally rehearse how to hold yourself and perform your best at whatever you must do during the day, and try to put yourself in line with becoming your best self and fulfilling the Daoist vows you have made for your life.

If you set out to do something in life (such as learn a skill) and improve yourself by 1% every day, by year end you will have improved yourself by 37 times. It is not hard to improve yourself a little bit every day, or make progress in becoming the person you want, if you use a disciplined system of measuring your progress and reinforcing the desire to practice to improve to help you accomplish this, which is what you have here. This is how you do so, but few people use this technique of daily review.

Benjamin Franklin used a practice of daily review in watching his behavior to eliminate mistakes to make himself a better and happier man than he otherwise would have been had he not used it. He showed how a person's life and character could become a noble one through constant self-assessment and personal work at transformation. Frank Bettger used a similar system that he wrote about in *How I Raised Myself From Failure to Success in Selling*. Yuan Liao Fan reported in *Liaofan's Four Lessons* that he entirely overturned his fortune because he tracked his efforts at changing his personality by also using a daily ledger system to track his progress and further his motivation. These methods should be used to help you change yourself, your fortune and accomplish your vows.

All Daoists must become committed to self-improvement and use a similar technique. This is the way to change your fate, fortune and destiny; the way to change your personality, conduct and behavior; the way to engage in more profitable activities for your life that will tend to go better; and the way to create a life of significance by working on fulfilling your vows.

Throughout his day Liao Fan practiced mindfulness in watching his thought-stream in order to cut off bad thoughts, create good thoughts in their place, practice good deeds and stop performing bad actions. The great Chinese Confucian Wang Yang-Ming spoke of the process of self-correcting saying, "This effort must be carried out continuously. Like eradicating robbers and thieves, one must resolve to wipe them out completely. In idle moments one must search out and discover each and every selfish thought for sex, wealth, fame and the rest. One must resolve to pluck out and cast away the root of the sickness, so that it can never arise again. Only then may one begin to feel at ease. One must, at all times, be like a cat catching mice – with eyes intently watching and ears intently listening. As soon as a single [selfish] thought begins to stir, one must conquer it and cast it out. Act as if you were cutting a nail in two or slicing through iron. Do not indulge or accommodate it in any way. Do not harbor it, and do not allow it to escape."[8]

Wang Yang-Ming taught that cultivating personal morality was the way that individuals within society could create social well-being and peace because in Confucian thinking the ordering of the world ultimately started with self-cultivation, meaning that it started with everyone adopting the personal aim of perfecting their own self behavior. *Daoists should adopt the same attitude!* The Daoist attribute of demonstrating excellent skills that look easy comes from consistent efforts at self-improvement rasher than from simply going along with naturalism. Goodness or virtuous ways in society do not just happen naturally either, even though some would like to believe this from reading *Laozi* and *Chuangzi*.

---

[8] *Confucian Moral Self Cultivation,* Philip Ivanhoe, (Hackett Publishing Company, Indianapolis: Illinois, 2000), p. 67.

To be sure, the evidence from the long history of China's dynasties shows that when you reduce taxation, leave the people alone and don't interfere with their lives this tends to produce tremendous prosperity for the country. However, despite a policy leaning towards *laissez faire* that unshackles productivity you still need laws, religion and social shaming to pacify the behavior of the populace. I always urge people to study history and large-scale marketing, advertising and public relations campaigns because social engineering efforts are being used on us all the time and these matters must be understood. Typically it is said that Traditional Chinese Medicine doctors, who learn five elements theory of Daoism and how one element can be amplified or checked by another element via their interrelationships, are the first to realize how society is always being manipulated by rulers and governments. A Daoist should understand this, namely what is going on to try to influence him in certain directions.

The point is that you must cultivate yourself and develop strong values along with a personal moral compass (strong moral bearings) to become qualified as a vessel for enlightenment, not to mention become able to change your life and fortune or the trajectory of your nation. Once enlightened, you are to become like the third of The Three Pure Ones (Taishang Laojun or Daode Tianzun) who masters himself, masters universal forces, and *devotes himself to helping humanity and saving the world through his actions based upon his Daoist vows.*

You can think of these actions as *"kindness and compassion"* that protects the people, eases their sufferings and difficulties, magnifies their spirit by serving their happiness and well-being and creates a brighter future for them. You can think of them as loving one's neighbor. You can think of them as *Karma Yoga*, the fulfillment of one's vows, or as the purpose of life being service.

I suggest that everyone follow a daily method like that used by Liao Fan and Benjamin Franklin, and review your own activities at the end of each day where you light a stick of incense and report what you did to Heaven (what good you have done during the day), remind yourself of your vows and or important mission in life, ponder how you might make progress, and then make a To Do list for tomorrow. The important point is to create a system where you track your behavior and use a daily review to eliminate the repetition of errors. You must also reaffirm your vows nightly to become a certain way, achieve a specific ideal, or work at something larger than yourself in order to keep your commitment to self-improvement fresh. In the morning you must also ask yourself, "What good shall I do this day?" and set the motivation for the day while always remembering the *raison d'etre* of your being. At the end of a week you should also review the entire week's activities, and also use some time to plan for the week ahead, which I explained in *Quick, Fast, Done.*

The basis of this daily repetition is simple. Every time you repeat the same action, follow the same path or activate a specific pattern it becomes more defined as a neural circuit in your brain, and it then gets closer to becoming your default behavior and way of being. Your entire life runs on the neural patterns and software in your brain, namely the algorithms of consciousness for how to think and do things. Your brain, wanting to be efficient, will take the easiest, most familiar mental route in producing thoughts and actions so repetition will make your efforts your natural way of doing things over time.

Similarly, our thinking algorithms possess the capacity to become convinced of anything you like - particular mindset, perspectives, or points of views - provided they are repeatedly and persistently influenced in the required direction. Advertising teaches us this principle, and it is used to program viewpoints in individuals according to the guidance of national leaders. At the same time, there are cosmological efficient causes that guide mankind en masse in certain directions as well and the sage both recognizes and applies the proper octaves of such forces in their teachings to point humanity in the right direction at opportune periods in time.

Sometimes it takes introspection and experimentation to see how to integrate new behaviors or strategies into your life, or stark reappraisal to replace old ways of reasoning with newer, more accurate methods and perspectives. However, once determined the repetition of your new ways will over time change your psyche or personality, your Qi energy or aura, as well as your astrological configuration for this and your next life. Every time you follow the same pattern you will activate those circuits again and pretty soon you will be that way. This is why you must create a system of corrective feedback and constant repetition to actualize what you value as personality traits, and shape your behavior to become the way you want that is your highest best self and enlightened ideal. Furthermore, when you consciously create a new image of your ideal self your brain and nervous system will automatically provide continual feedback to ensure that you "live up to" that preordained image you create.

CHAPTER 5:
DAOIST BODIES OF KNOWLEDGE
AND FIELDS OF DAOIST EXPERTISE

I've tried over the years to make a contribution to Daoism by producing information that was not available, and although it mighty seem like self-promotion I must definitely direct you to these books because they are usually the only source available on certain topics that are properly Daoist areas of interest.

For pure Daoist reading, however, I highly recommend the books by Eva Wong and some of Thomas Cleary's translations of Daoist texts.

Countless martial artists have written about *qi-gong* and inner *nei-gong* exercises but the most important features of Daoism are missing from these books, which are an understanding of the higher spiritual bodies and methods of highest cultivation training to achieve these bodies.

Daoists are known for fathoming the principles or laws of nature, which means to master the principles of cause and effect in various fields of knowledge. This applies to medicine, agriculture, governance, human relationships, warfare, health, longevity, astrology and many other areas of endeavor. If one wishes to become a Daoist sage it behooves you to become master of several areas of expertise other than just the field of spiritual cultivation so that, upon your enlightenment, you might help people in ways other than just by using wonderworking superpowers.

Daoists are taught to "go along with the flow" when trying to get things done, which means adjusting yourself to the forces of nature, the momentum of human affairs, and the cycles of heaven (astronomical and terrestrial forces). You adjust your actions to your body, the climate, human affairs, and larger scale national or geopolitical events. Daoist cultivation uses many forces, such as the natural energies of the body, weather and cosmic conditions, in order to achieve the higher spiritual bodies of ascension. The target objective of Daoism is to become a Daoist Immortal like Lu Dongbin because this will free you from the material world forever.

The sage Lu Dongbin serves as an example of Taishang Laozun (Taiqing) who is the "Highest Elder Lord" or "Grand Supreme Elder Lord." He is akin to the Bodhisattva of Buddhism who works on behalf of the people to help them in various ways. This is the true ideal of Daoism, which is to become just like a Bodhisattva savior rather than a self-centered Arhat who is interested only in his own salvation and affairs. All of your Daoist activity should be geared toward developing yourself – your skills, circumstances and personality – in order to take your place on the world stage as an Immortal with many unseen spiritual bodies who will use them to help people in all sorts of invisible ways. During this life you yourself should be working hard to become a Daoist sage just like Lu Dongbin and other Daoist greats of the past.

To become an Immortal you must cultivate the human virtues and the merit of good deeds because you will need to depend upon others for the process that takes you to enlightenment. You must also train to develop certain virtues, skills, and excellences that polish your personality and abilities while also enabling you to help

175

people in various ways, some examples being giving good advice or charity to others, offering a service like acupuncture, or other means of lending assistance. A basic principle of Daoism, as represented by Yaiqing (the third of the Three Pure Ones), is not only to become master of yourself but master of the forces of the universe so that you can use your mastery of causality on behalf of the people in various instances. A Daoist is always studying the interrelationships between phenomena, how they produce one another, and the patterns of cause and effect so that he can become expert at intervening in affairs at critical junctures to change the trajectory of what is unfolding.

Here are some of the bodies of knowledge that a Daoist typically familiarizes himself with and how you can start to learn about them.

I-Ching

Much of Daoist philosophy is based upon the *I-Ching*, which focuses on how phenomena change so I published a translation based on its earliest known version, the Mawangdui manuscript. Within this book you can see early Zhou and Shang dynasty thinking about various life topics as well as commentaries on politics, governance and military matters. Unbeknownst to people, many of the *I-Ching* hexagrams are simply retellings of the history of the Zhou dynasty's triumph over the Shang dynasty with the inherent message: Shang dynasty bad, Zhou dynasty good; Shang dynasty evil, Zhou dynasty virtuous.

This translation of the *I-Ching* references the earliest known manuscript and translates the hexagram lines according to several principles: that there is a storyline within each hexagram where the sequence of lines from bottom to top incorporates an increasing intensity or progression of a main theme, each line reflects yin and yang as well as the meaning of component trigrams, and many lines reflect the meaning of overlapping trigrams or the meaning of the reverse, inverse and complementary (opposite) hexagram lines. This is the truest meaning of the *I-Ching* you will find, which is basically sixty-four cleverly written commentaries on various topics, composed by following a special structure, that Daoists (in particular) later turned into fortune telling prediction methods.

Political Science and Geopolitics

At one time I asked Master Nan Huai-Chin "who was the best Chinese sage to guide modern western man?" and instead of Lao Tzu, Meng Tzu, Kung Tzu, Mo Tzu etcetera he said Guan Tzu. After giving me a lecture on *The Book of Master Guan (The Guan Tzu)* I worked with five separate translators to prepare the best translation of this classic possible and added commentary on the topics of rulership, leadership, economics, geopolitics and military affairs from such notables as Cyrus the Great, Lee Kuan Yew, Zhuge Liang, and many more notables. This is found in my book, *The Art of Political Power,* which is a translation of *The Book of Master Guan (The Guan Tzu).*

The Guan Tzu provides us with early Daoist geopolitical thought that transcends any materials by Sun Tzu or Confucius on such matters. It provides strategies on national security, how to manage your population, how to become the most important leader in your country, how to manage your state and build it into a superpower, how to win wars without resorting to actual military force, how to win an election, geopolitical survival strategies, and much more. Guan Tzu was the very first prime minister to combine Keynesian and Monetary policies in his strategies to conquer other states without resorting to warfare.

The Book of Master Guan is definitely a Daoist text that teaches a higher level perspective on how to manage a country and guide mankind. A lower level text might be something like *The Master of Demon Valley*, which was translated by Thomas Cleary as *Thunder in the Sky*. I also suggest *Lee Kuan Yew: The Grand Master's Insights on China, the United States, and the World* by Allison and Blackwill. In today's world we manage the population through laws, education, public relations campaigns (propaganda) and control of the media (which you can learn about by studying very large national advertising and marketing campaigns) which we'll get to in a moment. These fields belong to Daoism as they are applications of Daoist principles for influencing the masses without seeming to use any effort.

Two other individuals who were said to have become *xian* or Daoist immortals, and who were connected with relevant political texts you might study, are Jiang Ziya and Zhang Liang. Jiang Ziya, author of *Six Secret Teachings,* was a general, strategist and expert on civil affairs who helped Kings Wen and Wu of the Zhou dynasty overthrow the tyrant King Zhou of Shang. Zhang Liang, who was taught by Daoist Master Huang Shigong (author of *Three Strategies of Huang Shigong*), helped Liu Bang establish the Han dynasty but afterwards retired from state affairs to become a Daoist adept. Zhuge Liang is a third individual who was expert at warfare, geopolitics and state affairs and often venerated in Daoist temples as an immortal. His works and life should also be studied.

Yin and Yang Cycles

Daoist philosophy is about following the natural rhythms of life and emphasizes the fact that life unfolds as a constant movement between complementary opposites. Daoism espouses that we should move along the waves of great forces without fighting their inevitable flow because life bobs up and down along with these waves. Exercising a constant resistance against the natural ways by which the universe unfolds, on the other hand, is considered by Daoists as a stupid and wasteful way to live.

All situations are characterized by Yin and Yang, and Daoism teaches that Yin turns into Yang at its extreme just as the peak of Yang turns into Yin at its extreme. This means that situations eventually have the potential of turning into their opposites. This is seen in the cycles of history and specifically within the rise and fall of dynasties, countries, cities and civilizations.

Daoism especially focuses on the 60-year cycle sexagenary or Jupiter-Saturn planetary cycle as the heartbeat of civilization. This cycle explains many impulses in mankind's history, as do other outer planetary cycles. The Chinese sexagenary cycle has been employed by Daoists for centuries to predict the large-scale trends of the Chinese nation, the ebb and flow of living conditions, and how society transforms and develops in resonance with the cyclical interplay of these two major planets. As one simple example, Bill Meridian notes that Jupiter-Saturn conjunctions in Pisces relate to the Japanese, those in Libra relate to the Mongols, conjunctions in Scorpio relate to the Chinese and Turks, and the Russians are particularly affected by Jupiter-Saturn conjunctions that happen in Sagittarius.

I've summarized the principles behind the historical economic and political rise and fall of dynasties, empires and countries in *Culture, Country, City, Company, Person, Purpose, Passion, World: The Grand Strategies and Unifying Principles Behind the Groups Which Rise and Thrive.* Together with *Super Investing*, these are two of the most powerfully useful books for you and also two of my favorites. Governments grow larger and more complex over time whereupon they start robbing people through inflation and taxes on a massive scale to fund wars, social welfare goals or to fund the extravagance and debauchery of entrenched institutions and the elite ruling class that loses its moral foundations. These burdens and corruption become so great over time (especially when the number of elites becomes too great at the top and they fight over political power) that governments eventually collapse and are replaced by something else, which accords exactly with Daoist notions. This is all within *Culture, Country, City, Company, Person, Purpose, Passion, World* which explains how to use these cycles to create prosperity for whatever sized group of individuals you wish to help.

It is interesting to note that the planet Pluto, which tends to bring slow fundamental changes in social structures and politics, has an orbit of roughly 240 years around the sun and that the duration of many dynasties has historically been approximately the length of one Pluto orbital cycle. As an example, the Dutch ruled for 250 years, then the Spanish and Portuguese, next the British and now the United States has reached the same age where it is possibly nearing the end of its own supremacy cycle. The Chinese date these cycles using multiples of sixty years, which is the approximate age of Kondratieff waves as well. In terms of large scale planetary cycles, Neptune has an affinity with mass movements, utopian ideologies, fanaticism, deception, dissolution and spirituality while Uranus has an affinity with rational thought, invention, innovation and sudden changes.

Of all the books that I have written, *Culture, Country, City, Company, Person, Purpose, Passion, World* is my favorite because it teaches you how to create products and services, includes investment strategies you can use for the rest of your life, and it reveals several strategies that might help your career. It teaches you about the repeatable cycles of mankind and how to guide the fate of companies, cities and nations by focusing on the lessons of these cycles, where you are within them, and the specific economic principles they activate. *Super Investing* takes a different angle by teaching you how to accumulate great generational wealth throughout economic cycles, and once again contains information from four decades of research that you will not find elsewhere. These two books, along with *Quick Fast Done* and *Move Forward* should be given to your children.

All sorts of cycles influence human activity, an example being Alexander Chizhevsky's finding that peak sunspot activity triggers humans to act upon grievances and complaints en masse through wars, revolutions and revolts. A true Daoist studies to know this type of celestial influence on mankind.

In the field of investments the concept of Yin and Yang is similar to contrarian investing where one buys assets with depressed prices that are out of favor (when there is "blood in the streets" because people are fearful) and sells them when everyone is buying with euphoria (because soon there will be no more buyers left and then without any more buying pressure the asset price must fall). To accumulate great wealth you can either chase assets whose prices are moving fastest, which is *momentum investing*, or buy assets that are undervalued in price, which is *value investing*. Over my career in finance I've collected some of the best investment strategies ever invented that have actually worked consistently for over 100 years, and you are not likely to encounter them so I saved them within this book and *Buddha Yoga*. I also put them in *Super Investing* and *Breakthrough Strategies of Wall Street Traders*. *Super Investing* teaches you how to create generational wealth with tested investment strategies but you need enough time to use its methods to create and then compound your investment returns to millionaire status.

The famous Indian astrologer B.V. Raman has translated several Indian classics that use astrology to chart the mundane affairs of nations so that you can forecast their flow of Yin and Yang in politics and economics. There is a large "I vs. We" social impact on human life due to planetary cycles (see *The Pendulum* on the swing between one social extreme to another by Roy William and Michael

Drew) that becomes reflected in actual mass events, and Elliott Wave analysis is another technique that tries to formulize a mathematical understanding of these influences. Many Daoists study Elliott Wave analysis which is akin to a facial reading of the stock market.

Every year *feng-shui* masters in Hong Kong, Taiwan, Singapore, Malaysia and China publish a new almanac forecasting the events for the coming year by employing Chinese *feng-shui* and astrological principles. While Chinese culture tries to do this by employing the sexagenary cycle of heavenly stems and earthly branches with what they typically mean for worldly events such as the stock market or politics, I suggest you study the following works that, in line with Daoist leanings, teach you how to forecast mundane affairs through various western forms of planetary cycles:

- *Planetary Economic Forecasting* (Bill Meridian)
- *Mastering Geopolitical Prediction – Applied Mundane Astrology* (Bill Meridian)
- *Planetary Cycles* (Andre Barbault)
- *The Value of Astrology* (Andre Barbault)
- *Cosmos and Psyche* (Richard Tarnas)
- *Mundane Astrology* (Baigent, Campion and Harvey)
- *Mundane Astrology: The Astrology of Nations and States* (Green, Carter et al)
- *Mundane Astrology* (Stefano Stracuzzi)
- *Astrology Chart of the United States* (Richard Houck)

Based upon such work, there are several forecasts for upcoming decades that you should take note of:

- The Barbault index and Ganeau graphs reveal the potential for an intense world war (greater than WWI or WWII) starting around 2080-81 when, as Andre Barbault noted, a Jupiter-Saturn conjunction (2080-81) passes over a Uranus-Neptune opposition

- In 2030 there is a conjunction of Cupido and Chronos that Bill Meridian says "will challenge the individual to choose between God and Satan. Any government formed at this time (such as a one-world government) is likely to have evil intentions."
- Barbault notes in *Planetary Cycles* that there will be "no surprise if Japan experiences a new era of full prosperity with the Uranus-Pluto trine at the end of the decade 2020-30, but then has major challenges at the opposition of 2036-37"
- Strazuzzi in *Mundane Astrology* notes that Neptune's progression through Taurus in the 2040s may lead to the possibility of mankind's discontinuing its dependence on fossil fuels and until then you should ignore any "Green movement" nonsense that mankind can survive without fossil fuels
- Studies show that military attacks timed to have their major offensive as Mars hits its maximum daily speed (41 minutes daily) are usually most successful
- Barbault in *The Value of Astrology* notes that armistice and détente periods are historically pronounced (and thus possible) when there are Sun-Jupiter conjunctions (and trines to a lesser extent), which thus gives us timing indications as when to strongly press for peace or a halt to war
- Analyst Martin Armstrong reports that his Socrates program expects deep economic decline unfolding between May 7, 2024 and 2028. He also expects China to take over as the world's preeminent economic leader after 2032. If China's economic takeover were to happen it would probably coincide with the Saturn-Uranus conjunction of 2032 and the culmination of the current Saturn-Pluto cycle in 2035-36 by which time China may have consolidated its position.
- Strazuzzi in *Mundane Astrology* notes that a potential rebirth of Russian society might occur around 2026 when there is a Saturn-Neptune conjunction.

- Carlos Alegria (in *Economic Cycles, Debt and Demographics*) notes that from 2030 onwards the populations of the large emerging markets will start to decline

The planetary alignments of 2020, where we had a Jupiter-Saturn-Pluto conjunction in Capricorn, led to world events that captured the symbolic essence of this astrological sign, which stands for a structured, heavy and limiting nature. The COVID panic coincided with a wave of fear, promoted by officials, that lead to previously unimaginable acceptance of widespread restrictions across society.

The planetary alignments of the early 2030s suggest another period of incredible historical importance similar to the late 1700s when tremendous illuminist thought arose across the world. In this case society may come to new realizations that revolutionize the world because forbidden knowledge is no longer repressed or withheld, which might then cause a major collapse of various controlling societal or economic structures.

Martial Arts & Daoist Cultivation

Daoism emphasizes the soft martial arts, and in particular the martial arts styles of *taijiquan, baguazhang* and *xingyiquan* as well as various animal forms. What is missing in the modern training systems for these and other schools of martial arts is knowledge of the inner energy practices that actually purify our internal Earth Immortal subtle body so that it can emerge as an independent vehicle of life. This inner energy work is the central crux of Daoist cultivation that, when correctly practiced, will propel you to a higher level of martial arts mastery while also preparing you for the independent deva body attainment. The accomplished martial artist Sun Lutang, who became an Immortal at around age 27-28 (after twelve years) through his practice under Guo Yunshen (d. 1898), who was also enlightened as evidenced by his martial arts feats and the details of their overall story, has provided teachings on this.[9]

An individual who starts the micro-macrocosmic circulations in his

[9] At the beginning of the twelve year kundalini transformations of internal alchemy you simply wish that the internal Qi rotations (being performed by enlightened masters within you) would increase and the process speed up. By the third year of the process you are being used by all the local protect gods, enlightened masters and devas as a training arena where they accost you constantly, go into your brain, check your memories, and criticize everything you did in life. They practice giving you all sorts of thoughts and bring up all sorts of past wrongs and guilty behaviors to make you embarrassed and raise your Yin Qi. The end of the process is one of hardship where you pass through increasing painful physical attacks by spiritual beings who are trying to demonstrate such skills in the entire audience of devas at the same time, who are always assembled around you (desiring entertainment) because they wish to partake of the purification efforts being continually done to you. In order to pass safely through the process he went to Guo Yunshen at the three year mark who kept watch over him and protected him until he achieved the Tao. Then after this attainment he moved on (most masters move around to a new area after they achieve the independent subtle body so that the local guys can rest after spending so many years on you) to spend time at the enlightened master Cheng Tinghua's *baguazhang* school learning how to unify the powers of his deva body with his martial arts while cultivating to attain the Causal body of the Spirit Immortal. Instead of sitting motionless in meditation while masters would work on his body transformations, he would stand motionless in the stationary standing posture while cultivating to attain the next higher transcendental body. This is why those who practice the stable martial arts postures such as the Trinity Posture (*San Ti Shi*) of *xingyiquan*, the Eight Mother Palms holding postures of *baguazhang*, or various *shuzuang bu* (Tree Stump) postures usually show the most process as they are the equivalent of empty mind sitting meditation (*zazen*), sitting prayer or stationary yoga *asanas* (held while remembering Patanjali's aphorism that "yoga represents the absence of fluctuations within the mind"). During all these stationary positions devas will possess your body and try to transform your Qi while a master simultaneously works on them with his own *nirmanakaya* energies. Using the *garima siddhi* superpower of making one's body very heavy he practiced striking cannons with his palms until he could move them several inches, and then was able to defeat a challenger to Cheng's school by sending him out the window with a single palm strike. When this happened, Cheng Tinghua stood up and in happiness struck the bench he had been sitting on, which immediately split into two, to also demonstrate his own enlightenment skills that came from his spiritual body practice rather than physical strength, which is something most people don't understand. Many martial arts students hurt themselves (especially their hands and fingers) training to duplicate a famous feat of some master they hear about without realizing that he could only achieve it because he had attained the Earth Immortal's spiritual body and had the *garima* heaviness (Qi condensation) *siddhi*, so don't destroy your hands and knuckles in training.

or her teens usually achieves the enlightenment stage of a full Arhat before age forty, like Mohammed, at which time they are asked to take over a spiritual tradition if they are so willing. They go through twelve years of kundalini transformations to achieve the deva body (stage of the Earth Immortal), three years to achieve the Causal body (stage of the Spirit Immortal) and then three years to achieve the stage of the Supra-Causal body or full Arhat (stage of the Celestial Immortal). After this you must work to achieve the Immanence, Tathagata or Great Golden Arhat stage of the Universal Immortal. When some achieve the Earth Immortal body at a young enough age they will take on a heavenly wife to be their companion for the long journey ahead so the idea of *bramacharya* (celibacy) really only holds in most traditions for the earthly plane. Thus, many enlightened masters will stipulate celibacy to you but are really married "upstairs" and you just don't know it.

Sentient beings across the galaxy, and universe, all work to achieve the same stages of spiritual achievement. Most monastics achieve the subtle body stage of the Earth Immortal only at around age forty due to starting late. Many who do achieve the stage of the Earth Immortal at a young age, however, such as a Dilgo Khyentse Rinpoche (d. 1991) or Chatral Sangye Dorje Rinpoche (d. 2015) of Tibet, want to leave the world but at the requests of others they stay and teach subsequent generations and the public. If you enter into the realm of government matters and public affairs before you attain the capabilities of the Great Golden Arhat body, such as did Jesus, then it is easy to make strategic mistakes with your activities even though you are enlightened.

There are many individuals walking around in society who achieved enlightened through traditions or methods other than the standard paths of Daoism, Buddhism, Vajrayana, Yoga, Hinduism, Yoga, Sufism, Orthodox Christianity and so forth including through secret lineages in each country unbeknownst to the public!

Since this information on internal alchemy is largely missing, I put the most advanced teachings you'll ever find in *Neijia Yoga*, *Arhat Yoga*, *Internal Martial Arts Nei-gong* and *Correcting Zen* to fill in the missing gaps. All Daoists need to know the material in *Neijia* Yoga since it teaches you how to cultivate your meridians, *bindu* acupuncture points on the body, *dantian* (elixir fields), organs and appendages through various Daoist techniques. This information is mandatory if you are studying or living according to Daoist teachings. It is the basis of Daoism, martial arts and even Chinese medicine.

Hindu yoga focuses on "chakras" to help you cultivate your body in a seven sectional partitioning scheme while Daoism prefers the elixir fields schema that partitions the body into just three sections. Some cultivation schools partition body (Qi) cultivation into two halves while some use four or five body sections. You will encounter some of these schemes in the appendices.

Also, because inner cultivation is a method of inner Qi purification and of building your health, the Hatha yoga school of cultivation promotes six traditional methods of inner cleansing but they are not strong enough for us in today's world of chemical bombardment. Daoist medicine, such as various branches from the Wudang Mountains, has many "secret" herbal formulas to help cleanse the body but many are too weak for modern man. A successful manufacturer told me that his most successful formulas were derived by taking ancient classical Chinese formulas and replacing the ingredients with more potent alternatives from the West. This is something that most a top herbalist can do if he wants to create more effective products.

Three separate herbalists over the years, each from a different tradition, has told me that medical formulas that once lasted for centuries are less effective today due to the fact that our bodies have changed due to diet, environment and lifestyle changes. In particular, our vibratory rate, frequency, and various electrical potentials have changed drastically due to strong electromagnetic field exposure. One formulator who died years ago said that his herbal formulas would only remain effective for about fifty to sixty years before they would have to be reformulated because of the changing vibrational rates of the human body subject to those influences, which he always measured using multiple techniques to create his various formulas. Another formulator who would measure the blood pH, electrical, magnetic, Qi and other fields of the human body in all sorts of ways also told me that those averages were not remaining constant and this is why formulas would lose their effectiveness over time due to those changes.

I updated the various yoga detoxification methods in *Detox Cleanse Your Body Quickly and Completely* using stronger naturopathic techniques that have a Daoist flavor. While Daoism segments the body into the three major elixir fields for purposes of cultivation, the Hindu Upanishads and Hatha Yoga of India focus primarily on chakra cultivation. In order to clear up all the nonsense you hear and read about chakras you will find the first trustworthy explanation of chakras (and various related cultural goodies) in Appendix 1 as previously stated.

If you are interested in martial arts for sports purposes then in addition to *Neijia Yoga*, *Arhat Yoga*, *Internal Martial Arts Nei-gong* and *Correcting Zen* the book *Sports Visualization* might interest you. It is a single topic out of the larger book *Visualization Power* that I originally wrote because of reading stories of jailed individuals or prisoners of war who used visualization practices to improve their skills, so I collected countless visualization practices that you can use to improve various aspects of your life or that you can specifically employ for cultivation purposes. In general, however,

Correcting Zen, Neijia Yoga and *Arhat Yoga* are best.

One of China's top swordsmen told me that when he was young the Communist government forbid anyone from practicing *nei-gong*, but he realized that the only way he would be able to become better than all his opponents who were more talented than him or training harder was if he practiced forbidden breathing techniques of *qi-gong* and *nei-gong*. Hence *Neijia Yoga* has many *nei-gong neijia* exercises for martial artists and yoga practitioners as well.

Many spiritual schools use visualization practices but when using them practitioners neglect the most important principle which is to *engage all of your senses during visualization practice.* Visualizations are not supposed to be just stale mental imagery rehearsals without much emotional content. You should try to feel physical sensations during the session of mental rehearsal if you are visualizing yourself doing something. You must try to see and feel yourself doing it perfectly. Most important of all, you must try to stimulate your emotions during visualization and raise your energy in order to transform the quality of your Qi. This principle should be employed in all Daoist visualization practices.

Health, Anti-Aging and Longevity

Master Nan Huai-chin once recommended that I write a book on longevity so I combined the (1) Daoist methods of longevity with (2) the ten *xian* cultivation methods within the *Surangama Sutra*, (3) Siddha Medicine from ancient India, (4) modern scientific anti-aging approaches and (5) the Blue Zones findings as well as (6) house clearing detoxifying methods in *Look Younger, Live Longer.* This book lists the best anti-aging supplements that work and spotlights those which actually address all the biochemical theories on aging. For some reason, no one ever bothered to do this.

Unfortunately the internet suppresses advertising for this type of book and its companion volume, *Detox Cleanse Your Body Quickly and Completely* (also *Super Cancer Fighters*), so they are not widely known. However, if you are a Daoist interested in anti-aging I recommend them along with Ben Greenfield's book *Boundless: Upgrade Your Brain, Optimize Your Body & Defy Aging*, which is excellent. I firmly believe that every adult should engage in a brief detoxification routine every year using the fewest but highest quality products. I provided a list due to my own experiences and due to interviews with naturopaths, doctors and manufacturers that I put in this book.

If you are seeking optimum techniques for how to do things from experts you usually will not go wrong with any of Tim Ferriss's books such as *Tools of Titans, Tribe of Mentors, and The 4-Hour Body* and *The 4-Hour Chef*.

An important issue for longevity is how to prevent death by avoiding accidents and by eliminating harmful habits such as smoking, drug use, alcoholism and so forth. Another issue is to avoid the leading causes of death. At present the leading causes of death in the world, in order, are cardiovascular disease, cancers, respiratory disease, diabetes, Alzheimer's dementia, lower respiratory infections, neonatal deaths, car accidents, liver disease, tuberculosis and kidney disease. I have tried to make my contribution to eliminating these pains by publishing books of various natural remedies and cures that individuals often use:

- *Prevent and Reserve Atherosclerosis: Proven Natural Alternatives that Eliminate Cholesterol Plaque Without Surgery* (Stanton Reed) addresses blood clots, strokes and heart disease
- *Super Cancer Fighters* addresses natural healing measures for cancer (absent the latest information on ivermectin-

fenbendazole-tocotrienol protocols and information in *Life Force* by Tony Robbins)

- *Detox Cleanse Your Body Quickly and Completely* addresses all your organ systems but there are particularly good sections on liver disease, kidney disease and intestinal detoxification

Military Strategy

I am working on a manuscript about the most successful generals of all time and the strategies they used to win their battles. This too is a Daoist field of knowledge but you'll have to wait until this is published to see the most effective strategies of all time.

For an inkling of real politics, geopolitical strategy and military strategy you should read *The Fourth World War* (Count de Marenches and David Andelman), *The Evil Empire* (Count de Marenches and Christine Ochrent), and *The Book of Master Guan.*

Other tacticians, geo-strategists, mega-historians or related people of interest to study include Sun Tzu (*The Art of War*), Zhuge Liang, Han Fei, Clausewitz (*On War*), Thucydides, Kautilya (*Arthashastra*), Ibn Khaldun (*Muqaddimah*), Machiavelli (*The Prince*), Cardinal Richelieu, Talleyrand, Metternich, Otto von Bismarck, Camillo Benso of Cavour, Cyrus the Great, and Frederick the Great. Eventually military readers encounter Jomini, Corbett, and many other military strategists. For warfare you must also study the various teachings of the little-recognized genius John Boyd, who revolutionized modern air and ground warfare strategy with his emphasis on speedy reactions.

To understand military strategies and geo-political maneuvering you will be forever helped by reading the Chinese classic *Romance of the Three Kingdoms*, and watching the "more than excellent" 2010 "Three Kingdoms" television version available (with English subtitles) on Youtube in 94 episodes. Chinese friends had told me that anyone who reads *Romance of the Three Kingdoms* is forever "polluted" by the text, and so a friend and I watched the *complete* 2010 video series on Youtube. I could not believe it but must concur with them that your mind will be forever changed and start to think strategically after watching this masterpiece.

Astrology and *Feng-shui*

Daoism incorporates teachings on *feng-shui* and astrology into its philosophies because people should know their upcoming fate, know how to change it, and act in tune with the heavens to minimize problems in life. Knowing the fate or destiny of your life is a well-known ability of enlightened Daoist sages who, like all people who reach the stage of the Celestial Immortal or yet higher Immanence body, can see the future. Knowing how to change that future is what is difficult.

Daoism uses *feng-shui* remedies to try to change people's fortunes but frankly speaking, most are useless. When your future fortune is unfavorable there sometimes *are* various remedial measures (such as moving) available for changing it as revealed in *Liao Fan's Four Lessons*, but most people will not take the difficult road of using them because they involve changing your personality and conduct on a deep level and holding to wise principles of behavior that would truly change your fate. The famous astrologer K.N. Rao, who is familiar with countless astrological remedial measures, only advises Hindus to recite the Vishnu Sahasranam from the *Mahabharata*, which is the only Sahasranam that Sri Adi Shankacharya had written a commentary upon, and the "Narayana Kavacha" from the Sreemad Bhagavatha Purana (Chapter 8, Skandha 8). There is also a Lalitha Sahasranam.

The universal principle is that your personality and behavior create your fortune, so to change it you must act differently by going against the grain of your personality and behavior that have both an astrological natal foundation and predisposition due to your genes, education, as well as parental and societal influences. This is hard. Going against your fortune involves friction because your fortune is your natural inclination or predisposition, so the going is usually rough and difficult to change's oneself and one's fate. Thus most people don't want to make the effort or continue the effort. Nevertheless, most people do want to know their fortune; everyone wants to hear about upcoming good news if it is there.

Daoism employs several forms of Chinese astrology and fate forecasting such as *Bazi, Zi Wei Dou Shu,* and *Tieh Pan Shen Shu.* They all depend upon the principle that hidden forces, due to the planets, are at play within the human psyche and those forces help create events within people's lives. You can learn many essentials on how to change your fortune and destiny from *Liao Fan's Four Lessons,* which has a Daoist-Confucian-Buddhist flavor to it, and I've summarized this technique and put my own procedure for changing your fate and destiny (the 8M Method) in *Quick, Fast, Done* and the upcoming book *Self-Creation.* I also always recommend that people also read *Think and Grow Rich* by Napoleon Hill, *How to Win Friends and Influence People* and *The Autobiography of Benjamin Franklin.*

If you think that you will play a significant role in the fate of your nation to the extent of affecting the course of your country and its culture then your natal planets (usually the Sun) must overlap the zodiacal degrees that have been vital to the country (or affairs you want to affect) historically. I once attended a *Tieh Pan Shen Shu* astrology reading for the President of Taiwan where his name was kept secret from the astrologer, yet it correctly revealed the details of his life with one sentence saying that he would play a significant role in the history of his country. This just shows once again that at your birth time your fate for such things is already set. As another example, royals born on the day or within the day of an eclipse (Prince Charles, Prince William and Kate Middleton were born during eclipses) usually indicate the beginning or end of a dynastic line while Pluto-Sun and Saturn-Sun aspects are common in the charts of long-lasting political entities.

To note: the most difficult times in the careers of individuals are often when there is a Saturn-Uranus hard aspect (a square or opposition). Also several planetary configurations that accompany someone's fall from power include: (1) eclipses conjunct and opposite the Sun (and sometimes square), (2) second Saturn returns, (3) progressed full moons, (4) eclipses conjunct and opposite the Midheaven (MC), and (5) Saturn transiting over the Sun.

You can spend hours learning many different astrological principles like this along with different types of astrology (I recommend Vedic astrology over Chinese astrology) but no matter what you study I especially recommend Julian Lee's *The Geostel Brownbook* on relocation astrology because by simply moving to a new location to take advantage of different house rulerships and planetary progressions you can change your fortune tremendously. Much of my upcoming book *Self-Creation* concerns how you can change your fate and fortune or improve the fortunes of specific astrological houses by unusual methods.

As to astrology for setting up businesses, I want to pass onto you a simple technique from *Planetary Stock Trading* that originated with Charles Jayne, one of the best technical astrologers of the last century. This is important because many people want to know the most auspicious time to start a new business. Jayne said that when starting a business and trying to select a suitable date you must first determine what planet rules the new venture such as Venus for a beauty shop, Mercury for a cellphone shop, Mars for a martial arts dojo and so on. Then you should make the planet strong by selecting a day when that planet is conjunct or opposite the recent eclipse point since that will energize it. If that is not possible then select the day upon which the planet stations. Since there can be several choices, examine the other aspects for that day to make sure that they are also positive. This method in general highlights the power of the major function of the business that is represented by the relevant planet.

Marital Relations

Daoism espouses that couples should try to build a harmonious relation within their marriage. In an ideal marriage the two should be like a team where the parties support and help one another. I wrote *Husbands and Wives Were Connected in the Past* to summarize a lot of ancient thinking from China, India, and the Christian mindset on the secret of great marriages and families because I saw great interest on this topic in lectures I was giving in China.

Since I love the ancient Chinese quote that once hung above the imperial shrine in Hangzhou, "Husbands and wives were connected in the past. Whether for good or bad those connections never fail to meet again. Children are basically past debts. Some come to give and some come to collect," I touched upon this principle within the book.

Unfortunately, marriage today seems headed for extinction because women are being taught to choose life paths that go against their inner nature while men are being asked to enter into marriage relationships that are legally and financially biased against them. Master Nan Huai-chin told me that for this century marriages would almost cease to exist, and one might read *The Evolution of Desire* (David Buss), *The Rational Male* (Rollo Tomassi), *The*

Unplugged Alpha (Rich Cooper), *How to Stay in Love* (James Seton) to gain some ideas as to why.

This includes the fact that the essence of womanhood is declining in the west as women become more masculinized, which men don't find appealing since they don't want to marry someone who is like them. Also, today's family law puts men at a great financial and legal risk if they enter into a marriage that doesn't work out, which happens at least 56% of the time according to divorce statistics. Radical feminization has made most women unattractive to men where marriage now involves an extremely high legal risk to the men for losing any children they produce and most of their financial assets. For men the legal bond of marriage is therefore no longer considered a "good deal" but something not worth the burden and risks, hence they are pursuing alternative avenues for joy and peace and letting go of what they deem doesn't contribute positively to their life.

You can find information about the characteristics of your (future) spouse through Vedic astrology, Chinese astrology, or western astrology readings. There are many forms of fate prediction that can reveal characteristics about whom you are likely to marry. For instance, you might even be given their name or occupation (as well as personality description) in a Chinese *Tieh Pan Shen Shu* reading or in an Agastyr *nadi grantha* palm leaf reading from India. I searched for over thirty years to find a trustworthy source for *nadi grantha* readings and can recommend greentaracanada.ca where you can do the reading over the internet once they find your *nadi* palm leaf after some searching.

In *The Predictive Power of Eclipse Paths* the author Bill Meridian pointed out that your major eclipse path, or where it overlaps with ACG astrocartography lines, is sometimes related to major locations connected to your spouse such as where they come from or where you might meet them.

In *Astrology and the Authentic Self (Nicholas Hays, Florida, 2008)*, author astrologer Demetra George mentions that the names of your spouse are often connected to asteroids or minor planets that conjunct the sensitive points of your natal astrology chart: "And yet, in my twenty-five years of working with the minor planets, I have repeatedly seen how amazingly accurate these can be in detailing the specifics of people and places and mythic themes in an individual's life. Following are some striking examples from the charts of celebrities that illustrate this point. Prince Charles, for instance, has the asteroids Camilla and Parks conjunct his Venus within 15 minutes of arc. The name of his lifelong love and now wife is Camilla Parker. Bill Clinton has the asteroids Paula, Monica, Asmodeus (the Persian demon god of lust), and William opposite his Moon, and the asteroid Hillary conjunct his Moon as well as the asteroid Hilaritas conjunct his IC, the ground and anchor of the chart. Jacqueline Kennedy Onassis has the asteroids John and Aristotle, the names of her two husbands, opposite her Moon (within 1 degree), which, as one of the significators of marriage, is itself conjunct the asteroid Abunduntia, the Roman goddess of abundance. Her final life partner, Maurice Tempelsman, is indicated by the asteroids Maury and Temple, both on the degree of her Midheaven."

Agriculture and Rainmaking, Weather and Climate

Daoist masters are famous for making rain by climbing up onto a high platform and swinging a sword while uttering incantations. Actually, a more effective method involves using mirrors to stimulate the Qi within an area, and one researcher in China told me that he had tested various mirror methods and found them to be 80% successful at generating rain.

The absolute best information on weather engineering are the works of Trevor Constable such as *Loom of the Future: The Weather Engineering Work of Trevor James Constable*, "Etheric Weathering Engineering on the High Seas" (video), and his other videos. These materials show how to use very simple-to-construct esoteric devices for weather engineering whereas the U.S. government secretly uses microwave energy and very large-scale atmospheric heating devices such as HAARP.

Trevor taught me how to make and use his famous rainmaking tubes when visiting Hong Kong. On a trip to Hainan Island in China and during a trip to the Tenggri Desert in Inner Mongolia a group of us confirmed that they really work. We witnessed Trevor performing the impossible feat of stopping a typhoon in its tracks off of Hong Kong by using the repulsive power of a rain tube that kept it offshore. The mirrored tube also caused a strange pink aura in the sky at a 90-degree angle to its pointing direction, which I had never seen before as an atmospheric phenomenon, but it was foretold in his book, *Loom of the Future*.

While on Hainan Island he created a perfectly circular dark rain cloud by rotating a mirrored rain tube with his hand that eventually caused the cloud that he had formed to rain. He even punched the cloud at its periphery using another tube pointed there that then produced another perfect circle within it. I had never seen anything like this – a perfectly round but very black cloud directly over head that was formed by him rotating a rain tube with another hole inside it!

His rainmaking tubes create rain by creating a negative Qi pole within them (they push out all the Qi inside the tube due to mirrors reflecting it away so it cannot enter or stay inside) after which they can be used to push against oncoming atmospheric Qi until it bunches up into an agglomerated mass and then discharges as rain when the mass of accumulated sky water becomes too large. The tubes can be used to drag atmospheric phenomena from one place to another as well. Trevor has showed in his books how to change weather patterns by placing the ends of empty pipes in a running stream while pointing them correctly in the sky to draw energy to an area or push it away, which can also be used to push smog away from a region.

If I remember correctly, in a Youtube interview Juan O Savin once mentioned that some individual was able to create standing waves that prevented rain by somehow using a car battery along with old television antennas, but he didn't explain how the set-up worked. He simply said that the effect was unmistakable on weather maps so the U.S. government sent some men asking the individual to stop.

Why the focus on rain? This is a Daoist field of expertise due to its importance for agriculture. Daoists are concerned with agriculture since most people in olden times were farmers and if their crops did not grow then the people would starve. Therefore Daoists usually familiarized themselves with the best practices concerning soil health, seeds, planting (times and conditions), crop rotation, weed management, irrigation, weather (rainfall), fertilizer, pest control, and harvesting. Acres USA provides many books on these farming topics. TED talks also provide information on innovative, revolutionary farming techniques and you can find permaculture and other related videos galore on Youtube.

For instance, soil health and fertility can be improved through products like volcanic ash, the soil enrichment methods of William Albrecht, compost teas, earthworms, and by using radionics to identify mineral excesses and deficiencies that must be addressed. Dr. Arden Anderson is one expert who can do this. For some people the homeopathic-astronomical methods of Rudolph Steiner for pest control, as well as the fascinating radionics methods of

Galen Hieronymous might prove of interest.

Along the lines of radionics, devices such as the Quantum Tube broadcaster (if they work) might offer subtle energy solutions to farming problems, such as pests and fertility issues. Decreased irrigation costs and nutrient uptake can be improved through inexpensive water treatment methods such as Crystal Blue Water Structuring Units. Furthermore, various mantras for crop growth are available in Hinduism and other religions.

The big issue, however, is climate rather than just rain. In particular, Daoists are concerned with weather because it has a gigantic effect on human health and well-being. Extreme weather events, such as heat waves or cold waves, can result in human morbidity. Dr. Raymond Wheeler, who analyzed world climate and cultural activities over 2,000 years (his teachings are found in *Climate: The Key to Understanding Business Cycles*), found that there were four cycles of weather (Cold-Dry, Warm-Wet, Warm-Dry, Cold-Wet) that produced similar patterns of human mass behavior and thus similar events in history when the same weather phases were repeated. The worst wars, as an example, occur after Hot-Dry periods while Cold-Dry periods typically spell major unrests and civil wars.

If we look at the development of the world's empires we will also see that they usually developed borders that overlapped with climate zones because people living within the same climate easily develop a similar culture without even trying. Those living in the same climate zone survive by farming and hunting the same foods and live very similar lives due to experiencing similar hardships so it becomes easy for them to interact with one another, grow and thrive from common methods as well as unite together to defend themselves from outsiders. A common climate unites people by producing a common culture throughout its expanse. Thus it is often noted that Islam spread throughout desert regions while Christianity spread where olives grew!

When in the 80s I first read Wheeler's predictions that the United States would be entering a Warm-Dry period from the late 1990s to early 2020s I thought his work was probably wrong because this seemed implausible. I said to myself "It is impossible for his predictions to come true that the government would become authoritarian and despotic, a police state would emerge, personal freedoms would decline and there would be a collapse of the economic system." Boy, was I wrong!

Now the prediction is for a Cold-Wet period from the mid 2020s to late 2040s whereupon we should see a reemergence of individualistic philosophies, decentralizing and reorganizational trends in government and business, mechanistic education, simplistic and straightforward art, and an emancipation of natural behavior. Absolutist governments do not thrive in a Cold-Wet phase because the uncomfortable weather brings out increasing expressions of social discontent. However, during this time we should see an increase in birth rates, improved general health of the public, better mental vigor, mass migration movements to rural areas, economic prosperity, international trade and improvements in intercultural exchange. Martin Armstrong, who I greatly respect, has much to say about this on his blog, which I recommend.

Wheeler noted that more than 90% of leaders/rulers who have been titled "great" or "good" by historians (because they helped their people out of chaos) held tenure during the Cold-Dry nation-building phases of this 100-year weather cycle. Warm weather decreases human energies, human birthrates and brings about economic depression and social dependence.

Basically, the rise and fall of civilizations is tied to the climate due to agriculture. Civilization tends to expand during warming periods and collapses during cold periods due to reduced agricultural production and an increase in diseases so if you want more food you should prefer global warming (and CO2 because it is plant food). Wheat prices soared during the Little Ice Age because crops fail in winter, and the Black Death made its appearance during a global cooling phase too. You should actually prefer cyclical global warming to global cooling as long as it's within bounds.

Weather is associated with changes in birth rates, sperm counts, outbreaks of influenza and bronchitis, and of course it affects agricultural production. Weather affects spiritual cultivation as well because it becomes difficult to move your internal Qi when your body feels damp and humid, which cramps the internal circulation of energy. Thus the whole field of *feng-shui* is about the fight between water (dampness) and wind (Qi) in your body and environment.

You should realize that the idea of man-made global warming is a scam (backed by fake models and lack of evidence) since there is no statistical evidence for it whatsoever. The idea that climate changed is caused *exclusively* by mankind, CO2 or even the sun is also a hoax although the sun plays the major role. The records of millennia prove that CO2, for instance, does not cause temperature change at all. Climate change is cyclical, complex, and the current mantra of "global warming" and "climate emergency" is entirely nonsense being pushed on people through brainwashing. It's a scam, a hoax, an invented scare, a funded fraud. This is why the elites changed their focus from global warming to "climate change" since man-made global warming is fake news but everyone will go along with a mantra of "climate change" because it happens every day. "The weather is always changing so there must be climate change, sounds reasonable." Man has little to do with climate change, and there is no "control knob" cause and effect relationship between CO2 and temperature over the long history of the earth either. Weather is variable, cyclical, greatly dependent upon the *behavior of the sun* and other factors, and mankind is not doing much to affect it through fossil fuels usage, CO2 or nitrogen emissions. This is actually the majority view of scientists that governments and press lackeys are trying to suppress as they try to marginalize those who don't support the false narrative. Watch the 80-minute internet video "Climate: The Movie (The Cold Truth)" by Martin Durkin for the facts that they don't want you to know.

The public relations campaign going on about climate change has a political agenda behind it *is actually about world domination and power.* Governments are lying to you about climate change through psychological warfare in pursuit of funding and more power over you. They are waging an assault against your freedom and prosperity via a covert power grab using the pen. The objective here is to take over the world and use a fake, manufactured climate crisis to gain control over people to create a one-world government by claiming "humanity faces doom and it's beyond the power of a single nation to defend against climate change and reverse the trend so it's going to take all of us following a central authority. We must therefore turn control over to the UN." There is absolutely no climate emergency that requires the elimination of fossil fuels or destruction of farming, and it is ridiculous to say that the majority of climate change is all linear caused by humans or that CO2 is even a driver. Once again, the idea that humans are heating up the earth is a scam since the weather and temperature are cyclical.

A similar attempt is being made by the World Health Organization (WHO) that wants to take control of your healthcare for its own globalist agenda. The WHO agency is under the United Nations and wants to obtain the power to declare a pandemic in any country under any conditions it likes, thus robbing you of national sovereignty and personal freedom. The WHO wants to mandate vaccines on you for future pandemics and wants the right to withhold drugs and silence your doctor without any accountability for its actions. This, once again, is a political (and monetary) agenda. Certain elites want you to become a prisoner of their dictates. Remember that when governments criminalize the questioning or criticism of information or "police misinformation" (which is none of their business) it is usually because they are hiding some harmful agenda through contrived narratives.

"Local knows best" so you certainly know what is best for your own health and for your family. No one remedy fits all, and your country should be in control of its health policies instead of some unelected bureaucrats somewhere else who are unaccountable for ordering that you be injected with some untested foreign substance or undergo some unwanted medical procedure. This is a big scam in the making with your health and freedom at risk, but these people will never stop trying to gain power over you.

Martin Armstrong has models that project we are entering another "grand minimum" within a 300-year weather cycle. This "Maulder Minimum" will overtake the sun beginning in 2020 and last through the 2050s. The results will be diminished magnetism, infrequent sunspot production, and less ultraviolet (UV) radiation reaching Earth. The last Maulder Minimum took place from 1645 to 1715 when the sun's brightness declined and the number of sunspots collapsed; as sunspots fade away a solar minimum is produced. Parts of the world became so cold during this previous Maulder Minimum that it produced a mini-Ice Age within a larger "Little Ice Age" cycle that you can read about in works by Brian Fagan. This coming Maulder Minimum means we are facing a global cooling period on the planet that may span 31 to 43 years. Various governments do not want you to know this. The last grand maximum peaked in 1958 after which the sun has been gradually quieting down, and since then we have seen sunspot activity decline at its steepest in 9,300 years which is affecting weather patterns. There is nothing scientists can do to alter solar activity so all the hullabaloo about changing our behavior to affect the weather is nonsense.

Marketing and Advertising

Through its classics like the *Three Strategies of Huang Shi Gong* or *The Master of Demon Valley*, Daoism teaches us how to control, guide or influence a population by piggybacking a message on the trends of the times and using as little effort as possible (an economy of labor) to achieve a big result. Daoism instructs leaders to gently address the fundamental issues that lie at the foundation of daily ordinary human behavior in order to produce big changes in society.

Therefore, the skills of marketing and advertising properly belong within the field of Daoist study since they work this way. They can be used to permeate society with certain messages and memes, thus disseminating influences with very little human intervention to steer society in certain directions by perfuming it with certain ideas. Whether for good or bad, you can think of marketing and advertising efforts as guiding human affairs without it looking like you are personally doing anything at all.

If you want to learn what policies will guide nations to prosperity, which is also a Daoist field of study, I greatly recommend the Youtube videos of Hans Rosling. In "The Century of the Self" Youtube videos you can also see how the American elites used various policies and advertising to influence America along particular economic lines of development that the elites determined would spread consumerism in order to power the economy. For its own economic growth China has recently decided to similarly develop a consumer-based economy rather than an export-driven economy like Germany.

I have put some lessons related to this in *Culture, Country, City, Company, Person, Purpose, Passion, World*. In my book *Bankism* I have shown how the fields of banking and finance have become corrupted over time but can be corrected so as to bring prosperity back to nations despite the trends of over-population, over-capacity and over-production. The following videos deal with large-scale human behavioral issues and will help you understand what Daoism tries to teach in its various classics about guiding or ruling a nation:

- "Hans Rosling's 200 Countries, 200 Years, 4 Minutes – The Joy of Stats"
- "The best stats you've ever seen – Hans Rosling"
- "Don't Panic – Hans Rosling showing the facts about population"
- "How not to be ignorant about the world – Hans Rosling and Ola Rosling"
- "Hans Rosling: Debunking third-world myths with the best stats you've ever seen"
- "Religion and babies – Hans Rosling"
- "The Century of the Self (Full Adam Curtis Documentary)"

I also recommend you study the works of David Ogilvy, Leo Burnett and Hal Riney to see examples of atmosphere ads that set a tone to move the masses without asking people to buy anything. George Orwell once correctly wrote, "the energy that shapes the world springs from emotions" and advertisers recognize that purchasing decisions are usually made by emotions rather than by logic. Advertising is a way to influence the emotions of people to buy products and service *or think a certain way*, which then becomes the field of social engineering. Unbeknownst to people, enlightened beings are influencing people all the time with *nirmanakaya* emanations that give thoughts trying to influence them to virtue, charity and better behavior. I recommend you watch these

Youtube videos to develop a higher-level understanding advertising by paying attention to the methods used to move the masses without overtly asking them to buy anything:

- The Real Mad Men of Chicago – A Chicago Stories Documentary
- A conversation about advertising, with David Ogilvy
- David Ogilvy: Essentials
- Classic Commercial – "The Crocker Bank" 1970
- Hal Riney "You've Only just begun" Commercial for the Crocker Bank
- Hal Riney's "Morning in America" (1984) Ronald Reagan Campaign Ads – Art & Copy Documentary
- Ronald Reagan Train Commercial (1984)
- Unsung Hero (a Thai Life Insurance commercial)
- Tear-Jerker Commercials Create Internet Challenge ("Giving" commercial created for the Thai phone company)

Related books you might profit from:

- *Positioning: The Battle for Your Mind*, by Ries and Trout (and all their marketing books)
- *Ogilvy on Advertising, Confessions of an Advertising Man* (David Ogilvy)
- *Reality in Advertising* (Rosser Reeves)
- *Tested Advertising Methods* (John Caples)
- *My Life in Advertising, Scientific Advertising* (Claude Hopkins)
- *Jump Start Your Brain, Driving Eureka!* (Doug Hall)
- *How to Create a Million Dollar Unique Selling Proposition* (Bill Bodri)
- *Influence: The Psychology of Persuasion* (Robert Cialdini)
- *Quick-Start Copywriting System* (Anthony Flores for Clayton Makepeace)
- *Breakthrough Advertising* (Eugene Schwartz)
- *Thinking, Fast and Slow* (Daniel Kahneman)

The following is related to this field of marketing and advertising as well as the challenge of business survival since most new businesses only last a few years. Doug Hall found that the most predictive measure for the success of a new product or service (innovation) is its meaningfulness (it matters) together with whether it is new and different. As a businessman, if you are offering goods or services in the marketplace you want them to seem "new" and be "meaningfully unique" where they are different from everyone else in a significant, meaningful way so that you do not have to compete with other products on price alone.

The meaningfully unique benefit promise of a product or service is related to its positioning for advertising purposes, and is called its "unique selling proposition" or USP. I wrote *How to Create a Million Dollar Unique Selling Proposition* to help businessmen find this for their products and services so that they can advertise this benefit to increase their sales rather than simply waste their advertising dollars. The book contains ten ways to create a USP, which is the highest number of methods you'll find anywhere in print. It also contains unique marketing tactics along with how to create an elevator speech and personal brand message for yourself! It's packed full of helpful information for businessmen and professionals on their own.

At one time I put this information into a lecture together with the fate of cultures, countries, cities and companies and it became the most popular of all my talks in China. Businessmen and heads of companies would come up to me afterwards and ask me to come to their firms to help with innovation efforts based on what I told them. Because of those requests this information became the initial basis of *Culture, Country, City, Company, Person, Purpose, Passion, World*, which I think people will find highly useful, especially its review of supremacy cycles and what cities, nations and even businesses must do to stay alive and thrive.

This book is probably the most useful for businessmen and layman who are not interested in spiritual cultivation. *Buddha Yoga* would also be highly useful for many individuals even if they are not interested in spiritual cultivation because it teaches you how to find a greater life purpose and how to raise money for charitable causes or invest so that you have ample money to fund churches, temples, monasteries and so on.

Businessmen who are not interested in spirituality must still avoid becoming what Nan Huai-chin called "errant men of business" due to overly materialistic profit-seeking ways, so the very helpful short book *Color Me Confucius* was written to show people how to avoid this fate. We are not here on this planet to make money, which is certainly necessary in life, but to improve our human beinghood.

You should be cultivating elegant, skillful, consummate conduct during your life. You also need to find your North Star - a constancy of life purpose that allows you to enjoy life despite its sufferings, while also engaging in meaningful activities that help others with positive influences that impact their well-being. The reward is not monetary but a happiness, a kind of inner fulfillment. You are always evolving in some direction, and the best course of action is to take an active role in this process to evolve into your highest and best self to become the kind of person you highly approve of and deeply admire in terms of character, thoughts, behavior and activities. You need purpose for fulfillment and to give meaning to your existence.

Daoist philosophy is all fine about going along with the flow but you also need to find a purpose for your existence, an outlet for your activities that brings fulfillment and deep satisfaction. The issue is how to use it. Thus you need to determine a significant purpose for your life to provide it with more meaning and fulfillment rather than just maintain your living protoplasm.

Finding your life purpose is so important that I have emphasized this topic again and again in:

- *Buddha Yoga*, Chapters 3 & 9, "Life Purpose" & "Minimizing Life Regrets"
- *Arhat Yoga*, Chapter 16, "Arhats, Bodhisattvas and Buddhas"
- *Color Me Confucius*, Chapter 10 & 11, "Errant Men of Business" & "Your Life Purpose and Purposes Within Your Life"
- *Correcting Zen*, Chapter 8, "Making Buddha Vows, Cultivating Relevant Skills and Performing Acts of Service for Society"
- *Quick, Fast, Done*, Chapters 5-7, "Yearly Goal Setting" & "The Eight M's" & "Service to Humanity Versus Profits"
- *Culture, County, City, Company, Product, Person, Passion, World*, Chapter 9, "Passion and Purpose"
- *The Art of Political Power*, Chapter 6, "Life Purpose and Political Power"
- *How to Create a Million Dollar Unique Selling Proposition*, "Branding Yourself with a Personal USP and Elevator Speech"

A relevant lesson is the common regret spoken by those dying: "I wish I hadn't worked so hard." People near death often lament that they had shackled themselves to the treadmill of their job and did not have the courage to do more in life outside of their work or career. This has relevancy to marketing and advertising, becoming an "errant man of business," and wasting your life in uselessness.

Many people work so hard all their life that their family and friendships suffer and at the end of life they grieve that they should have worked far less. "What was it all for? What did I ultimately accomplish?" they ask. No one has ever had "He wrote a great business plan" carved on their tombstone. What should matter most in your life are your family, relationships, health, joy (bliss), life purpose, and spiritual cultivation.

Linds Redding, a New Zealand-based art director who had worked at BBDO and Saatchi & Saatchi, both advertising firms, recognized this just before his death when it was too late. He wrote the famous essay, "A Short Lesson in Perspective" after he was diagnosed with lung cancer that eventually killed him. Instructive for its insights on his life as a creative in advertising and on working so hard in general, Redding wrote as follows:

> Perhaps I am not alone in this assessment. Many people have their own idea of a person's life, without knowing what really goes on, on the inside. Some even envy the lives of their friends and colleagues, without realizing, their lives are much better. Now that I am out of that life, I am able to have a different perspective of my old life.
>
> And here's the thing.
>
> It turns out I didn't actually like my old life nearly as much as I thought I did. I know this now because I occasionally catch up with my old colleagues and work-mates. They fall over each other to enthusiastically show me the latest project they're working on. Ask my opinion. Proudly show off their technical prowess (which is not inconsiderable). I find myself glazing over but politely listen as they brag about who's had the least sleep and the most takeaway food. "I haven't seen my wife since January, I can't feel my legs any more and I think I have scurvy but another three weeks and we'll be done. It's got to be done by then. The client's going on holiday. What do I think?"
>
> What do I think?
>
> I think you're all fucking mad. Deranged. So disengaged from reality it's not even funny. It's a fucking TV ad. Nobody gives a shit.
>
> This has come as quite a shock I can tell you. I think, I've come to the conclusion that the whole thing was a bit of a con. A scam. An elaborate hoax. ...
>
> Countless late nights and weekends, holidays, birthdays, school recitals and anniversary dinners were willingly sacrificed at the altar of some intangible but infinitely worthy higher cause. It would all be worth it in the long run ...

This was the con. Convincing myself that there was nowhere I'd rather be was just a coping mechanism. I can see that now. It wasn't really important. Or of any consequence at all really. How could it be. We were just shifting product. Our product, and the clients. Just meeting the quota. Feeding the beast as I called it on my more cynical days.

So was it worth it?

Well of course not. It turns out it was just advertising. There was no higher calling. No ultimate prize. Just a lot of faded, yellowing newsprint, and old video cassettes in an obsolete format I can't even play any more even if I was interested. Oh yes, and a lot of framed certificates and little gold statuettes. A shit-load of empty Prozac boxes, wine bottles, a lot of grey hair and a tumor of indeterminate dimensions.

It sounds like I'm feeling sorry for myself again. I'm not. It was fun for quite a lot of the time. I was pretty good at it. I met a lot of funny, talented and clever people, got to become an overnight expert in everything from shower-heads to sheep-dip, got to scratch my creative itch on a daily basis, and earned enough money to raise the family which I love, and even see them occasionally.

But what I didn't do, with the benefit of perspective, is anything of any lasting importance. … Economically I probably helped shift some merchandise. Enhanced a few companies bottom lines. Helped make one or two wealthy men a bit wealthier than they already were.

As a life, it all seemed like such a good idea at the time. …

Pity.[10]

You need to understand advertising and marketing to understand how others are trying to influence you, and you need to use them to sell your products or services and keep your business alive. They are tools you must master without becoming an errant man of business where you use various methods to cheat people. At the end of your life you are going to look back at everything you did and give yourself a rating whose score you already know as you are performing those activities or projects in real time. Take the high

[10] Linds Redding, "A Short Lesson in Perspective," Accessed July 19, 2018, http://www.lindsredding.com/2012/03/11/a-overdue-lesson-in-perspective/.

road of ethics - don't engage in activities or behavior that are C's, D's and F's.

You must also swallow the "red pill" of realization that reveals how governments (or other big players) try to manipulate you with social engineering messages against your welfare. A Daoist, like a Buddhist, tries to open his own eyes and eliminate personal ignorance about what is really going on in the world. You need to understand how governments use propaganda against you by controlling the press and by constantly pushing messages to promote wars or to convince you of falsities like global warming, safe vaccines, voting integrity, controlled immigration, white supremacy and the like that are all nonsense promoted for some political agenda.

Governments do this because they have ulterior motives to control you in various ways. You need to wake up from ignorance about the fact people are trying to manipulate you constantly, hence you need to study these topics so that *you* are not so easily hoodwinked against your best interests.

Daoist Medicine - Waidan

The Yellow Emperor of China provides one of the main models for Daoist medicine. Daoism had a profound influence on the development of Chinese medicine, and there are countless courses and books available on this subject. For your health I want to recommend the following.

First, *Blood Chemistry and CBC Analysis: Clinical Laboratory Testing from a Functional Perspective* by Dr. Dicken Weatherby and Dr. Scott Ferguson should be in your home so that you are able to discover the real cause of some ailments whose diagnosis physicians might miss. I have sat down with many people who, with their blood work in hand, looked up the optimal ranges for their blood work in this book and found diagnoses and solutions that ended their suffering after tens of thousands of dollars of doctor visits. It is invaluable because the book sometimes offers vitamin-mineral cures as interventions for clinical issues.

Jonathan Wright and Alan Gaby's *Nutritional Therapy in Medical Practice: Protocols and Supporting Information* – and many other sources – can teach you how to intervene naturopathically for various medical issues. In the near future the "Health Ranger" Mike Adams will be releasing a natural medicine AI app which will do this for you and thus enable you to bypass the censorship instituted by Google and other web browsers that prevent you from easily finding naturopathic cures, remedies and approaches for your health issues. I suggest you use it when it is released at www.brighteon.ai.

Second, I also recommend an annual short, self-directed detoxification program for your body, which is why I wrote *Detox Cleanse Your Body Quickly and Completely* to help guide you. Yoga talks about cleansing the body but its approach is insufficient for today's world so I updated the protocols you might use to support your organ systems and detoxify your body in total. You can find remedies for various organs that might "save them from the scalpel" and by visiting naturopathic, Chinese and ayurvedic physicians you might be able to find cures that doctors do not offer.

Third, I've researched specific remedies for cancer, heart diseases and other conditions to cover as many of the top diseases as possible. *Super Cancer Fighters, Prevent and Reverse Atherosclerosis (Reed),* and *Look Younger Live Longer* contain specific protocols as does *Detox Cleanse Your Body Quickly and Completely* since it offers protocols for the kidneys, liver, intestines, heart and lungs that match with blood work findings. No other book does this.

I always recommend that a Daoist interested in medicine should familiarize themselves with the following bodies of health knowledge:

- Diet and Nutrition
- Vitamin-mineral, nutritional and naturopathic supplements
- Herbal medicine (Traditional Chinese herbal medicine, Indian Ayurveda, South American and western herbs) – the key is learning the functions of herbs and how to use them, in particular what herbs to combine in what measure, how to prepare them, and how to adapt a formula over time since no formula maintains top effectiveness for decades
- Detoxification and internal cleansing
- Environmental remedies to create a healthy home such as air filters (ex. Pure Air Doctor equipment), EMF radiation protection, water filters, etc.
- Bodywork modalities such as massage, lymph drainage, strain-counterstrain, chiropractic therapy and other muscle manipulation therapies like Egoscue, cranial sacral work, IMT, Rolfing, AMIT method, etc.
- Homeopathy
- Acupuncture, Acupressure points and Marma Points
- Nutripuncture - a new modality similar to homeopathy that uses microdoses of minerals
- Energy modalities (Reiki)
- Alternative medicine diagnosis methods – Chinese pulse taking, tongue diagnosis, iris diagnosis, VEGA and Asyra electrodermal screening machines, kinesiology muscle testing, reading blood work, etc.

Daoism focuses on your health and longevity because in ancient times medicine was not readily available to the public. Therefore the Daoists developed a philosophy for living in a way that would preserve your health so that medical visits could be avoided since they would not be available. Here is a collection from experts of some helpful approaches (not medical advice) for some specific health problems that is so valuable that I am excerpting it from my upcoming book *Self-Creation*.

I am not a doctor or physician giving you medical advice. Do not take this information as such. I am simply providing information like a medical journalist and am certainly not diagnosing you, dispensing medical advice nor recommending that you use any of these approaches to treat yourself. This is just information. If you have a health condition, please go see a doctor for treatment. These approaches as well as all others mentioned in this book simply tell you where to begin your own research for health conditions. The information might give you some helpful clues for solving various ailments:

- Glucosamine sulfate and collagen peptides (Collagen 2 or Collagen 1&3) can help repair the cartilage in worn knee joints and heal (or prevent) knee problems;
- Stem cell treatments can help repair a torn meniscus and other joint problems (stem cell enhancing and supporting nutrients/foods include colostrum, chlorella, curcumin, marine phytoplankton, aloe vera, coffeeberry fruit extract and moringa;
- Peptides, prolotherapy, cow thymus injections, platelet-rich plasma injections and placenta delivery options mimic the anti-aging effects of stem cells); Tony Robbins' book *Life Force* provides many stem cell treatment therapies that are like miracle cures for different conditions;
- Physical therapies that may help heal or repair your body in general include chiropractic treatments, acupuncture, AMIT, Feldenkreis, Pilates, Rolfing, strain-counterstrain, Graston technique, stem cell therapy, cryotherapy, prolotherapy, vibration therapy (Power Plates), magnets, hyperbaric oxygen, far infrared saunas, deep tissue

massage, Egoscue, EMS electrical muscle stimulation and pulsed electromagnetic field therapy, photobiomodulation, fasting, nutrition and diet and herbs, and proteolytic enzymes (ex. Vitalzym). For more ideas see *Boundless: Upgrade Your Brain, Optimize Your Body & Defy Aging* (Ben Greenfield), *Life Force* (Tony Robbins) and *The 4-Hour Body* (Tim Ferriss);

- HCG (human chorionic gonadotropin) is used to help people lose weight but together with colloidal platinum (Purest Colloids) the two might help regenerate (severed) nerve tissue – more research is warranted;

- Dr. Roy Taylor reports that people who lose 22 pounds and keep it off for 2 years usually escape type-2 diabetes;

- Intermittent fasting together with a low-sugar diet will help you lose weight, but I offer two more powerful weight loss protocols in *Husbands and Wives Were Connected in the Past*;

- The absolute best vitamin E supplementation is A.C. Grace's Ultimate E (you take your complete daily dosage at once); nutritional clinicians and manufacturers themselves have told me that the best CoQ10 brands are Jarrow and Bio-Quinon Pharma Nord CoQ10;

- Gin-soaked raisins can often reduce arthritis nodules in the fingers and associated finger pain;

- An old naturopath told me that the herb quebracho is a very old American remedy for asthma conditions that he used to give his patients while chanca piedra is commonly used to dissolve kidney stones; Mannose and cranberry juice are used for urinary tract infections while black cherry juice is used for gout;

- Nebulized hydrogen peroxide or nebulized Mesosilver (colloidal silver from Purest Colloids) are used by people for respiratory tract infections;

- Vitamin B6 can sometimes alleviate tendonitis and carpal tunnel syndrome;

- The famous homeopathic *Arnica montana* can help speed the healing of bruises while the miracle Chinese formula Tienchi powder can help stop bleeding, reduce swelling and pain, and eliminate blood stasis; Chinese *Ching Wan Hung* is good for burns; plant extracts good for varicose veins and leg circulation include Horse chestnut, Butcher's Broom, gotu kola, hesperidin, diosmin, ginkgo biloba, nattokinase; Edgar Cayce hot castor oil packs can alleviate many internal conditions;

- CoQ10 can be a great help for congestive heart failure (Jarrow QH + PQQ or Bio-Quinon Pharma Nord CoQ10); full spectrum A.C. Grace Unique E and magnesium are also helpful;

- Fenbendazole in combination with Ivermectin (taken with food) and tocotrienols (also with Chaga tea, Essiac Ojibwa tea, Carnovira and C-60) are used in alternative medicine cancer cures, as is laetrile, and GcMAF is a possible cancer cure that has been suppressed; Essiac Ojibwa tea, Carnivora, colloidal platinum and low dose naltrexone are adjunctives; an AMAS or GRAIL blood test can help to spot cancer; BEC5 or Curaderm (composed of solasodine glycosides and the Australian Devil's Apple) has an incredibly high skin cancer cure rate; Low-dose naltrexone can help modulate immune health issues – see my book *Super Cancer Fighters* for many at home adjunctive cancer therapies;

- Florida Urologist Dr. Fernando Bianco has invented the Focalyx intense heat or cold technology for treating enlarged prostates or prostate cancer; phototherapy (pioneered by Nobel Prize winner Dr. Niels Finsen) can help many types of skin condition while far infrared saunas can help with body detoxification;

- Suramin (used for African sleeping sickness and river blindness) is reported to work for autism; it has been reported that 50% of sudden autism cases in children happen within 3 days of some type of vaccination; a former police detective in a major US city who handled over 250 sudden infant death syndrome investigations over 7 years recently reported that 50% of SIDS cases happened within 48 hours after a vaccine and 70% within one week of a vaccination;

- Nattokinase and EDTA chelation therapy or rectal EDTA suppositories (i.e. Detoxamin) together with bromelain can dissolve blood clots and arterial occlusions ... possibly addressing mRNA vaccine blood-clotting issues; ACZ Nano is an excellent zeolite detoxifier for heavy metals;

- Dr. Peter McCullough (*J of the Assoc of Am Physicians & Surgeons Fall 2023 issue*) reports that spike proteins from the COVID vaccination are not broken down by the body or pharmaceuticals but can be dissolved via the following protocol: nattokinase 2000 IU 2X, bromelain 500 mg 1X, curcumin 500 mg 2X; other medical professionals additionally recommend NAC 400 mg 2X (and EDTA) to also help whereas the most common protocol is just bromelain and NAC together;

- Dr. Bryan Ardis has found that nicotine helps neutralize venom and the spike protein in COVID vaccinations since it interacts with nicotinic acetylcholine receptors (nAChRs) – nicotine gum or nicotine patches cut up into six sections are said to help neutralize the toxins while a product called "Foreign Protein Cleanse" contains many ingredients intended to do so;

- Candisol together with Physician's Strength Oregacillin can kill Candida while PC123 is a very effective parasite remedy (as are Methylene Blue drops for some parasitic conditions); Oregano oil can kill skin fungal infections;

- Resveratrol and cinnamon help manage blood sugar levels (bitter melon extract, berberine and apple cider vinegar are also blood sugar stabilizing nutrients) as well as chromium-coffee (and nicotine patches or gum);

- NeuroCranial Restucturing (bilateral nasal therapy), also known as Cranial Facial Release, can open blocked sinus passages and eliminate recurrent migraine headaches;

- To protect against the effects of aging, carnosine eye drops (ex. Can-C) protect your eye lens from cataracts while SkQ1 eye drops (ex. Visomitin) protect your retina. Also, 20% or 40% DMSO eye drops in saline with vitamin C are also used to treat cataracts when taken immediately after application of carnosine drops to help them penetrate to the lens; high dose bromelain is an alternative therapy sometimes used to help eliminate eye floaters;

- According to Edgar Cayce, psoriasis and eczema are usually caused by a thinning of the intestinal walls and can be cured through chiropractic adjustments, a more vegetarian diet, American saffron tea, and slippery elm powder tea (see *Healing Psoriasis* by Dr. John Pagano); colostrum and the liquid supplement RESTORE (with lignite) can help heal leaky gut intestinal permeability; Biogenesis "Intestinal Support Complex" and Pure Encapsulations "Epi-Integrity Powder" are also designed to help heal the intestinal wall;

- Buhler's Advanced Muscle Integration Technique (AMIT) can be used to reactivate muscles that have been "shut off" due to accidental damage and which have therefore shifted some of their weight-bearing functions to adjacent tissues;

- *Nauli Kriya* and plank hold exercises will help to prevent hernias in men; leg splits, yoga exercises and *Mula bandha* will help open the pelvic muscles;

- The *Knees over Toes* Youtube channel of Ben Patrick will help you eliminate knee pain or repair damaged knees with simple exercises such as a tibialis raise and backwards walking (retro walking) or "sled on turf walking backwards" that safely, in a pain-free manner, cause blood flows to reach the knee to help regenerate cartilage; his book *Knee Ability Zero* also contains the exercises that will help you heal bad knees;

- "Powerbatics" and similar natural bodyweight training exercise modalities (capoeira, animal forms, primal flow, GMB Elements, yoga, Pilates, Ginastica Natural, *Yijin Jing*, Z-health etc.) will help you train your body for greater flexibility, strength and mobility; you want to cultivate a lean and muscular body with balanced and symmetrical proportions;

- An Elgin Archxerciser will create flexibility for the bottom of the foot as will Z-Health foot exercises that

press on vital spots in the foot that stretch and
strengthen the foot muscles and tendons;

- An Ultraflexx foot rocker (or cheap equivalent) can be
used to stretch your Achilles tendons, and Buhler's
Advanced Muscle Integration Technique (AMIT) can
reset inhibited Quadriceps, glutes and lower back
muscles to help fix sprained or torn Achilles tendons
damage *permanently* because if Quadriceps muscles are
not reset the tears will usually reoccur;

- The Medlight 630-PRO healing device emits near-
infrared light to penetrate tissues to help heal injuries;
Wein Products produces some of the best ion generators
while the Aranizer is one of the best ozone generators;
Weston Scientific has devices that produce clustered ions
to kill germs in your environment as can UV light;

- Acupuncture and deep tissue massage can help restore
the functionality of damaged muscles but first you want
to adjust your bone alignment to optimality and restore
full muscle functionality such as with deep tissue
massage and Buhler's AMIT therapy;

- Terry Laughlin's Total Immersion method of swimming
instruction can teach you to move through water more
efficiently ... these are some of the physical techniques
you might use. Countless others are available.

You want your sense organs to work as accurately as possible and
want to interpret their input as accurately as possible too. You want
to continue refining them during life but must always remember
that your sensory perceptions can never capture all the dimensions
of the environment nor are they ultimately accurate without
distortions. There are several commonly known helpful remedies
for improving the functioning of your sense organs:

- Zinc supplements usually help restore the sense of taste
and smell that weaken as you age;

- Lion's Mane mushroom or Bacopa extracts *(bacopa
monnieri)* can sometimes help restore hearing

deterioration. Lion's Mane mushroom can help improve memory too (as can phosphatidyl serine or PS);

- Lutein, zeaxanthin, vitamin A, beta carotene, nattokinase and the Bates method, Z-Health Vision Gym (or eyeglasses) can help restore declining eyesight; Can-C carnosine eyedrops and SkQ1 eyedrops (ex. Visomitin) may help with specific eye issues;

- DHA, good oils and non-oxidized micronized lecithin (derived from organic micro-milled non-GMO soybeans) can supply the purest nutrients to help build a great brain since it is mostly composed of fat.

Daoist Cultivation Practice (*Neidan* or *Neijia*)

I have written many non-denominational books on spiritual cultivation demonstrating the unity of religions and explaining how their paths help you cultivate to attain the higher spiritual bodies. Within them I lean towards using Buddhist, Daoist and Hindu explanations since they have the best vocabulary and huge repertoire of related teachings. The books that can best help guide you through these matters include:

- *Hidden Teachings in Hinduism* to see similar but more advanced information like this book but for Hinduism
- *Arhat Yoga, Buddha Yoga* and *Correcting Zen* for cultivation theory
- *Neijia Yoga* and *Nyasa Yoga* for techniques (instructions)
- *Correcting Zen* for practical cultivation methods and personal practice schedules
- *Meditation Case Studies* and *The Little Book of Hercules* for explaining spiritual phenomena and measuring progress
- *Color Me Confucius, Self-Creation* and *Quick, Fast, Done* for cultivating elegant consummate conduct and goals
- *The Little Book of Meditation, Easy Meditation Lessons* and *Correcting Zen* for learning how to meditate

- For Daoism: *The Secret Inner Teachings of Daoism, Neijia Yoga, The I Ching Revealed, The Art of Political Power*
- For Buddhism: *Buddha Yoga, Arhat Yoga, Correcting Zen*
- For Hinduism: *Hidden Teachings in Hinduism, Nyasa Yoga, Neijia Yoga, Correcting Zen*
- For the physical body: *Detox Cleanse Your Body Quickly and Completely, Look Younger Live Longer*

These few books will replace decades of Buddhist, Daoist, Vajrayana, Yoga and Hindu study that you would be forced to undergo in a Buddhist monastery, Daoist monastery or Hindu matha. They teach you the common basis of Daoist *nei-gong,* inner alchemy, kundalini yoga, *kriya* yoga, *nyasa* yoga, *boran kammatthana, anapana* practice and more.

The most effective forms of *nei-gong* involve moving the Qi of your body in various ways via your will (thoughts), or breathing pressure or sounds (mantrayana) or visualization concentration through other methods so that you can continually wash your tissues with Qi and thereby eventually prepare to attain the immortal body of the Earth Immortal. Once you reach that stage of attainment then you can begin the road of true cultivation practice to attain yet higher spiritual bodies.

Liu Huayang (d. 1799) wrote the *Scripture on Wisdom and Life Destiny (Huiming Jing)* that broke the alchemical process of purifying your body's Qi into eight stages. Different schools partition the sequences of the path differently but his is a recognized Daoist approach. The main initial focus in Daoism is usually about connecting your body's governing and conception channels which you can do by spinning, revolving or circulating your Qi (however you wish to word it) up the back of your body and down the front (or middle) of your body in a circular-like orbit that passes *through* the brain (not across the top of the head) so that the body's main upper energy circuit becomes more connected. This is activating the waterwheel or microcosmic orbit of Daoism but just a very minor, initial stage of transformation.

Obviously many other inner energy practices should be practiced besides this basic exercise that most every Daoist learns. There are, for instance, other exercises that focus on "coalescing the embryo of the Tao," which means washing the Qi of your entire body with similar techniques so that its entire matrix, which is the actual "holy embryo" rather than some small type of fetus within you, can emerge as a radiant spiritual being – the Earth Immortal.

This whole process of internal washing or purification is called "cultivating the purity of your subtle body" (rather than an actual spiritual embryo inside your abdomen) until you eventually attain its release from your human shell. At that point you have "manifested the transformation body," which is the independent subtle body attainment that makes you an Earth Immortal or lowest level Arhat.

Your physical body also becomes purified during this process, which is why many saints exhibit incorruptible bodies or *sariras* after their death. Many incorruptible Christian saints, including several Catholic popes, demonstrated incorruptible bodies because they achieved enlightenment at a young age, continued allowing their bodies to be used for teaching devas, and during those times their physical nature was continually being purified yet further (past the necessary twelve years) by other enlightened masters working on those devas by giving them all inner alchemy kundalini rotations through *nirmanakaya* emanations. Countless spiritual traditions provide tantric pictures of deities within human bodies in order to prepare you for this truth as to what is necessary for spiritual ascension. Because of so many years of continuous inner *nei-gong* work rolling through their tissues their bodies achieved incorruptibility, which commonly happens to Tibetan masters and many enlightened Buddhists because as we know they too frequently exhibit incorrupt bodies after death.

People never check if Daoists attain this but they achieve this too because it indicates that you activated the inner Qi circulations that kept revolving to transform your Qi, thus purifying your physical body so that its corpse does not easily disintegrate. From the Earth Immortal achievement onwards you are cultivating to attain the stage of the Spirit Immortal (Causal body), next the Celestial Immortal stage (Supra-Causal body of the full Arhat), and then the Immanence body which is typically not discussed in Daoism even though everyone who gets this far works usually attains it.

As stated, Appendix 1 shows you how to partition your body into different sections for *neijia* (*nei-gong*) inner energy cultivation. Daoism focuses on the upper, middle and lower *dantian* partitioning scheme of three sections but knowledge of the other schemes, and methods used by other spiritual traditions to purify the Qi within them, will help your Daoist practice immensely. The principle is to *use what works!*

It takes many years for a tradition to adopt the cultivation practices from other schools and make them their own, but once done everyone uses them. Skip the delay and just use whatever works regardless where it comes from. Electric lighting, antibiotics, mathematics, science … you shouldn't care where these things originated but just use them. The same goes for effective cultivation exercises from other religions that purify your Qi. Shugendo has them and Shintoism has them and both traditions are similar to Daoism. Buddhism, Yoga, Hinduism, Jainism, Sufism, Catholicism and Orthodox Christianity have them too. Countless schools have very effective Qi purification exercises and it is just that few people bother to search them out and use them.

APPENDIX 1:
WHAT ARE CHAKRAS REALLY?

This is an excerpt taken from my book *Correcting Zen* that has been appended with additional examples. Similar information can be found in *Neijia Yoga*:

Most chakra visualization techniques use a seven-part scheme to segment the body into seven segments for energy work, yet since people don't know the real meaning of the chakras they don't know what these segments are. Hence, here is the lost information that can be used for the purpose of cultivation practice.

The four-petalled *Muladhara* root chakra, often symbolized by a four-sided square, four-legged elephant or four-armed deity, represents the bottommost section of our torso containing the perineum. This is supposedly where the power in our body torso comes from. When visualizing this chakra you are actually supposed to be focusing on the flesh, bones and energy within the pelvis in order to wash these tissues. The reason that an *elephant* is sometimes used to symbolize this chakra is because male genitalia are similar in appearance to the head of an elephant.

Power is symbolized by an elephant, and hence we have another reason for the symbol of an elephant since this region of the body is said to be where our torso's power originates. The reason that this chakra is also often represented as a *square* is because a square represents the foundation of a building and the major muscles around the perineum form a square of four sides. In mandalas, a foundational four-sided square with doors represents this chakra and its four muscles. Seen from below there are two ischiocavernosus muscles that form a corner of a square, the diagonal is the superficial transverse perineal muscle, and the ileococcygeous muscle forms the rest of the square. On the internet you can find pictures to confirm this and see the square.

This chakra simply represents the lowest section of our torso, and our energy is supposed to originate from this area although it doesn't produce any special energy generation. The idea is just an analogy although in the martial arts the power of our legs below has to pass through this region to get to the upper body. Buddhist mandalas have four sides to represent the energy within this part of our torso, and Buddhist deities commonly have four arms to represent the power of this region as well with the insinuation that the energy is used for virtuous celestial purposes.

The *Svadhisthhana* six-petalled sacral chakra corresponds to the sacrum. This chakra is often represented by a crocodile because rough crocodile scales remind people of the bony protrusions of the sacrum, and its six petals refer to the six nerves protruding from each side of vertebrae S1, S2, S3, S4, S5, and C0 within the sacrum. If you look at a picture of the sacrum from the internet and find these nerves you'll quickly see why it is said to be composed of six petals.

In Indian culture the goddess of the Ganges River, Ganga, is represented as having four arms (representing the four-petalled root chakra) and riding a crocodile-like creature called the makara (the six-petalled sacral chakra) on the river. The overall symbol represents the Qi/Prana running from the pelvis (containing the two chakras) and traveling up the spine.

In the *Surangama Sutra* Samantabhadra Bodhisattva stated, "World Honored One, I always use my mind to listen in order to distinguish the variety of views held by living beings. If in a place, separated from here by a number of worlds as countless as the sands in the Ganges, a living being practices Samantabhadra deeds, I mount at once a six-tusked elephant and reproduce myself in a hundred and a thousand apparitions to come to his aid. Even if he is unable to see me because of his great karmic obstruction, I secretly lay my hand on his head to protect and comfort him so that he can succeed."

This is actually referring to *nirmanakaya* emanations where Samantabhadra's "six-tusked elephant" represents his pelvis (waist), thus meaning his entire person, because the six tusks represent the sacral chakra and the elephant's head represents the root chakra and both are in his pelvis. When he says he rides an elephant *it just means he is standing there resting on his pelvis*. Buddhism has encoded the chakra lessons into this one image but this information has become lost over the ages.

The ten-petalled *Manipura* navel (solar plexus) chakra corresponds to the section of the body served by the left and right nerves protruding from the L1, L2, ... L5 lumbar spinal vertebrae, and represents the lower *dantian* belly of the body. It is basically our body's abdomen within which are the intestines used to draw energy from food and excrete wastes. The twelve-petalled *Anahata* heart chakra corresponds to the regions of the body controlled by (the body section in front of) the T1 through T12 thoracic vertebrae nerves, which includes the heart and lungs in the chest region. The sixteen-petalled *Vishuddha* throat chakra is the set of C1, C2, ... C8 cervical vertebrae and their surrounding tissues of the neck, face and upper chest ruled by the nerves extending out of those vertebrae.

The two-part "third eye" *Ajna* chakra represents our brain stem and the two halves of the brain that have left and right, Yin and Yang sections, and thus in Hinduism this synthesis of masculine and feminine energies is represented by *Ardhanarishvara* (a form of Shiva conjoined with his consort Parvati). The male-female deities of Harihara, Jumadi and Vaikuntha Kamalaja also represent the two-part brain stem that we say is partitioned into a

Yin and Yang side. It is ashamed that no one knows this. Even the Shiva linga represents the brain stem, which gives us consciousness, and that is why it is worshipped. It is the wish-fulfilling jewel of the human body.

The famous Indian legend of Garuda the magical bird being ridden by Vishnu also symbolizes the brain stem controlling the two wings or halves of the brain. Incidentally, garudas are said to "eat dragons" because your Qi rises up the spine into your brain stem (garuda) and this Qi is a snake or dragon. In Hinduism, the deity Skandha is known as "the rider on the peacock" to symbolize the brain stem surrounded by the web of neurons in the brain that are symbolized by peacock feathers.

The top chakra is the thousand-petalled *Sahasrara* crown chakra that symbolizes our brain with all its neurons and nerves, which are also often represented as colorful peacock feathers or the hairs of Yang-type animals. The *Sahasrara* crown chakra is not located above our head but instead represents *the brain and all its neurons* inside the skull! Its nerves can be seen in modern DTI diffusion tensor images that you can and should use to guide internal Qi rotation patterns that you perform to "wash your brain" to help open up its Qi channels.

What most people don't know is that our brain also represents Kamadhenu, the wish-fulfilling cow of Buddhism. As can be seen from pictures of Kamadhenu, she becomes the Sphinx of Egyptian mythology and the Chimera of Greek mythology (where the tail is the spine with its triangular sacrum and its fiery breath is the kundalini hot Qi necessary for some of the purification processes involved in the processes of spiritual transformation). The Tibetan Wind horse (Lung-Ta) that carries the wish-fulfilling jewel of enlightenment, which is the brain stem, is also a symbol of Kamadhenu and the brain as well. In the Hindu epic *Mahabharata* the warrior Arjuna meets the mythical creature Navagunjara (a manifestation of Vishnu) who also represents the human brain and spinal cord.

This information should cause you to have greater faith in your cultivation practice that absolutely should include inner energy techniques such as the white skeleton visualization sadhana, or even Qi rotational schemes using chakras and appendages as body sections. It is no crime to use tantric yoga or Vajrayana methods as well since the goal is enlightenment and such methods are virtuous and clean. This is why many people use the Indian partitioning scheme of seven chakras based on spinal vertebra, and in *Neijia Yoga* you will find an eight-part sectioning scheme based on fascial planes within the body that is even better since it is more relevant to Qi flow inside us.

This is an excerpt from Chapter 7 of *Neijia Yoga* ("Cultivating the Body's Qi in Sections") and teaches you how to cultivate your body in sections:

Fixing your Qi for a long time at various points within your body, and holding visualizations at those points or simply washing them with Qi, is one way to cultivate the Qi of your entire body in sequence.

If you partition your body into logically defined sections such as torso segments, body cavities, limbs, muscles, glands, internal organs, bones, etcetera then you can subsequently work at cultivating your entire body by using your mind-guided Qi to wash all such areas one by one. Eventually you can link the purified Qi of all those body segments into one undivided whole and thereby create permanent power. Power becomes permanent after sufficient internal Qi cultivation work to cleanse and unite your internal energy, whereas force (the usage of power) is temporary.

There are several ways to work on purifying and transforming the Qi of body sections. Using your mind you can try to feel the Qi of an entire region by concentrating on internal sensations within it, and simply hold onto the feeling of the "energy" or "substance" of that section. You might also mentally wash it with a visualization of bright sunlight or moonlight while pushing your Qi around within that area.

You can use your mind to push your Qi energy throughout all your various body parts and sections. You can ultimately guide it in this way to wash all the sections of your body and their interior components. However, it takes time to learn how to perfect mind-guided movements of your Qi. Bodhidharma's "marrow cleansing" technique within the *Xi Sui Jing* follows this principle as applied to bones. Daoism has various systems of inner washing as well and Hinduism has the method of Nyasa Yoga to wash body parts step by step.

You can also recite mantras or *bija* sounds on body sections, or as if from within body sections to stimulate/activate their Qi and thereby wash them through excitation. Furthermore, you can recite *bija* sounds on top of strategic *bindus* (points) such as acupuncture points, pressure points, *Dim mak* points, or marma points because by emphasizing those points you will affect the Qi connected to its network of associations. Reciting a sound as if at a point or upon a point will stimulate all the Qi around it, thus serving as a force for Qi activation and frictional purification.

While performing such practices you can try to arouse positive (Yang) or negative (Yin) emotions within yourself in order to stimulate the Yin Qi or Yang Qi of your body, and in particular you must then try to feel the Qi in this way within that section. Emotions can used to stimulate, arouse, excite, energize, invigorate, and transform the Qi within your body as they change its quality or tonality and all the possible tonalities of your Qi must be washed in this way. Martial artists and yogis tend to think that you should only cultivate your Yang Qi but your Yin Qi must be cultivated and purified as well.

Here are some classical ways to partition the body into various sections so that you can work on transforming the Qi within each segment.

TWO SECTIONS:

Left side, right side; Top and bottom; Front and back; Up the spine and down the front of the body through the *du mai* and *ren mai*; Up the spine and down the Alimentary canal (the tube from mouth to anus) and everything surrounding it ... these are some ways of partitioning the body into two parts.

The Buddhist and Hindu sutras recommend that you use the sounds of Om, Ah or Ram, or recite the Rah-Vah (also Ram-Vam) mantra, within the different body sections in order to transform the Qi of your underlying energetic nature. This work will help to improve Qi flow throughout your body, which is essential for the highest level of martial arts proficiency.

Leading your Qi upwards or downwards in your body, or to the left or right, or in a clockwise or counterclockwise direction, or in spirals or in caressing bones or limbs or organs, etcetera are all ways of moving your Qi internally to wash your tissues.

Traditionally the right side of your body is considered Yang and the left side is considered Yin. The traditional cultivation method of Buddhist Arhats is to concentrate on feeling heat and fire on one side of the body (that is envisioned with the color red), and feeling cooling water on the other side (which is envisioned with the color blue or white). After sufficient practice, the hotness and coolness (Yang Qi and Yin Qi) are switched to the other side of the body. This is practiced within the top and the bottom sections of the body, and for the left and right sides of the body.

This is essentially the Daoist practice of *Li* and *Kan*, which is working to purify the Yin Qi and Yang Qi of your body. Yogis and the supreme martial artists use a variety of methods to cultivate the Yin and Yang energies of their bodies. Rather than using the visualization spur of fire and water to change the texture or quality feel of your Qi, you can practice feeling the energy of the sun on one side of the body and the energy of the moon on the other, and then switch them.

Another martial arts practice is to feel that one half of the body is empty while the other is heavy, and then to switch sides again with those feelings. Or, you might try feeling that one side of your body is light while another side is darkness, and so on.

This sort of technique is like practicing under a cold rushing waterfall and then in a hot spring or dry sauna.

THREE SECTIONS:

Head with neck and arms, chest and middle torso, thighs and legs to feet; Head and neck, arms and chest and trunk to pelvic waist, legs and feet; Head, chest and arms to waist, thighs and legs to feet; Backside of the body running upwards, front side of the body running downwards, inner core of digestive organs and alimentary canal ... these are some of the ways to partition the body into three sections that you tackle one-by-one through inner Qi washing exercises. The most famous three-part sectioning scheme is the three *dantian* of Daoism.

Om-Ah-Hung, Om-Ah-Hum, Om-So-Hum, Om-Aum-Hum and Hreem-Shreem-Kleem are some of the three-syllable mantras used to stimulate and purify the Qi in each of the three body sectional schemes. Each syllable of these mantras is to be recited within a different segment of the body so as to vibrate the Qi within it.

For instance, Samantabhadra's mantra of "Om-Ah-Hung" is used extensively in the Esoteric school of Buddhism. To use this mantra to transform your body's Qi quickly you would recite "Ah" while trying the feel the Qi of your head, neck and arms. This is the upper part of your body according to one partitioning scheme. You would then recite "Ah" while trying to feel the Qi within your arms and torso. This is the middle section of your body. You would then recite "Hung" or "Hum" while trying to feel the energy in the lower section of your body from your waist down to your feet.

Other three-syllable mantras are available to be used in a

similar manner.

Daoists concentrate on feeling their internal energy within the three *dantian*, but few realize that one reason to favor this tripartite scheme is because each section contains organs with the most nerves, and nerves are responsible for consciousness.

The upper *dantian* contains the brain, which is the major organ of consciousness. The middle *dantian* contains the heart, which has lots of nerves and neurons that can also store memories, which is why heart transplant recipients often start exhibiting the likes and dislikes of their heart donor that were impressed within the heart tissues as memories. DTI (diffusion tensor) images of the heart easily show these nerves. The lower *dantian* contains the intestines (alimentary canal), gut or "second brain" that can also store memories although to a lesser degree. Through these and other mechanisms people often carry over their own personality tendencies and even fears from a past life.

If you arouse attitudes or emotions within these sections then those neural tissues will become imprinted by them and they can be more easily carried forward to subsequent lives. Hence you can use "dominant attitude" meditation to not just transform the Qi of this body but help design the personality of your next incarnation. Even now, you can alter this life by altering your attitudes of mind.

FOUR SECTIONS:

Head, neck and arms, arms and chest (middle torso), lower abdomen and pelvis, legs and feet; Upper left quadrant of the body, upper right quadrant of the body, lower left quadrant of the body, lower right quadrant of the body … these are just some of the ways to partition the body into fours.

Om-Ah-Vah-Lah, Om-Hreem-Shreem-Kleem, and Sah-Rah-Vah-Nah are some four-part mantras that apply for the head, chest, abdomen, and waist to legs. One can also use the five-syllable mantra Ah-Vi-Ra-Hum-Kham where the first four syllables are apportioned to four sections of the body while the final "Kham" should shake the Qi of the entire body in total, or just be used on the spine.

FIVE SECTIONS:

While the body can easily be partitioned into five sections, your Qi can be partitioned into five different qualities or categories as well.

According to the five Vayus (winds or Qi-types) principles of Hinduism our head and arms correspond to the ascending Qi called *Udana*; the region of the chest with lungs and heart corresponds to *Prana*; the mid-trunk of body containing digestive organs corresponds to *Samana* Qi; the lower abdomen and pelvis corresponds to the Qi called *Apana;* the entire body is pervaded by *Vyana* that is especially located in the legs to the feet. Some yoga schools differ on this attribution scheme, so this is just one of the many ways to partition the body into five parts.

Om-Ah-Vah-Lah-Hum is one of the many five-syllable mantras you can use to cultivate your Qi in these five body sections. Another is Om-Ah-Vah-Rah-Hum.

Besides the five Prana, martial artists are often taught to evoke different internal feelings in their training that correspond to different flavors of Qi. They must not only learn how to make their Qi surge, ebb, be stored and be guided to wherever their mind directs, but must be able to change the quality of that Qi. The quality, flavor, feeling or nature of your Qi is often represented by the characteristic temperament of an animal such as a snake, monkey, tiger, dragon, crane and so forth. Thus, students are sometimes taught to practice the spirit and movement of a Yin or Yang animal in order to master particular movements as well as temporarily transform the quality of their Qi.

Similarly, you can also recognize for each of the five elements – earth, water, fire, wind and space – a different type of Qi energy within your body. Each type of element Qi can be purified through a different type of Qi training. In fact, you can practice Qi purification exercises for your Yin and Yang Qi, a different Qi feeling for each of the five elements of your body, a different Qi feeling for the planets of our solar system since they affect us, a different Qi feeling for each season or for the 28 lunar mansions, and other partitioning schemes that segment Qi into different types. To do this, you must focus on feeling that type of energy within your entire body, perhaps by first stimulating it, and hold onto that Qi sensation so that it suffuses the segment with some type of mild or overt excitation.

Earth represents the solidity of your body, is especially felt within your flesh and bones, and is usually cultivated by imagining that your body becomes solid, heavy, yellow earth. Often masters teach students to merge with a boulder, mountain or wall that they train next to (or feel its energy) in order to help them cultivate their earth element Qi.

Water represents fluidity and the Yin Qi of the body, which is 70% water, and is cultivated by imagining that your body's entirety becomes cool blue water, or simply white in color. Often Daoist and Buddhist masters teach students to train next to a lake whose energy they might feel or try to merge with in order that they cultivate their water element Qi or Yin Qi.

Fire represents the heat and Yang Qi of your body, and is cultivated by imagining that your body becomes a raging fire.

Wind represents just the Qi or vital energy of your body, which is often referred to as the wind element, and is cultivated by imagining that your body loses its structure and is just a matrix of coursing energy everywhere.

Space represents the ultimate nature of your body that is empty like space, and is cultivated by imagining (and feeling) that your body becomes like an empty sack, or is abandoned entirely and becomes universal empty space.

A practitioner should progress through these contemplations

one-by-one to purify the Qi of their body and end them by abandoning all notions to rest their mind in emptiness by imagining that they become empty space.

The *Visuddhimagga*, or great treatise of Theravada Buddhist cultivation written by Buddhaghosa, has teachings on cultivating the five elements within the body through concentrations, called *kasina* meditations, but these lessons are incomprehensible without this information. You should not just concentrate on merging with a certain type of element but on feeling the energy or Qi of that element within you. This is how you wash the Qi of your body with different flavors or textures.

In the martial arts, special attention must be paid to each of the elements within five elements cultivation. For instance, the earth element represents an integral combination of all the elements together (they all exist within the earth element). It is the embodiment of both Yin and Yang essences combined together.

For martial arts it is important to practice the earth element cultivation method of feeling rooted in your feet so that you develop firmness in your stepping. You practice feeling the earth element below your feet united with the Yin Qi in your foot. Or, you can practice sinking your Qi into your legs and feet as if the entire Earth empties its weight into your shape, and then mix this feeling in your feet with the Qi of the Earth. When martial artists practice heaviness in the legs or feet in order to develop this firmness, they must make sure that the feeling doesn't transform into sluggishness. Nevertheless it is common and proper to imagine that your foot becomes very cold, like Yin Qi, and to spin that cold Qi within it to wash its tissues. This is superior martial arts as well as superior Buddhist and Daoist cultivation.

SIX SECTIONS:

Heart, lungs, stomach, liver, kidneys, and triple warmer ... this is one of the ways to partition the body into six internal organs.

The organs correspond to the Daoist six healing sounds Haa (heart), Szz (lungs), Hoo (stomach), Shoo (liver), Foo (kidneys), and Shee (the three sections of the upper, middle and lower warmer). Different traditions will use different sounds for the organs, and the proper sounds are the ones that help you feel or move the Qi of the organs. While practicing, you can try to feel the positive or negative emotions associated with each organ.

SEVEN SECTIONS:

The body can be partitioned into seven sections using a symbolism of "seven chakras," which corresponds to body sections delineated by spinal vertebrae and their nerves. The top chakra is the thousand-petalled *Sahasrara* crown chakra that represents our brain with all its neurons and nerves. Its nerves can be seen in DTI diffusion tensor images, and those pictures should be used to guide any internal Qi rotation practices that you perform to "wash your brain" and help open up its Qi channels. This will result in higher mental quietness, clarity, and speedier reflex responses over time.

Incidentally, the brain is Kamadhenu, the wish-fulfilling cow of Hinduism and Buddhism (that becomes the Sphinx of Egyptian mythology and Chimera of Greek mythology)[11], and the Qi channels within it must be opened through countless Qi washings. The Tibetan Windhorse (Lung-Ta) that carries the wish-fulfilling jewel of enlightenment, which is the brain stem, is also a symbol of Kamadhenu and the brain as well.

As stated, Kamadhenu has its equivalent in the Sphinx of ancient Egypt who could ask questions of humans since the Sphinx symbolizes the brain. The hairs of the Sphinx represent the nerves or Qi channels in the brain, its wings represent the two brain lobes, the four paws represent its four sections and the tail of the Sphinx represents our spinal cord.

The Lamassu or Sadu of Mesopotamia (Sumerian and

---

[11] See *Nyasa Yoga* and *Buddha Yoga* for details.

Akkadian mythology), which looks like the Sphinx (and Kamadhenu), also represents our brain. Furthermore, the strange creature Navagunjara that the warrior Arjuna meets in the Hindu epic *Mahabharata* represents our brain as well, which is a fact unknown to scholars.

The Greek Chimera also represents the brain through its many lion hairs that are the brain nerves, its two wings that are the two brain lobes with neurons (feathers), the two goat horns that are the two protruding nerve bundles that ascend upwards from the spinal cord, the snake tail that represents the spine and cobra head-shaped coccyx, and its fire represents the *kundalini* energy necessary to transform it.

The two-part "third eye" *Ajna* chakra symbolizes our brain stem that has conjoined left and right, Yin and Yang sections like the Shiva-Parvati *Ardhanarishvara*. This is the "muddy pellet" of Daoism, and the hump on the back of Kamadhenu the wish-fulfilling cow. Its two horns represent two ascending spinal nerve bundles that reach from the spine to the top of the head. The great sage yogi Gorasknath named Kamadhenu's four teats Ambika (mother), Lambika (eyes at the summit), Ghantika (sound) and Talika (clapping) in order to represent the two nodes of the superior colliculus and two nodes of the inferior colliculus in the brainstem that process visual and auditory information.

The sixteen-petalled *Vishuddha* throat chakra is the set of C1, C2, ... C8 cervical vertebrae and their surrounding tissues of the neck, face and upper chest ruled by the nerves extending out of those vertebrae.

The twelve-petalled *Anahata* heart chakra corresponds to the regions of the body controlled by the T1 through T12 thoracic vertebrae nerves.

The ten-petalled *Manipura* navel (solar plexus) chakra corresponds to the section of the body served by the left and right nerves protruding from the L1, L2, ... L5 lumbar spinal vertebrae, and represents the "*hara*" of Japanese martial arts or lower *dantian* of Chinese medicine.

The *Svadhisththana* sacral chakra corresponds to the sacrum. This chakra is often represented by a crocodile because rough crocodile scales remind people of the bony protrusions of the sacrum, and its six petals refer to the six nerves protruding from each side of vertebrae S1, S2, S3, S4, S5, and C0.

The four-petalled *Muladhara* root chakra, often symbolized by a four-sided square, a four-legged elephant or a four-armed deity, symbolizes your pelvic girdle muscles along with your asshole, perineum and genitals (male genitalia are symbolized by the head of an elephant).

The major muscles around the perineum form a square of four sides because seen from below two ischiocavernosus muscles form a corner of the square, the diagonal is the superficial transverse perineal muscle, and the ileococcygeous muscle forms the rest of the square. Hence, mandalas have four sides to represent this area of our torso, and Hindu deities commonly have four arms to represent the power of this region as well. In other words, the four-petalled chakra just represents the bottommost section of our torso.

Power-possessing Hindu deities are shown with four arms to represent the muscles of this square that is the primal source or foundational basis of power for all the muscles above. The center of the square contains the perineum or *huiyin* DU-1 acupuncture point, which is the *haidi* or "bottom of the ocean" from which Sun Wukong retrieved his staff. Thus the pelvic region in general is usually symbolized by the root chakra together with the sacral chakra, which are sometimes together represented by an elephant (who symbolizes great power). The Goddess Ganga, who is symbolized as having four arms and riding a crocodile in the Ganges River, also symbolizes the pelvis, sacrum and spine together. The Ganges River she rides upon represents Qi ascending through the *du mai* into the brain.

All of these sections can be washed with Qi that can be

vibrated by traditional *bija* sounds recited within them. You have to vocalize various sounds to see if better ones than those used in your own tradition can be found to vibrate/affect the Qi in various body sections.

The *Mahavairocana Sutra* of Buddhism and *Yoga Yajnavalkya* recommend the same set of sounds to help wash each body part with Qi, which is called the "disposition of letters" or "disposition of syllables." However, these are not to be taken as definitive. The best mantra sounds to use are those that vibrate the Qi within the section being concentrated on, and sometimes you can find sounds to do this that have not been recorded in ancient scriptures. If a tone vibrates the Qi channels within certain sections of the body, it is considered a *bija* or root sound for that body part and you can use it.

Daoism needs to do some research work on this to find the best sounds for vibrating the Qi within each section of your body. After those sounds are discovered, they can be turned into mantras that you recite to vibrate/wash the Qi of specific body parts in sequence. This type of mantra recitation will help you make progress in purifying your Qi even if an enlightened spiritual being is not there to help you was your Qi at the same time through one of his *nirmanakaya* projections. Whenever you recite a sound you would focus on feeling the Qi of the body part with which it has a vibrational association, *and possibly add a strong emotion to each sound as well*, to wash the Qi of that section as you proceed from one region of your body to the next.

Each spiritual cultivation school in the world recommends different *bija* sounds to help resonate the Qi within separate body parts, and that information is usually incorporated into mantras or prayers. Sometimes a mantra is designed to vibrate the Qi of your body, and sometimes it is designed to call for the assistance of a Buddha, deity or Immortal to use their own Qi to work on purifying the Qi of your body segments and cleanse the underlying subtle body within them. You might inquire of a master as to which mantra may work best for you.

EIGHT SECTIONS:

Another torso partitioning scheme[12] of eight sections can be made using seven fascial meridians or meridians of latitude called "bands" that segment the body into eight parts. While the seven sectional scheme based on chakras is delineated based on nerves and spinal vertebrae, this sectioning scheme is based on fascial planes within the body, and hence is more relevant to the Qi flow inside us.

The first meridian is the eye band that is a horizontal plane starting from the bridge of the nose and running to the back of the skull. The section of the body delineated by going upwards thus contains the eyes and the brain.

The chin band is the angular line formed by the bottom of the chin slicing upwards to back of the skull. This band to the eye band contains the bottom region of the head including the nasal cavity, teeth, tongue, palate and cerebellum. As with all other body structures, these parts must all be washed over and over again by revolving your Qi inside them in many diverse ways.

The collar band is a strap running around the bottom of the neck centered on the clavicle (collar bone) and continuing towards the back on the upper border of the shoulder blade (scapula) ending at the junction of the cervical and thoracic vertebrae. The body region delineated contains the neck with thyroid gland.

The chest band is the area just below the nipples running horizontally as a band around the body. This band running upwards to the collar meridian contains the heart, lungs, thymus gland, shoulders and arms.

The abdomen (belly or umbilical) band starts at the belly

---

[12] Dr. Louis Schultz and Dr. Rosemary Feitis discovered these horizontal bands within the body's myofascia, which are thickening in the deep layers of fascia and connective tissue. See *Anatomy Trains* by Thomas Myers for illustrations.

button and then wraps horizontally around the body. This band upwards to the chest band contains the internal organs of stomach, pancreas, spleen, liver, gall bladder and kidneys.

The inguinal band runs across the lower abdomen starting at the back of the buttocks and running atop the pelvic bones until falling at their front, slightly dipping downwards, thus taking the shape of an inverted arch. From the inguinal band to the umbilical meridian are the bulk of the intestines.

The pubic band extends from the pubic bone (pubic symphysis) in the front of the body across the groin to the bottom of the buttocks in the back. From the pubic band to the inguinal band above it is the region containing the sacrum and coccyx as well as the genitals.

The lowest section of the body below the pubic band contains the legs and feet. This section starts from the public band that stretches like a gentle arch from the pelvic bone to the bottom of the buttocks, thus defining the beginning of the legs.

APPENDIX 2:
DAOIST FIVE ORGANS, FIVE ELEMENTS
AND ORGAN-MERIDIAN PRACTICE

A common type of Daoist internal cultivation is to focus on the "Six Healing Sounds" that stimulate the Qi of the six major internal organs of your body through sound resonance.

A related method is to identify emotions associated with each organ, the acupuncture meridians of that particular organ system, and then focus on holding onto those emotions while impressing that Qi route with those dominant attitudes.

As an example, the liver channels (on both sides of your body running down to your feet) can be stimulated (pulsed with Qi or just both halves of your body focused upon) when you are holding onto and trying to be more optimistic with a dynamic positive attitude since this corresponds to liver energy. You can focus on the heart channels when you are trying to be very happy, generous, kind or gregarious.

In Traditional Chinese Medicine the heart is associated with love and joy and fire, the lungs with justice and the metal element, the kidneys with courage and water, the liver with anger and Qi, and so forth. There are other lesser known associations as well of virtue-organ correspondences that you might want to cultivate in yourself.

Normally you can just hold onto deep but inspiring emotions

(including sunniness, happiness or cheerfulness) to impress the energy of that dominant attitude into your nerves and inner Qi body when you perform an activity. You can view whatever activity you are performing as having a higher ultimate purpose that is worthy, uplifting and fulfilling – *especially if it represents greater service to society* – and hold those elevated emotions in your mind when performing that activity so as to affect the Qi of your entire body. You choose your own attitudes as to how to make sense of the world, and by reframing your activities as having higher meanings with strong emotional connections you will add higher intentions to those activities that will transform not just your behavior but your personality too. By doing this you can create your own intrinsic motivation and satisfaction.

By concentrating your intent with a dominant attitude/emotion during the performance of an activity you can embed your actions with a higher meaning by seeing them as having a more elevated purpose. This is how you can "purify" or "elevate" even ordinary activities, and thus make your behavior more noble and majestic. You do this by instilling them with a higher meaning and by strongly feeling this new interpretation within you to the extent that it affects the Yin or Yang quality of your Qi as you engage in those behaviors. This practice is a way to gradually *beautify your personality and behavior, and your Qi as well,* similar to the way that the Four Immeasurables meditation of Buddhism works. You interpret unique activities you engage in with a higher meaning of service, thus spiritualizing them, and when participating in those activities you practice holding onto that interpretation with concentration, including the amplified *positive* emotional feeling of what you are doing. You let strong attitudes or emotions permeate or suffuse your being and thereby purify its Qi during that process.

As advanced Daoist practice you can alternatively try to feel the meridians corresponding to certain emotions when you hold onto that dominant attitude, or the Qi surrounding the meridian lines in greater measure. For instance, the heart Qi meridian runs down the arm into the palms of the hands so whenever you engage in acts of giving, generosity, feel tremendous joy and so on you can focus on sending energy down this meridian. However, you should use the opportunity to color the entire energy of your arms and hands, rather than just the Qi along the meridian line, and then especially feel it run to *all the fingers of the hand rather than just the middle* and last *digits that pertain to meridian lines.*

In other words, whenever you feel joy or generosity, which are emotions that involve the heart, the positive feelings can be projected from your heart center and on through your arms during expression.

You can do this with all the positive emotions of your internal organs to help open up meridians, strengthen the organs, and amplify your personality especially when you practice holding immeasurably large dominant attitudes. You focus on feeling the energy sensations of a (related) internal organ while holding onto a special emotional intent related to the standard organ-emotion correspondences noted in Traditional Chinese Medicine.

There are a variety of emotions and dominant attitudes related to our internal organs so you can select the Yin or Yang emotions you want to cultivate during an activity, support that impetus through an affirmation that amplifies your emotional emphasis, and thereby elevate your participation in any activity by holding onto strong attitudes during participation. You can create countless types of meditations or visualizations to transform your Qi by focusing on the internal organs, their emotional correspondences, their Qi channels, and to the elements (water, air, fire, earth, space) they represent or activities they perform.

Here is a list of several organ-emotion-attitude correspondences and how they can be used in cultivation methods:

STOMACH & PANCREAS – grounded physicality of the body, careful industriousness, discipline with restraint and steady pacing, modesty and humility

- Physicality of the body (muscles); solid, stable, steady, grounded; simple
- Practical, industrious; prudent and careful; responsible, reliable; dutiful
- Self-discipline, abstinence or renunciation; temperance (discipline and self-restraint or self-control) in the face of pleasure; autonomy and command of oneself through willpower, discipline and resolve; diligently puts plans into action, paces oneself
- Straightforward, honest; principled with proper conduct; trustworthy
- Modest, humble, respectful
- Friendship; nourishes others

If you want to think of friendship and nourishing others with food you can concentrate on feeling the stomach meridians and projecting that energy to the rest of your being while also radiating it outward as your aura. If you want to feel the entire physicality of the body (its earthiness and solidity) you can concentrate on feeling the stomach and pancreas and related meridians and then try to sense the feeling of all body tissues, cells and then atoms as a *bodied single unit*. The stomach is related to the earth element so you can use the color yellow if you use accompanying visualizations. Related to this is when you feel the usefulness in doing things (which is a feeling of practicality), or when you are doing things diligently, or when you feel you are being straightforward, honest or direct are times you can concentrate on those dominant attitudes and the feeling of the stomach and stomach meridians along with your whole body's solidity energy.

Related to this are the feelings of being humble and modest because of limited capabilities. When you feel humility or humbleness you should feel it at your core and extend that feeling to the energy of your whole body. When monks are walking in a line to collect food alms, for example, they should be concentrating on the Yin feelings of humbleness and humility in order to use that opportunity to wash their Yin Qi. When Daoists are performing ceremonies of repentance they should try, with all their power, to feel great humility, sorrow and contrition (Yin emotions that will wash their Yin Qi) for their misdeeds as they confess them to Heaven and ask for help in changing themselves.

The blood sugar within your body is regulated by the pancreas to produce stability, and the stomach churns all sorts of different foods that come to it making it suitable that the earth element, represented by the stomach, symbolizes the harmonious conglomeration of all five elements in the universe (emptiness, wind, fire, water, earth). To perform an earth element meditation you can imagine that your body becomes just a collection of (solid) atoms that are separated from each other by space, and therefore you cannot tell where you body actually ends because space and the earth element continue throughout the universe. Thus the elements of your body actually constitute everything in the universe (you can try to feel that expansiveness as your single body). Or you can try to feel the actual physicality of your body and make efforts to push that deep solid energy into moving.

Some Daoists go into caves or face a wall in a meditation posture, relax their mind, and meditate to feel the solidity of their body and that all its parts separate to become atoms, then the energy of the atoms, next expansive fields of energy and then the emptiness of space in which they all rest. They start with form and then imagine becoming formless (empty) like *infinite empty space*. The goal of this is to achieve a meditative state of an empty mind. As an earth meditation you can also imagine that your body becomes golden in color or bright yellow like the color of a GAGG lumogarnet under UV light.

HEART & SMALL INTESTINES – Fire Element – Joy – cheerfulness and joyous, friendly, generous, kindness
- Cheerfulness, happiness; feeling alive with joy; thrilling and exhilarating; feeling glorious or like dancing, elatedness, euphoria; fun and delight, joy and laughter; enthusiasm; glow and shine
- Friendliness, gregarious; outgoing spirit, good-willed sociality; warm-hearted, comforting; making contact with and bonding with others
- Generous, magnanimous; liberality with sharing your possessions and giving of oneself; a magnificence in charitable giving
- Kindness, loving-kindness; compassion, merciful and forgiving; softness, gentleness, tenderness; intimacy

When feeling joyous or cheerful you can feel the energy extending from the heart (chakra) or preferably the entire chest region out through your arms, and even through your entire body and also into your aura since you want that bliss to always be felt everywhere (that blood flows); you make the feeling of exuberance, euphoria, or blissful gloriousness felt everywhere within you, but especially radiating from the heart outwards in order to impress the heart neurons with this energy and offer that joy to others. As *friendliness and the warm-heartedness of brotherhood kinship* constitute factors of happiness for human existence so you can practice feeling friendliness, warmth and good-will centered in and extending from the heart out through your arms and aura (while also feeling this in the rest of your body to affect its energies and impress its neural cells with the memory that this is the natural way for you to be).

When practicing charity and being generous/magnanimous you can also practice feeling warmth spreading out from your heart on through to your arms (and aura) via the heart/pericardium meridians. While the Buddhist practices of infinite joy and infinite kindness should energize all the cells of your body and your aura extending to infinity, you can, while performing these meditations on feeling uncontainable boundless joy (or kindness), also imagine that this extends from you infinitely in a red light that *interpenetrates all beings* and gives them joy as a gift.

The heart pumps the blood within your body to give you warmth and life. Blood has a hemoglobin molecule with iron at its center whereas the structure of chlorophyll (plant blood) is exactly the same but with magnesium at its center. Since red is the color of blood then it is used in meditations to represent the heart as well as the planet Mars and fire. To cultivate the fire element in your body you can start with special pranayama or *tummo* techniques and by imagining a bright reddish flame in your lower *dantian* that grows bigger until it subsumes your entire body with energy so that your body becomes just a raging inferno shaking with fire energy, and you should simultaneously imagine that your body feels uncontainably joyous (the joy energy cannot be held in check because it is boundless) to add further stimulation to this energy. The point is not to evoke a feeling you can contain but generate feelings you cannot contain *totally outside your comfort zone of control, like the wild Indian goddess Kali,* in order to violently flood the energies of your body with positivity beyond the norm. This, for instance, is experienced during orgasm or by people who practice bhakti and totally forget themselves in adoration of a religious deity.

Remember, this is just a method used to arouse your Qi with a different quality than it normally has and then to knead that energy throughout your body via various methods of churning and turning. You should imagine that your body's energy becomes warm and then hot just as if you were sitting near a fire and felt its warmth penetrating you, and you can use special breathing methods in coordination with these efforts. You must give into letting these energies totally take you over infinitely so that you forget yourself but the energies still course within you producing purifying churning (don't be scared but joyous) while imagining that your body is red in color, and the energy constantly moves like flames do. Reciting the sound "Ah" or "Rah" or "Ram" may help stimulate the energy sensations during fire element cultivation methods. You can practice the fire element meditation in front of a fire or by imagining that your body become red in color as bright as a ruby under UV light.

LIVER & GALL BLADDER – Wood/Wind Element – Anger – optimism and positive activity, perseverance and persistence in doing, calmness, courteousness and good tempered

- Optimistic positive attitude; "can do" pioneering American spirit; bold and dynamic; vibrantly moves forward and initiates; creates ambitious change; freshness, growth and development; like vitamins
- Determination, perseverance, willpower of steadfastness, one-pointed concentration or purpose; diligence in hard work; activity with purpose and movement with direction; patient endurance
- Peaceful, calmness, serene, not moody; has control/domination over one's urges and desires; patience and forbearance; anti-excessive
- Good-tempered, slow to take offense, courteous, kindness, benevolence

If you want to develop the trait of optimistic initiating activity that has a vibrant boldness and freshness to it then concentrate on feeling this inside the liver and along the two meridians on both flanks of the body, or just impress these feelings in the two halves of your body while ignoring the meridians. To develop determination, steadfastness, *the desire to persevere in moving forward for a purpose while bearing difficulties* then also concentrate on feeling the liver and liver/GB meridians on the body's left and right flanks. Because the liver stands for anger the feelings of calmness, serenity, patience and control over one's moods and desires can be cultivated by holding those antipodal emotions along with great clarity while concentrating on the liver/GB meridians and the body divided in two halves.

Jujitsu coach John Danaher suggests that before an aggressive sports competition (that would evoke liver energies) you should avoid worry and excitedness but focus on being very calm and clear because you are well prepared, have the mindset that little will go wrong because you've practiced well enough to know how to handle any situation, and permit the attitude that it is safe for you to be aggressive in your actions with the calm attitude "this contest is non-exceptional" because you've practiced this hundreds of times.[13] Despite the liver's ability to get ruffled you can concentrate at other times on feeling good-temperedness, kindness, unflappability, calmness and courtesy by focusing on the liver/GB meridians and impressing both sides of your body with those feelings to help change your attitudes and behavior.

The liver is responsible for blood filtration and detoxification, makes proteins necessary for the body's functioning activities and stores vitamins and minerals (like providing a rich soil for plant growth). It symbolizes the wind element of energy in our body (our life force or Qi) as well as the planet Jupiter that represents expansion, growth and

---

[13] When interviewed about gun fighting in 1910, the famous frontier police officer Wyatt Earp said, "I was a fair hand with pistol, rifle, or shotgun, but I learned more about gunfighting from Tom Speer's cronies during the summer of '71 than I had dreamed was in the book. Those old-timers took their gunplay seriously, which was natural under the conditions in which they lived. Shooting, to them, was considerably more than aiming at a mark and pulling a trigger. Models of weapons, methods of wearing them, means of getting them into action and operating them, all to the one end of combining high speed with absolute accuracy, contributed to the frontiersman's shooting skill. The sought-after degree of proficiency was that which could turn to most effective account the split-second between life and death. Hours upon hours of practice, and wide experience in actualities supported their arguments over style.

"The most important lesson that I learned from those proficient gunfighters was that the winner of a gunplay usually was the man who took his time. The second thing I learned was that, if I hoped to live long enough on the frontier, I would shun flashy trick-shooting - grandstand play - as I would poison.

"When I say that I learned to take my time in a gun fight, I do not wish to be misunderstood, for the time to be taken was only that split fraction of a second that means the difference between deadly accuracy with a six-gun and a miss. It's hard to make this clear to a man who has never been in a gunfight I suppose. Perhaps I can best describe such time taking as going into action with the greatest speed of which a man's muscles are capable, but mentally unflustered by an urge to hurry, or the need for complicated nervous and muscular actions which trick shooting generally involves. Mentally deliberate but muscularly faster than thought is what I mean.

"In all my life as a frontier peace officer, I did not know a really proficient gunfighter who had anything but contempt for the gun-fanner, or man who literally shot from the hip. In later years I read a great deal about this type of gunplay, supposedly employed by men noted for skill with a forty-five. From personal experience and numerous six-gun battles which I witnessed, I can only support the opinion advanced by the men who gave me my most valuable instruction in fast and accurate shooting, which was that the gun-fanner and hip-shooter stood small chance to live against a man who, as old Jack Gallagher always put it, took his time and pulled the trigger once." Source: *Wyatt Earp: Frontier Marshall* by Stuart N. Lake (Pocket Books, 1994).

abundance. To perform a wind element meditation you can concentrate on feeling your breathing push the energy around inside your body, which is *anapana* practice or wind-based rather than mind-based *pratyahara*. Pranayama techniques are wind element cultivation methods.

Oxygen is energy to your body so when breathing you can concentrate on feeling the flow energy throughout your body knowing that your body of atoms is actually energy that has been crystallized into solidity. You are actually liberating your energy nature from its solid casing when you push various energies around your body during cultivation in order to cleanse and purify its energy nature. When you practice *kumbhaka* pranayama by retaining your breath this gradually causes your body to develop more capillaries which will in turn help your cultivation. You can concentrate on the color green or blue when doing wind element practice, like the bright green of an emerald, the bright blue of a blue sapphire or dark blue of a kyanite gemstone.

KIDNEYS & BLADDER – Water Element – Fear – the clarity of a pristine mind, strong confidence, a steady voice that expresses one's entire energy, composed and comfortable, flexibility

- Presence with pristine awareness; *mental clarity, acuity and mindfulness;* clarity of discernment in evaluating affairs; insightfulness; the hearing skill of being able to listen to others deeply and intently; empty infinite detached awareness
- Confident composure; comfortable & at ease; self-confidence; brave and courageous; not shy
- Expressing oneself flawlessly and fearlessly with truth to one's words; steadiness of voice in harmony with one's whole energy revealing the truth of one's authentic self through self-expression; personal magnetism in being attractive to others
- Suppleness, flexible, adaptability; able to accept change quickly and gracefully because of being comfortable and at ease

When cultivating the state of presence with calm, clear awareness-knowingness of your thoughts that never ignores the perceptions of your environment (awareness resides in the experience rather than robotically does things mindlessly through inattention), you can try to also focus on your kidneys and kidney/bladder meridians that form the microcosmic circulation along with the leg meridians. Try to center your Qi when cultivating mental clarity and open the back of your head. You are composed of 70% water, ruled by the kidneys which clean your blood of impurities, so when speaking from your physical self try to feel the entire energy of your water body and especially the kidney/bladder meridians.

Because you are essentially water, you should practice expressing the authentic energy of who you are (how you have colored your water through your personality) from your whole body and show your authentic self by focusing on the feeling of your entire body while feeling the kidney/bladder meridians. To become more supple and flexible as in yoga practice, dance or the martial arts, always imagine that your body and energy are flowing water that can twist and turn in any way, and when exercising try to feel the meridian lines or imagine flowingness. When settled let your mind be like a calm pool of peacefulness.

To perform a water element meditation it is common to go to a clear lake and sit in a location where you can view the placid, calm and peaceful nature of water. You patiently let your mind become still without random thoughts so that your awareness is like pristine clear water where you can see all the way through to the bottom. This is the true nature of your mind and what consciousness is, so the target is to forget about your mind and body to achieve a calm but pristinely clear state of mind like crystal clear water.

Another method is to imagine that everything around you – above you, below you, in front and back of you – becomes water and then you become one with the sameness of that water element since you are essentially a bag of water. The water element is symbolic of fields of energy that span universally across the cosmos flowing in various ways, and you are actually a unified part of this. Therefore you should remember that you can safely let go of holding onto your identity when you realize this mindset because those flows of cohesion will always still produce you. Another water method is to imagine cool water entering the top of your head, or coming up from the bottom of your feet, and then guiding its travels around inside you washing all your tissues.

Supple, soft and adaptable is the nature of water and yet it is the strongest element because through gentleness it can wear away mountains. Laozi therefore taught us to practice influencing people through softness, such as pleasing words and behavior, which is a type of water and kidney cultivation. You can imagine that your body becomes cool and white, dark blue or black in color when you do water visualizations so as to transform its energy. The important principle is to feel the energy within your body as being cool like moonbeams or pearl powder. Then let your inner Qi energy move around like currents of water washing everything inside you in various ways.

You can also imagine that your entire body becomes like water and its various modes – surging waves, choppiness, smooth flowing, rippled running, deep stillness, etcetera – in order to wash your tissues with various types of Qi friction. In Daoism there are several different types of water currents mentioned in the *Zhuangzi* and *Liezi* (which refer to movements of Qi within a master's body) such as whirlpools, waterfalls, lakes (still water), damned water turned back to its source, swift currents, water bubbling up from the ground, water dripping from above, water slanting away as it falls off from a cave, water which drains to a marsh, multiple streams that divide from one source, ... and they all empty out into deep pools of stillness and calm. The idea is to practice many such movements internally and then afterwards rest in a stillness of mental peace and calm. You can watch bodies of water that surge or flow in various ways (with ripples, smoothly, violently, etc.) *and try to imitate those movements within your body's internal energy* so that the friction of internally moving your Qi in rugged ways where it rubs or laps against other Qi will also help to purify it.

LUNGS & LARGE INTESTINES – Metal/Space Element – Sadness/Grief – truthfulness and authenticity in your vocal expressions, fairness and righteousness, exuding a vibrating sparkle of energy that influences others, tolerance and patience, focused clear attention

- Honesty and total integrity, no lying; truthfulness in self-expression and trustworthiness in dealings
- Righteousness and rightness, fairness and justice; proper indignation
- Inspirational vibrancy that impresses others by natural projection through your breathing and speech that motivates, refreshes, clarifies, heals and uplifts others in a pleasing influential way; energetically influence your surroundings without thinking; refresh others with energy that sparkles, enervates, calms or protects
- Tolerance of other people and their values, acceptance, openness
- Focus, intense attention for clarity's sake

Your breath affects your Qi, which is your life force, so you want to be expressing your authentic self with honesty when speaking and doing things. When your activities involve the arms you can especially try to feel your breathing all the way to your abdomen as well as through your arm meridians since the arms are the instruments of doing (as are also the feet *and penis*). When thinking of justice, fairness and righteousness you should also concentrate on your lungs and on feeling your life force (Qi energy) throughout your body since this how you want to be along with the bodies of all present as they are one human organism. Justice must be enforced within society, even though penalties are involved, in order to establish fairness and harmony for all. Your life force, which represents you, must naturally fully express virtue and ethics so feelings of righteousness must be impregnated within your lungs, their meridians, your aura and personality (which issues from your entire body).

When speaking you can modulate your voice to express your entire beingness of energy, and thereby influence people and the environment energetically as far as your speech energy of pure intentions extends with its modulations. You should train your Qi when it is resting during states of mental calm with steady respiration to patiently accept/tolerate the speech or presence of others that intrudes upon it. When focusing with intense attention you should adjust your breathing to become smooth where it also permeates your entire body with a natural (non-artificial, non-contrived, non-controlled) rhythm, which takes training in sitting meditation practice. The object of your knowingness, and your mind, must both become very clear whenever you are experiencing a natural state of knowing, mindfulness, cognizance or awareness.

In Daoism the lungs represent Venus and the Metal element, which is known as the space element in other traditions. This element is represented by the color white, bright white light, (shiny) silver or clearness. To perform a space element meditation you can try to feel that your body is like an empty sack, or that you become bodiless *like an infinite boundless sky* while retaining an awareness that cannot hold onto anything since you are perfectly bodiless just like space. You can imagine becoming bodiless space that contains all sorts of things *without you being able to touch anything* because you are just pristine awareness, and hold onto that feeling (which is like the samadhi of infinite space from Buddhism). You can visualize that your lungs become filled with bright white light as you breath in which travels throughout your body as the pumping of your lungs causes you to breath out.

When possible, you can even strive to feel the energy meridians of the organ systems that might be related to any affirmations, dominant attitudes or emotional energy work you are using in your cultivation. For the purposes of purification it is very beneficial if you intentionally impress your neural cells (in the brain, heart, alimentary canal, spine and other nerves) with elevated attitudes, positive intentions, and Qi sensations as you do things. As recommended, you can turn higher intentions into affirmations or aphorisms to mentally recite while holding onto relevant dominant attitudes that come from your core.

When you reinterpret your activities with a different type of framing you shift your outlook on the world, and thus you gradually change your fortune if you maintain a new perspective because a new way of looking at things will cause you to make different decisions and act differently as if you had a new natal astrological chart. If you can find a proper new perspective through reframing then it is a way to uplift most of your mundane activities. You simply deeply identify your activities with a higher goal or meaning than before, thus making them become "more alive," and hold onto strong dominant attitudes connected with those ideals while you perform those activities. This will elevate you and them.

We can use the meridians together with dominant attitudes to also cultivate our personality and our Qi in yet another way. This new methodology will be applied to examining some of the famous qualities of Lord Krishna, who is adored in Indian culture and taken as an ideal model of behavior. This same method can be applied to Daoist greats, Buddhist greats, Christian greats, etcetera including even famous actors you admire if you are trying to develop a personality trait that they strongly represent. We should always be living in our innermost ideal that is the *raison d'etre* of your being, and this is one way to move towards that goal. You want there to be the progressive manifestation of your highest self in the forms in which it dwells.

In the case of Lord Krishna, he is known for several magnificent characteristics as listed below. Bhakti devotees mentally imagining that they are Krishna flood their Qi energy with the dominant trait of interest in a profuse manner believing that they possess that trait in abundance. This washes their Qi. You can cultivate personality transformation in this way, and going further you can concentrate some of your energetic focus on your meridian lines as below:

Talks pleasingly – kidney/bladder and lung meridians
Effulgence – heart and stomach meridians
Truthful – stomach and lung meridians
Highly learned – brain (& spine) meridians
Highly intelligent – brain (& spine) meridians
A genius – brain (& spine) meridians
Artistic – kidney/bladder meridians
Extremely clever – brain (& spine) meridians
Grateful – stomach and heart meridians
Firmly determined – liver/GB meridians
An expert judge of time and circumstances – brain (& spine)
    meridians
Self-controlled – stomach and liver/GB meridians
Steadfast – stomach and liver/GB meridians
Forbearing – stomach meridian
Possessing equilibrium – lungs and kidney/bladder meridians
Magnanimous – heart meridian
Heroic – liver/GB meridian
Compassionate – heart meridian
Respectful – stomach and heart meridians
Gentle – heart meridian
Happy – heart meridian
Well-wisher – heart meridian
Popular – lung and kidney/bladder meridians
Very attractive to women – kidney/bladder meridians

As stated, you can use this same technique to imagine that you become like famous actors you admire when you are trying to develop a personality trait that they strongly represent, such as ones they are famous for exhibiting. You hold onto the energy of possessing the personality characteristic of the actor you want while strongly feeling certain meridians too:

Gregory Peck – moral and physical strength – lungs and stomach
    meridians
Shirley Temple – happiness & sparkle energy – heart and

kidney/bladder meridians

Paul Newman – strong willed, fiercely independent – liver/GB and kidney/bladder meridians

James Stewart – easy going, always rose to the challenge – heart and liver/GB meridians

Gary Cooper – humility, hardworking, self-confidence – stomach and kidney/bladder meridians

Cary Grant – elegance, class, charisma, charm – kidney/bladder and heart meridians

John Wayne – adventurous headstrong leader, rugged and macho – liver/GB, stomach and lung meridians

Sean Connery – assertiveness and practicality – stomach and liver/GB meridians

Bruce Lee – quickness and confidence – kidney/bladder meridians

Clint Eastwood – assertive badass who gets justice – liver/GB & lung meridians

Jason Stratham – non-nonsense assertive, confident action hero – stomach, kidney/bladder and liver/GB meridians

Robert Downey Jr – overly confident smart guy – kidney/bladder & brain meridians

Vin Diesel – ambitious, adaptable, enthusiastic physicality – liver/GB, kidney/bladder, heart and stomach meridians

The whole point of this discussion is to teach you that you can help develop a personality trait in yourself by cultivating the Qi flow along your acupuncture meridians, or the Qi of your entire body while stirring your emotions with visualizations or mental enactments that you possess such traits. You must also take steps to embody the traits you want in regular life.

Instead of using emotions to vibrate or energize your Qi while you try to wash it with mind-guided circulations, you can also imagine the energetic texture of the five elements and use that to create entirely different sensations within your body to wash its Qi for the purposes of subtle body purification. Yes, you are supposed to do this! That's the point or purpose of these types of exercise.

Different sensations evoke different emotions and therefore stimulate different Qi qualities to arise, so this principle of "your mind (thoughts) and Qi are connected" within you is used to activate different types of Qi within you – different types of inner energy feelings impregnated with attitudes or emotions – which you might call qualities, textures or types of Qi. The purpose is so that all the various types of energies of your body, or energy states, can be washed when you hold onto different energy modes and simultaneously try to churn those energies at the same time. The churning washes your Qi through the friction of rotational contact and that's what eventually cleanses your inner subtle body that can eventually leave your physical nature. This is what happens during the twelve years of internal alchemy microcosmic and macrocosmic circulations that eventually produce the independent subtle body stage of the Earth Immortal. Naturally, you can also do this to help change your personality as stated.

A second benefit to meditations on the five elements is to prepare you for the perspective, view or "mind of enlightenment" that you start to develop when you finally reach the stage of a full Arhat, or Celestial Immortal, whose Supra-Causal body vehicle has gone past the Realm of Form and now belongs to the Realm of Formlessness. It is at this stage that you realize that your body, being composed of energy, is merged with the rest of the universe with no mediation. It is "oned" with the cosmos seamlessly where you are part of a single fabric of oneness in manifestation (Tawheed). Therefore you are not a body but the universe, at least in terms of manifestation because the real you, your real Self or absolute self-nature is a changeless, unmoving pure and eternal substratum that underlies and permeates the universe. This understanding, of what your body and consciousness truly are, is "self-realization." Many religions try to help you attain this very understanding.

When you attain the stage of the Celestial or Universal Immortal the composition of your body is of an energy level realm that spreads throughout all of dense matter, permeating it everywhere. You understand you are part of a seamless fabric of the universe where all of the universe "makes you" through an infinite interdependence involving every iota of it, and so you are not part of the universe or a portion of it but *are* the universe. Your true corporeal body *is* the universe and it's just that your consciousness has not yet caught up to this fact due to a wrong perspective and because physical sensations from your nerves extend no further than your physical nature. But soon you will be able to sense doings within the universe everywhere.

Hence, everything you see around you – the universe – is you. You are just a small process of embodied consciousness that appears within a giant ocean called the universe where its entirety gets into the act of producing you through various agglomerations and cohesions. You are the universe rather than something made by the universe that stands apart, and you just happen to have the property of consciousness due to your structure. You are a process with consciousness so you are part of the consciousness of the universe! You are like a node of the universal consciousness where communication and *nirmanakaya* emanations connect you with others. You are not separate from Nature but part of Nature because you are Nature. Your fabric of beingness is the universe instead of something small and separated from everything else by space. Your true Self is the fundamental unmovable essence that transcends all of Creation from which Creation is born, or it is *all of Creation* if you talk about its manifest aspect that is continuously changing to show a new face or personality every moment. Knowing what you are along these lines is called "self-realization."

One realizes this *experientially* rather than just intellectually when one becomes an Arhat, or Celestial Immortal, because by virtue of having a body composed of energy within a cosmos of energy – where some parts of the cosmos appear as more condensed or solidified tangles of energy than others (e.g. matter or atoms) – you can now (through your energy body) sense the thought energies of human beings, or hear sounds, or feel vibrational movements and so on in the lower realms of frequency/vibration/purity. Kuan Yin can "hear the cries of the world" because he has the higher transcendental bodies whose very composition, because they correspond to etheric energy realms that transcend ours, can sense the vibrations in our realm instantly. It is similarly said that if you address the enlightened Krishna, who could expand his body into many *nirmanakaya* so that he could be coupled with each and every *gopi*, your calling upon his name also immediately attracts his attention. It is so with all high stage enlightened individuals.

By virtue of the etheric composition of your body (its transcendental plane of existence of which it is composed) you attain a pervasive awareness of the consciousness workings and movements of sentient beings in all directions because they constitute vibrations. Kuan Yin can "hear the cries of the world" and a Daoist master can similarly hear when students call out his name or recite his secret mantra (which is like a phone number) because he has attained a Celestial Immortal or Universal Immortal body made of energy that can perceive these fluctuations in the cosmos. Only when you get to these two high levels does this become possible because it is not possible for the Spirit or Earth Immortal (the subtle-bodied or Causal-bodied beings).

Now that you understand this fact you can realize one purpose of the Daoist five element meditations from a greater perspective and understand how they are connected to various Buddhist sutras or the teachings of Hinduism and other religions. It is all about self-realization, namely realizing what you truly are composed of, and what what you truly are, instead of the mistaken perspective that you are an independent, intrinsic, self-so, homogenous sentient being that is somehow separate, independent or different than the universe. You are part of a universe of oneness.

The Daoist state of flow is achieved when you act in tune with the realization that you are not different from the universe, whose events are flowing in certain ways or directions, whereas with other viewpoints that focus on you being a "self" all sorts of tensions build up between the concept of "me" and "experience," which Buddhism calls "self" and "other."

EARTH ELEMENT

In the earth element meditation where you imagine that your body becomes just an aggregation of atoms separated from each other by space, the point is that this is the nature of the material universe and your true physical matter body extends everywhere. If the atoms of your body are separated by space then you cannot really tell where your body ends because space and the earth element extend everywhere.

The size of your body must include everything physical in the universe so during meditation you are supposed to *feel the solidity of your small body, and then the solidity of that massive expansiveness, and then ultimately the emptiness of that expansiveness* to help you let go of the ingrained image/perspective within your mind, formed due to the ever-present sensations of your nervous system and body consciousness where you feel its shape, that you are just a small body rather than the truth that you are the entire material universe, and also ultimately its essence.

Let's pretend that your body is just composed of atoms that cannot be decomposed into anything smaller like quarks and muons and so forth. Furthermore, let's call the atoms "particles," "quanta" or "simples." The *Diamond Sutra* of Buddhism calls all these small particles "specks of dust." While we say that your body is composed of atoms, or simples, you have to realize that atoms never aggregate into anything definite. We mistakenly conceptualize an aggregation of atoms into a body but this is a false conclusion. Atoms don't compose anything so although separated by space they just keep aggregating together to become larger wholes until the whole universe is involved because there is no ultimate pattern. The atoms together never compose any (lesser) wholes because (1) objects (wholes) don't truly exist as ontological patterns or self-so things but are only discriminated by a mind, (2) any whole you can discern through your mind can always be considered part of a bigger whole so it isn't anything definite itself and can always be considered incomplete, and (3) the atomic composition of wholes is itself always changing.

This is the concept of mereological nihilism, which is that *the building blocks of matter never compose any wholes, and so no "composite objects" exist.* Due to conventional analysis we think we are surrounded by macrophysical objects (wholes) that are composed of smaller objects like atoms as their proper parts. For example, we perceive objects such as cars that appear to be composed of other objects such as wheels, seats, metal, etcetera which in turn appear to be composed of still smaller objects such as atoms. Those in turn are composed of quarks and so on but we're just leaving the conversation at the atom stage to simplify matters. But basically, every material object that we perceive appears to be composed of smaller parts.

Now, when you think deeply about the composition of material things it must therefore be the case that there are no composite material objects. There are only fundamental physical simples like atoms (which compose objects) that are arranged in various spatial patterns that that our mind then calls objects. Actually, there are just aggregations of atoms in front of you. We make up these extra meanings of shapes when there are just atoms there. Atoms don't really aggregate into patterns with any ontological existence.

If you see a car it is really not a car because there are only simples there - atoms. It is our minds that arrange them into a pattern we identify as a "car." Without a mind there are just atoms. There is only a pattern there because we have consciousness; without consciousness there is no pattern, just atoms in the car, on the ground, in the air, everywhere. It's the same as looking at the wall of a building where you see nothing but bricks, which are composed of atoms. There really is no pattern there. There are just atoms.

The components of a car are all just atoms that aren't cooperating in producing a car but just situated in a spatial pattern that we call a car, yet on analysis it is just a collection of atoms. You can call what you see a "car" but that is nothing but a name, a designation, an expression, a simple word because there is no car there. There are just atoms. To the universe there is only a group of atoms in a sea of atoms and there is no real pattern to it, or to anything at all in any smaller section, since the entire universal sea of atoms is in a constant turbulent state of motion and transformation. There are only fundamental physical atoms spatially arranged and causally interrelated as a momentary group in such a way as to cause our minds to have a car-like perceptual experience because of our prior mental conditioning. If you did not have special prior conditioning then you would not see it as a "car" because of perceptual blindness. For example, lions on a safari will not attack a man on a truck to eat him because they see the two together as a single larger body.

Our minds make the atomic arrangement into a car so there isn't really a homogenous object called a car in front of us when we see one. We are just applying a mental name and label to a pattern developed by our consciousness, but there isn't any such real thing as a car with an inherent car own-nature or core that is self-existent.

"Composite objects," such as a "car," are therefore simply a conventional way of speaking to indicate things. They don't truly exist but we talk this way for ease of communication. What is really there is only the absolute substratum that appears as something with qualities in our minds. What appears is part of the entire expression of the personality of the universe at the moment in time we used our minds to carve out that object from the whole.

Our body is an agglomeration of atoms in the same way. It exists within what is ultimately a universal soup of uncountable atoms that itself doesn't have any fixed, definite pattern since everything is changing every moment. Hence, what pattern? An infinite number of galaxies composed of atoms are just atoms instead of galaxies and that's the universe. The universe is just a big soup of particles, which the *Diamond Sutra* of Buddhism calls "dust," and its homogenous nature of one taste is not made up of atoms at all.

The universe is your true physical material body because you are the manifest universe of physical matter and space, yet this still is not your real absolute body. Some people might therefore say that they are all form, or that they reside within form, or that they possess form because you encompass all realms of existence. Actually, there are subtle mistakes in all these conclusions but we'll leave this discussion aside. For convention's sake you can say you are a body, or *Taiji* (the Saguna Brahman of Hinduism or Triple Realm of Buddhism) but you are really *Wuji* (the Nirguna Brahman of Hinduism or absolute self-nature of Buddhism).

As to the fact that our physical body is composed of a collection of atoms, the way we handle its maintenance is through food, and the best way to make sure we avoid nutritional deficiencies by taking in the atoms we need for our proper construction, growth, and health is through the Daoist practices of excellent nutrition.

We can also deconstruct a galaxy of atoms, or the entire universe, into a big soup of surging energies together with atoms always transforming into different combinations and positions. This in turn can be decomposed into a big soup of fluctuating quantum fields underneath the material agglomerations/consolidations that appear as waves and currents headed in particular directions because of the aggregation of forces. In turn, this can be decomposed into just quantum vibrations, vibrational wiggles and virtual particles that appear and disappear everywhere as the micro-components within the water-like wind vectors of fields moving in all directions.

The many ways of conceiving the universe can all *eventually* be resolved or deconstructed into an immovable, single, pure, fundamental foundational substrate that never moves, is self-so because it is not constructed of anything else and never came from anywhere, and is pure, immortal, changeless, everlasting. Somehow a universe that possesses a facticity of cause and effect relationships seems to appear to our consciousness but ultimately everything we perceive does not truly exist in the way it appears to us. Everything is vastly different than how our minds make things appear, and objects or forms are ultimately empty of a true, stable, unchanging core existence of solidity except for their ultimate essence.

To achieve each new body of spiritual attainment is similarly like this process of decomposing matter into its most absolute components. However, in this case each purification of a lower, denser body separates from within itself a new and more purified, refined or transcendental body composed of higher vibrational energies that still retain the original body's cohesive shape. Each new body is a purified part of the "life force" of the old body that had been animating it and keeping it alive.

That is why we say that the subtle deva body (stage of the Earth Immortal) is the "soul" of our physical nature even though it can be further deconstructed into higher components until we come to the *ultimate absolute soul or true self*, which is the absolute unchanging substratum of the universe. However, the highest true person, soul, *jiva* or *atman* is the core stage within us of the Universal Immortal, Immanence body, or Tathagata body or Perfect and Complete Enlightenment.

The atoms of our body always remain atoms separated from each other by space, and since there is really no border to any pattern of atoms since their spatial separation eventually connects with other atoms, eventually you have an entire world of atoms agglomerated together that includes all the beings upon its surface moving here and there doing whatever they do. Seen from far away you can only see a planet and none of the human beings upon it, so *they should just be considered part of it rather than separate entities … especially since they are composed of it.* Then, of course, the earth itself is an atom within the galaxy while galaxies are part of larger agglomerations and on and on it goes. There is no human whatsoever on this scale of conceptions as you are just an atom in a universe of worlds.

The whole idea of the earth element meditation is to get you to realize that you are made of the earth element, it stretches across the cosmos, and if you consider yourself a physical body then you are really the entire universe of atoms and space. Be that and let go. That's the meditation feeling that you want – to let go of the feeling of the body and be empty of solidity because your body stretches everywhere. That is not our true spiritual self, or self-nature, but a worthwhile meditation for various reasons. You are actually bodiless, so use the meditation on being a vast body to then connect with the opposite feeling that you are essentially bodiless.

WATER ELEMENT

As to the water element, it stands for agglomeration and flowingness. Agglomeration means things are pulled together through forces of cohesion. Magnetism, gravity, and the weak and strong nuclear forces stand for the water element because they do this. Water droplets congeal together with other water droplets to form a larger mass of water just as droplets of mercury congeal together, and what determines the course of water in its agglomerations and flows are the physical laws of cause and effect that specify transformations and movements.

If you consider yourself all of the physical matter of the universe dissolved into its underlying energies flowing here and there in waves and currents like the water element, with the trajectories of those currents subject to the aggregation of forces in each location and cohesions producing the forms of apparent phenomena, then you end up with an entire universal ball of coursing energies surging in rolling waves.

You are that, and there are various types of water meditation where you try to feel your body as a compendium of surging internal energies, or smoothly circulating inner energies, or descending inner energies, and so forth. In water meditations you try to move the currents of inner energy within you in certain ways to wash all the areas of your body. Or, you try to excite into movement various inner currents by arousing *emotions strong enough to provoke sensations within you that stimulate various Qi qualities and movements*, which is the basis of sexual cultivation.

Thoughts can move your Qi, but emotions are usually more powerful at evaluating internal sensations that can influence your entire Qi body. Visualizations and willpower can move your Qi, but sound vibrations are more effective. What is better than reciting sounds to move your Qi is reciting *rhythmical sounds* that can produce a resonance of vibrating Qi energy within you. Reciting rhythmical sounds while arousing strong emotions (that stimulate your Qi) AND while also visualizing stimulating scenarios is even more powerful as a package than any single cultivation method alone. This is the basis of many cultivation techniques to wash your Qi.

There are many ways to stack various spiritual practice methods together to produce very powerful processes of Qi purification and transformation like this.

Naturally you can guide the Qi energy within your body to wash all its tissues, which is the basis of much Daoist *nei-gong* practice. You can also imagine, by *simultaneously trying to feel it inside you to make it happen*, your internal energy surging everywhere within you like a river, surging sea or the gigantic forces moving within the universe - in order to frictionally rub your Qi against itself in a random violent manner or in waves of purifying friction. You can also try spinning your Qi (by guiding it with your mind) around all your organs, limbs, appendages and overall structure and try moving it in the standard Daoist patterns of whirlpools, circular orbital circulations, rushing rivers, ascensions from the feet upwards, droppings from your head descending downwards, splurgings out of your sides inside you and so on.

In our own lives, the water element corresponds to our life trajectory or fortune which is a path already determined by the forces of the universe and its karmic agglomeration of energies.

How do we change our fate, fortune and destiny? I've detailed the "8M" method in several of my books and directed you to the stories of Liao Fan, Benjamin Franklin and Frank Bettger who have all written books on this topic. To truly change your destiny you must change yourself – your character, way of doing things, and activities that would have caused a fate you did not want. This is akin to changing your natal astrological disposition. The Daoist view is that only by transforming yourself – your personality, thinking, conduct and activities – can you change your fortune.

FIRE ELEMENT

If you examine the fire element, where heat and light flickeringly arise during the continuous transformation of molecules into entirely different molecules while heat, light or other energies are released (such as wood burning to become ash while giving off smoke, heat and light), then you can realize that the entire universe is always just an on-going process of transformations of elements and energies, and *you are also just that on-going process of nothing definite.*

You are one big ball of entropy where everything is changing always and every moment into something else. You are the single universal vat of continuous matter and energy transformations where the contents never remain the same because everything is always transmuting to something else.

The universe is always on fire. It is always burning with ceaseless transformations. That is what you are.

Can you imitate the feeling of fire within you by stoking the feeling of heat and flickering flames within your body? Can you generate the feeling of heat within yourself through breathing methods and visualization practices so that hot Qi energy arises and purifies your tissues? This is one type of fire element meditation popular in

Buddhism that also requires coordination with your breathing to stoke the warmth. Inner warmth is another way to purify your Qi.

Matter is always vibrating and always transforming into other forms of matter while energy is always flowing and transforming into other forms of matter since $E=mc^2$. There are always processes of destruction and construction going on where things are always changing into something else, and these sequences are called change, impermanence, entropy, cause and effect, indeterminacy or complex interaction. As regards fire it needs oxygen or air, and so breathing methods are essential for anyone practicing fire element cultivations that produce inner purifying Qi transformations based on warmth.

In our own lives, after a certain age our bodies are always degrading in a negative way due to aging, which is entropy, and the only way to counter this are the Daoist methods of health and longevity or the attainment of the higher and longer-lived spiritual bodies of the upper realms.

You must also understand that from the perspective of the fire element there is no such thing as reincarnation. Although you think of yourself as a "homogenous" self-being you are a "composite" or conditional being whose every part is always transforming while coming from somewhere else that is non-self (non-you), and thus you are an entirely different being from moment to moment that lacks a steady core. You lack a permanent, unchanging soul or "I-self." Consequently, no permanent part of what you take as "you," your "I" or self gets passed from life to life through reincarnation.

There is no such thing as a unified, homogenous, permanent innate core that is "you" that gets passed from incarnation to incarnation. Yes, there is indeed a process of transformation or transmutation that occurs, but no "self" reincarnates because we are not an unchanging self. Rather, a collection of attributes is passed and transformed during the transition process of reincarnation.

We are a temporary collection of aggregates like a car, and no part of us is unconditionally, innately, inherently, intrinsically self-existent on its own. There isn't a single speck inside of us that serves as an unchanging core I-self. Since everything is always changing within us then when there is reincarnation, which indeed does exist from a relative or conventional perspective, it is not the transformation *of an unchanging core self* into a new life. There is just some process in the universe occurring as some non-homogenous aggregation transforms into something else, which is happening every moment anyway in the universe.

How can you then say that a *permanent* self gets passed from life to life? There is just a process involving an agglomerated composite body having a property called consciousness that is transforming into something new just as it does every moment, only this change seems more significant.

From the ultimate perspective of the singular ground substratum, or absolute unchanging essence of the universe, no such thing as a transformation is going on. There are no movements, no comings or goings or energy fluctuations, no flows or phenomena in its perfect, pure essence. There is no change, no worlds, no sentient beings, and hence no such thing as consciousness or reincarnation. They are all just transient inventions in the illusory world of manifestation.

Whatever you are seeing in front of yourself right this moment essentially is just *Wuji*, the Great undifferentiated formless Tao where nothing is happening because there is just *Wuji* without any existence of *Taiji*. *Taiji* is just an illusory appearance of *Wuji* that shows a new personality every moment. All that your mind is seeing right now is actually just the all-encompassing, nameless fundamental substratum *Wuji* that is unfathomable because it is devoid of qualities, attributes or manifestations. However, you do perceive a manifested world in your mind of consciousness, but its mental productions are based on limitations of its anatomy. Through your mind you see an apparent universe that is Lingbao Tianzun, "The Celestial Worthy of Numinous Treasures."

This is actually because your senses and consciousness create a fiction for you. You are not a true self but just a process of the universe that thinks it is a self with something called consciousness that is true and accurate, and through consciousness you create internal representations of yourself and the outer world which don't truly represent reality in the way it really exists. In other words, reality does not exist in the way it appears to us.

You can see through to the Truth, but what you are seeing as the conventional world is actually an imagination or illusion that works for your survival at your stage of matter-energy condensation within the great realm of the cosmos. The universe is actually something other than what you are envisioning in your mind but you certainly see a realm of facticity because that is how our species has evolved … otherwise it would have died out.

What you are perceiving in front of you is actually Yuanshi Tianwang or Yuanshi Tianzun, the Heavenly Worthy of Prime Origin, the formless primordial nature or ground state material of the universe, of which all things are composed, that appears to us in a certain way only because we have sense organs and consciousness.

Hence there really is no such thing as reincarnation since the ultimate essence doesn't change into anything else, but in the conventional sense there actually is reincarnation just as there are rocks and trees. If you take a bar of gold and make it into all sorts of ornaments then from the standpoint of the gold they are all gold whereas you see them as ornaments. That is the situation. Ornaments are what we see but there is just one gold element there that represents the primordial substratum.

WIND ELEMENT

If you next look at the wind element it represents movement or energy in the universe, something that is born seemingly out of nothingness just as so-called "virtual particles" are constantly being born out of a perfect vacuum winking into and out of existence.

Energy itself can be further decomposed into fluctuating quantum fields. For cultivation purposes we can (1) use the image of energy inside us as being like a current of water or wind you can guide as sensations inside your body when you start to meditate. You can circulate the life force Qi of your body, or "wind element," around inside yourself like water or wind to wash your tissues and your inherent subtle body made of Qi. (2) You can imagine internal vibrations like the wobbling, spinning and shaking of atoms to energize us everywhere internally with bliss as a means of purification. (3) You can also use breathing exercises to push your Qi around inside yourself to wash those tissues.

The only important thing in this discussion, and the discussion for all of the five elements, is how to use your body's Qi to wash its tissues. You must use your imagination (thoughts/mind) to link with your Qi in order to stimulate your energy into changing its qualities while moving it to wash your tissues. This is what is important because this practice will eventually gain you the stage of the Earth Immortal and higher bodies, and thus freedom from the lower realm of matter. That's what is important rather than whether any description of manifest reality is accurate or not.

We've gone over various meditations or visualizations that you can use to make progress in stimulating your Qi to have a different feel or tonality, and then mentally linking with your stimulated Qi to move it around your body to wash your tissues while holding onto strong emotions. That is how you attain the first spiritual body.

In Daoism you normally just use your mind to guide your Qi through various circulations but you should realize by now that what you are really trying to do is change the whole flavor of your entire body's Qi energy as a single unit – typically by using arousing emotions, sounds, visualizations, or other imaginary cognitions to strongly stimulate your Qi – and then you rotate that energy everywhere to wash your inner subtle body. That is true *neijia, neidan, or nei-gong* but no one bothers to explain this to you unless you read and decipher the lessons of the *Surangama Sutra*, the hardships of Lu Dongbin or Naropa and other pertinent lessons. This is the crucial information that has been kept secret.

No one knows the true origin of wind, namely how and where it arises from, because it is produced from so many pressure systems near and far away that are always moving and mutually interacting with one another. The same goes for the energy of the universe. No one knows where *Taiji* comes from, meaning no one knows *how* the energy and formations of the universe originated from the changeless, stationary, non-moving, permanent *Wuji*. All that we know is that the universe is always moving, constantly moving, everything is in ceaseless vibration and indeterminacy except for the briefest quantum moment of time between changes of state, which shows that the whole thing is just an illusion of appearances like the step-by-step frames of a motion picture that seem real when viewed in series.

The manifest existence of the universe is a set of instantaniations, like a set of frames in a movie linked to one another giving the appearance of a smooth continuity when all that is there is a sequence of instantaniations creating a passing show that is a hollow illusion. The time slice when there is no movement is smaller than the refresh rate of the universe (the smallest time slice between instantaniations) that it uses for stepping through time. During that gap there is no movement to the appearance at all, so continuous movement is actually fake too. In Buddhism, this stationary moment is sort of like the "samadhi that is neither thinking nor no-thinking," neither movement nor not-movement.

Typically we say that the universe is never in a state of rest but since its overall movements are an illusion then even the quanta refresh rate gap is not real. From large waves on the ocean down to zones (layers) and micro-currents and the shaking of atoms and energy components within them, just think of everything moving on a vast fractal scale. This movement is the *life force of the universe* from which all its transformations arise including "evolution" thus happens due to complex interactions. Both life and consciousness can only exist due to continuous movement, but both life and consciousness need periods of rest in order to replenish and refresh themselves. If you tap into this energy by sleeping or by letting go and meditating with detachment then such meditation can renew you. That is the Daoist way; rest your mind from thinking, let go, and let the energy of the universe, its life force, renew you.

The Tibetan master Tilopa advised, "Don't recall. Let go of whatever has passed. Don't imagine. Let go of what has not come. Don't think. Let go of what is happening now. Don't examine; don't try to figure anything out. Don't control; don't try to make anything happen. Rest your mind. Relax."

If you realize that absolutely, positively everything in the universe (including you) is always changing (transforming) into something else, everything is always vibrating with indeterminacy so that what it is cannot be locked down, that you can never perceive the fluctuating universe truly with your senses and mind, that all things lack a core permanent essence which is *a fact that includes you*, and that even your cherished self concept (of being a self or small "I") is just a delusive process in the universe that your anatomical organism automatically generates in its consciousness processes for them to work, then it becomes easy to detach from clinging to mental events to experience a state of clear presence where your consciousness is calm, without concern, but there is clear focus and clarity. If you truly let go to openness and wonder you will *feel fully alive with beingness and presence*, but it takes time to actualize this to the fullest. Zen tries to teach you to do this, and Daoism as well.

In terms of *sat, chit, ananda* you still want to exist *(sat),* with consciousness, awareness, luminosity of cognizance of presence *(chit)* and knowledge (which means skills and understanding) but you also want to experience bliss *(ananda),* which can be found in positive emotions or in the state of flow where you are fully engaged with focus and attention on your activities but not clinging to them. That is truly the state of presence or beingness that people seek on the road of spirituality comprised of existence, consciousness, and a peaceful clear bliss. What would you then do with your life? That is *ikigai*, or life purpose. You need the guidance of a constancy of purpose to give meaning to your existence.

SPACE ELEMENT

Lastly, while we cannot tell whether the manifest universe is large or small because it is a single thing where there is nothing else to compare it to, we can say that all its events or contents are occurring within the container of space. The "womb of space" holds everything in existence, all manifest realities. But since space can get warped by matter, which Einstein says is just condensed energy because $E=mc^2$, space isn't the ultimate substrate of the universe. Since space can bend it is therefore an object of form.

Perhaps space is made of quanta components like most everything else such as time, energy or matter, or perhaps *energy somehow makes space* in a process of physics that we don't yet understand. In any case, because it can be warped then space is not the ultimate foundational essence of the universe even if space were a perfect vacuum empty of all things. It can change so it is not changeless and immortal.

Nevertheless, the image of space can be used in meditation to help quiet thoughts by reflecting on the fact that space is like the fundamental substratum of the universe that lacks any qualities. When you let go of your thoughts they will eventually quiet down and during that state of emptiness or non-distraction, where awareness remains alive, your consciousness is becoming more like the true nature of the universe. During that time you are not moving the Qi of your body (because of its linkage to your thoughts) so enlightened spiritual masters can use *nirmanakaya* at that time to enter it and rotate its Qi using their own energies without much opposition. That is one of the secret key benefits to emptiness meditation practice. One of its purposes is that it makes it easier for higher beings to enter into you to purify your subtle energy via *nirmanakaya* emanations.

It is funny to realize that when you are walking you experience space passing right through you. You don't walk through space and it parts. You walk in space and the space passes right through you without hitting anything. If you meditate on the image of this it can help you realize that your body is ultimately empty of concrete existence and you are ultimately not a body. This realization of space passing though you can also help you learn detachment.

Space must exist within something, and that *ultimate something* is the absolute nature which permeates all of space. It must also be the fundamental essence of space - its ultimate substance or substrate. How can you form a mental image of that primordial substrate if space is but one of its features or creations? You cannot because it has no attributes or qualities, which is why Islam says not to make any image of Allah.

You can turn off all your thoughts, like in deep sleep or the samadhi of nothingness, and say that when you have no consciousness you know It. If you are annihilated and no longer exist then through wordplay we can say you know It too but of course those states of non-existence are worthless. We want *sat, chit, ananda*, and *ikigai* instead of non-existence. Right now the fundamental substrate of existence is here in all you are seeing and experiencing through consciousness, which is the great miracle of existence, so you don't have to become annihilated to know your true nature. You are always It. Enjoy life and appreciate the beauty of it all just as Daoism urges.

Some Daoists meditate on clear space or the color black when cultivating the space element. As to making images of empty clear space we need not say much but blackness meditations (other than darkness retreats) should be explained. Here you imagine that everything around you is blackness and only blackness without any light. You imagine that this blackness extends everywhere when you want to meditate on the space element, so essentially you have no concept of dimensions when doing this since there is only blackness. You imagine that the universe is an evenness of empty blackness but because there isn't any light you don't know how big it is or is not, which is just like the fact that you cannot imagine (visualize or mentally represent) the original nature.

You can look at the color "vantablack" on the internet if you want to see a black that can retain 99.965% of light, thus removing the various colors of the spectrum so that all you see is black. The shade "black diamond" is even blacker. Go look at internet pictures.

When practitioners engage in black color meditations they can remind themselves of aphorisms like, "I am meditating on nothingness, the unmanifest fundamental substratum, the universe before existence … for this is the essence of what I am." Meditating on being the color black infinitely, without a body, has the intent of stimulating one type of Yin Qi experience while meditating on clear emptiness to represent vast and formless infinity is another type of space meditation that tends to prompt a different feeling of Qi to bathe in.

Of course, you need to let go of concentrating on feeling your body while doing these sorts of meditations (so that enlightened beings can work on your more easily) as well as any thoughts that naturally arise in your mind. You must gently push them away to rest in formlessness every time there is a distraction. What is there to worry? That is what you are. Just let go of everything and see what you turn out to be. The agglomerative forces of the universe will still cohere to uphold your physical existence without you disappearing, so let perfectly go and experience an imagination of bodilessness if you can.

Meditating on the color red while feeling the warmth of a fire (because you are sitting next to it) and energy flicker inside you, as done in Shingon, can be used as one type of fire meditation. Meditating on the color blue or blue green can be used for water meditations although these are sometimes used for the wind element while black or white are often used for water visualizations. The truth is that you need not stay with standard correspondences but should basically use whatever works for your own psychology in rousing your Qi.

The important point to all these organ, meridian and five element meditations is, as already explained, threefold:

(1) To help you develop a certain personality characteristic by maintaining an infinite version of that attitude (e.g. infinite kindness) during practice that is so *big and boundless* that it breaks your comfort zone, pervades your self without restraint (you cannot hold it off or contain it), and is unbounded beyond anything you would normally experience. Always try to make the emotion stronger than your ordinary daily conceptions of it in order to arouse your Qi and break your mental boundaries of that attitude.

By thus giving into this exceedingly large emotion or attitude (beyond the bounds of cognition) and holding onto that feeling with continuous maintenance to wash yourself in it you will radically energize the Qi of your body for purification purposes. This practice is a way to gradually *beautify your personality, behavior and your Qi* similar to the way that the Buddhist Four Immeasurables practice works, *but only if you also try to execute that new attitude by actively bringing it into regular life whenever you can. If it is virtuous, also become more that way in regular life!*

You must use some effort to make yourself a little more in the way of the trait you desire, but that's the point because the purpose is to actively become that way rather than just feel an emotion, such as joy, by taking it to a state of elation, ebullience or exuberance for the temporary thrill of savoring and then forgetting the experience. You can indeed use this as a mental exercise for washing your Qi during a method that you abandon thereafter, such as during sex, but a higher purpose is to select emotions, qualities, or attitudes that you sincerely wish to cultivate in your persona.

(2) By greatly stimulating all the positive emotions associated with your internal organs you can help open up the related organ meridians, and strengthen those organs or improve their health especially when, as explained, you practice holding onto immeasurably large dominant attitudes and try to hold those feelings within your organs and their related meridians.

An advanced Daoist practice is to try to feel your body's meridian lines when you hold onto specific dominant attitudes, or the Qi throughout the appendages or body sections crisscrossed by the meridian lines. While walking you can even be concentrating on stimulating the energy flows of specific Qi meridians and should be strongly impressing these pathways with specific attitudes or emotions, as is done in martial arts like *Har Gar*. *Har Gar* practitioners use sounds to try to stimulate the traditional Daoist six organ energies along certain acupuncture meridians when practicing their martial arts.

(3) By performing any of the five element meditations you can realize that you are composed of an element that stretches across the manifest universe – whether matter, energy, transformations, quantum fields, space, etc. – but this is not your true self. No composite, conditional, cause and effect, non-homogeneous way of looking at your composition is your true self. Nevertheless, since you are connected to the rest of the universe without mediation then you are one with the universe, you *are* the universe, the universe is you. You are the universe because all of it creates you and your manifest substance is linked, entwined or entangled with every iota of manifest substance in existence. We are interconnected inseparably with universal energies but people cannot perceive or understand this.

However, since the universe is ultimately *Wuji*, the primordial substrate that hasn't manifested into anything, you are essentially *Wuji* which Hinduism calls Brahman (alternatively Nirguna Brahman, Parabrahman), Buddhism calls the fundamental nature, Christianity calls God, Islam calls Allah and so on.

Understanding this is understanding the *Mahavakyas* of Hinduism that are the basic principles of Advaita Vedanta: "I am That," "That you are," "All of this is Brahman," "This verily is that," "I am Brahman," "This self is Brahman," "Brahman is one without a second," and "Brahman is consciousness."

You basically are the universe whether you think of it as space and matter, a ball of continuous transformations, as flowing streams of force and matter that have congealed together, as a ball of effervescent vibrations, as infinite emptiness, or whether you use the image of a changeless emptiness of attributes to represent our fundamental substratum.

The universe is essentially its fundamental substrate of which it is composed, which is Brahman, and you are ultimately nothing other than this Brahman as well. Everything is composed of Brahman so everything is Brahman. You are *Wuji* because everything is *Wuji*. You are the primordial nature mentioned by Buddhism because everything is that primordial fundamental essence, the absolute ground state of existence.

"Self-realization" means understanding the true nature of your selfness or beingness, who and what you really are, so it means understanding these facts. All your spiritual bodies, as high as they can go, are still really just the original nature. However, they can maintain very long existences of *sat, chit* and *ananda* that are preferable to the lower realms. *Ikigai,* or the purpose of your existence so that it has meaning and significance and fulfillment, is up to you. Without it a long life becomes meaningless. Hence

Immortals fill their life with works of kindness and compassion to help others who also have consciousness and thus are brothers and sisters in manifestation.

Thus the *Mahavakya* aphorisms of Hinduism are the basis of self-realization, which is the "mental" enlightenment of finally understanding what your self-nature is, what your source nature is, what your core Self ultimately is. This is *what you are* rather than some type of independent homogenous spiritual self or soul inside a small body that you probably take yourself to be.

In order to achieve this understanding many Indian sadhus, yogis and monks are taught to disconnect their mind from the concept of being the doer of actions because the universe itself is doing everything as a single entity. You are not the doer because you have no intrinsic self; the universe is the doer. Similarly, you might say that the Self that is its underlying substratum is the ultimate doer of everything (even though it never moves or changes).

Sometimes they are taught to unite their minds with God since He is the ultimate cause of everything as its absolute essence, so He is the real (ultimate) doer in their life. Thus, to help them learn detachment, they are taught that they should surrender themselves completely to God (either a deity like Ishvara or the absolute universal substrate that is *Wuji*-Brahman) and offer Him everything they have including their thoughts and behavior so that they can live their lives in peace.

They are taught that they are not the physical body so *they should live like someone without a body* in order to once again become detached and attain a serene nature of peace. All these mental perspectives are meditation methods that give enlightened masters a chance to work on you and purify your Qi for ascension.

Some are taught to disassociate from all mental objects that their mind fabricates and to focus their continuous attention on the sense of "I," which is the center of our thoughts and perceiver of our perceptions. If you focus on the I-sense and stop consciousness from connecting with all exterior phenomena then the individuality of the I can no longer exist, so it will have to withdraw and disappear ... and you can then realize the inherent unreality of our concepts of being a self. The idea is to cultivate a practice so that all sense of "I" is interrupted but without blocking the I-sense via other thoughts held with attachment.

Some are taught not to identify with their ego-self (I-ness) or their thoughts (emotions, desires, urges, attachments, sufferings, will, etcetera) or perceptions or any relative aspects of their active beingness. They are taught not to identify with their body, mind, thinking (discrimination), emotions, will, or their sensory perceptions of the manifest universe that surrounds us. They are taught to practice giving up the I-concept to achieve an unattached state of formlessness, or "emptiness," because we are all just the thoughtless Supreme Nature, *Wuji*, the fundamental substratum. This is your True Self, your ultimate and absolute true-nature of purity. They are taught that if they detach from their thoughts, desires and emotions in their spiritual practice they will find an internal peace as if nothing exists, and that this peacefulness is the bliss men seek.

Therefore many are taught that if they give up their ego and remain absorbed in God then they will experience peace or bliss, which happens because they consequently start quieting their mind and gradually touch upon degrees of inner peacefulness since this type of mental absorption is a form of emptiness or formlessness meditation. Of course it is actually impossible to "give up your ego" because consciousness needs it to operate as a central point for its workings, otherwise without a self-concept consciousness could not operate and without consciousness you would be mindless like the natural world.

Actually, the idea is to let go of connections and attachments in order to better experience mental peace, and it doesn't really matter how you achieve this because countless virtuous practice roads are available. Christian monks and priests are told to "find peace in the contemplation of God" in order to receive the same benefits of peacefulness, mental stilling, or the "bliss of emptiness" and its attendant states of Qi transformation that help purify your inner subtle nature. Daoism has its own traditional practices and ways.

Some people are taught that they are empty of an intrinsic, inherent, non-conditional self and lack all the attributes or qualities pertaining to a self, and that objects are free of an intrinsic self-nature too. The purpose of such perspectives is so that they achieve a type of release from mentally stationing themselves (clinging to or identifying) in identifying with self or form and thereby achieve peacefulness through this angle of practice.

These instructions on detachment are called *Vairagya* and serve as various types of meditation practice for individuals ordinarily walking around or busy in daily activities. A stationary equivalent are the sitting meditation practices (empty mind meditations) of Daoism or Zen. Also, we have the practice of standing in the Trinity Posture (*San Ti Shi*) of *xingyiquan*, the Eight Mother Palms holding postures of *baguazhang*, or standing in various martial arts *shuzuang bu* (Tree Stump) postures while maintaining a patient empty mind. These too will lead to inner Qi transformations and great *gong-fu* attainments because during these times, if you become truly empty through detachment then enlightened beings will have great success in purifying your Qi without stubborn push back.

Daoists should know about these practices. You should know

about the principles of cultivation practice and how different schools approach the task of cultivating the body and mind (consciousness) to purify them. For consciousness you want to learn how to control your thoughts, how to handle afflictions, how to transform emotions, how to maintain focus, attention and concentration, and how to develop countless mental skills or abilities such as counting in your head, visualizing a mental rehearsal, using logic and reason to deduce conclusions, mentally moving your internal Qi energy in various ways, developing a super memory using mnemonics, how to become absorbed in a state of flow, how to use your breathing to change your biochemistry and mental state, and so forth.

Vairagya detachment techniques are similar to Daoist ideas of meditation and flow, and Daoist ideas of detachment and letting go. Therefore intelligent Daoist masters who wish to learn from other traditions can in time absorb these other methods into the Daoist corpus to develop methods that produce spiritual progress in the quickest manner possible. The right practices can help you open your mind and lessen your mental burdens of egotism and desire.

Such attitudes are similar to what Daoists, monks and yogis should be practicing in their daily activities. All your experiences are conventionally real, but ultimately illusory and groundless. They are neither perceived *correctly* through your senses nor are they understood properly since you have adopted an entirely fictitious reference frame of what they and *you* ultimately are. When you achieve the Celestial Immortal and Universal Immortal stages of spiritual bodies then you will realize this more fully.

Therefore another reason you perform these meditations is to try to understand and prepare for the mind of enlightenment. When you attain the stage of a Celestial Immortal or Universal Immortal, which are equivalent to the stages of being an Arhat or Great Golden Arhat, the compositional plane of your body is so etheric and refined that it transcends all the denser realms of matter. One can see how matter is joined with energy seamlessly in one big ocean of matter-energy that is ultimately energy, or fields, or quantum wind, ... or a single substance substrate.

The realms of the Celestial Immortal or Universal Immortal are already so etheric that we cannot even sense them with scientific equipment. At those stages your form exists as a bodied-being that is almost pure energy that can then feel all the vibrations in the lower realms of existence across the universe (after training) AND you can also experientially realize that your body is seamlessly united with the many fields of energy that interpenetrate the universe. The universe is energy, you are that energy and the universe is the thing making you out of its single fabric of one taste. Ultimately there are no phenomena or different forces and energy types. There is just the one universe *Taiji*. Transcending *Taiji* there is just the single *Wuji*, the fundamental permanent ground substance.

At the highest stages of enlightenment you therefore recognize your unity and oneness with all of creation, and recognize that all men are brothers. You have an apparent existence dependent entirely upon an infinite number of factors that constitute the entire universe, which is the teaching of the Hua Yen school of Buddhism. All of the universe participates in making you because you are an essential part of its single body. Even your consciousness is a dependent construction instead of something that belongs to a single independent being. Climate affects it, your circumstances affect it, events affect it, even planets affect it. Where is there a person in its operations? There is none, and yet understanding is there in its Knowledge making.

These principles of interdependent origination, unimpeded infinite interpenetration, simultaneous (conditional) arising and perfect interfusion mentioned within the *Avatamsaka Sutra* of Buddhism is also taught by the Christian Meister Eckhardt, Jewish Abraham Abulafia and Moslem Ibn Arabi. Everything is dependent on everything else, everything is connected in a unity, nothing is separate or self-so (everything is empty of an intrinsic existence and only exists conditionally as a composite appearance of causes and conditions). All spiritual schools teach this because this is the truth of the universe as to what you really are.

Because of infinite interdependence, *when anything within the universe manifests the entire cosmos gets into the act.* When one iota of the universe changes the entire universe changes too, and when one part changes it is because the infinite interfusion of all things caused it to change.

The appearance of any one thing within the universe is an *unfoldment* of cause and effect that fully encompasses the entire universe into a *localized enfoldment* or appearance. That is to say, the existence of any single thing depends on the total network of all other things, which are all equally fused with each other, interdependent upon one another, and simultaneously mutually determined by each other to produce their appearances. Since everything is perfectly fused with everything else this forms one single manifest substance, which is what you are, and its absolute underlying nature is *Wuji*, the undifferentiated source essence of existence. All things merge in It.

The entire universe gets into the act to produce both you and the events and circumstances that you will experience in life which are all parts of the universe, seamlessly connected to everything else, as can be sensed by viewing the "Quantum Cloud" sculpture made by Antony Gormley (check the internet). Therefore your life trajectory or destiny is called karma since everything cooperates in producing that fate. Most of our karma, since it includes our environment and the world we enjoy, is collective destiny that we either enjoy or suffer from.

Thus you have seen in Chapter 2 the essence of self-realization, and in this appendix have realized what your body is as well. Whether a collection of all the atoms in the universe, or a ball of transformations, or a ball of congealed flows, or an effervescent, indeterminate shaking of energy bits, however you wish to think of the manifest universe it is still all you. And what does the human being want? You've seen that in Chapter 4. And how do you change yourself to become what you want, experience what you want or act to achieve what you want? I've explained this in many books such as the upcoming *Self-Creation (The Superhuman Protocol)*.

Your manifest self and life are thus the universe. However your core, unchanging, stable or permanent self-essence is the pure and eternal universal substrate, which is all that you really ultimately are. You are not this flimsy body-mind complex that flits around during life pursuing this and that for maintenance, pleasure and survival. You are the very universe itself and ultimately the one absolute Self that it actually is.

You also have a trajectory or fate already determined within the universe, but you can also change it so that you can even escape from the lower realms of existence by devoting yourself to the Daoist road of spiritual cultivation, or other spiritual roads should you so choose.

Daoism provides a guide for both living a good life and for escaping the lower realms. I've provided explanations for various aspects of this and have concluded revealing many of the secret inner teachings of Daoism.

ABOUT THE AUTHOR

Related books of interest by the same author:

Hidden Teachings in Hinduism – read this next and *Arhat Yoga*
Neijia Yoga – highly recommended
Arhat Yoga – read with *Correcting Zen*
Correcting Zen – read with *Arhat Yoga*
Color Me Confucius – highly recommended
Internal Martial Arts Nei-gong
Buddha Yoga – highly recommended
Nyasa Yoga
Bodhisattva Yoga
Meditation Case Studies
The Little Book of Hercules – recommended
The Little Book of Meditation
Easy Meditation Lessons
Twenty-Five Doors to Meditation

Also related to spiritual cultivation:

Visualization Power
Sport Visualization for the Elite Athlete – recommended
The I-Ching Revealed
Detox Cleanse Your Body Quickly and Completely – recommended
Look Younger, Live Longer – recommended
Quick, Fast, Done – highly recommended
Move Forward: Powerful Strategies for Creating Better Outcomes in Life
Culture, Country, City, Company, Person, Purpose, Passion, World –
super highly recommended !

Mundane Affairs:

Super Investing – highly recommended
Breakthrough Strategies of Wall Street Traders
High Yield Investments, Hard Assets and Asset Protection Strategies
The Art of Political Power
Bankism
How to Create a Million Dollar Unique Selling Proposition

Made in the USA
Coppell, TX
11 August 2024